POLITICS AND THE MILITARY IN ISRAEL 1967-1977

By the same author

Military and Politics in Israel 1948 - 1967

Egypt the Praetorian State

Military and Politics in Modern Times

POLITICS AND THE MILITARY IN ISRAEL 1967-1977

AMOS PERLMUTTER

FRANK CASS

First published in 1978 in Great Britain by
FRANK CASS AND COMPANY LIMITED
Gainsborough House, Gainsborough Road,
London, E11 1RS, England

and in the United States of America by
FRANK CASS AND COMPANY LIMITED
c/o Biblio Distribution Centre
81 Adams Drive, P.O. Box 327, Totowa, N.J. 07511

ISBN 0 7146 3079 9

Photoset in Baskerville by Saildean Limited.
Printed in Great Britain by offset lithography by
Billing & Sons Limited, Guildford, London and Worcester

To the memory of
my beloved father
Moshe Perlmutter
1905-1975

CONTENTS

PREFACE

The 1967 war precipitated by the adventurous and aggressive Egyptian praetorian ruler, Gamal Abdel Nasser, changed the nature and structure of war and the military in the Middle East. The protracted state of war between Israel and Egypt until 1967 changed into a permanent state of war of attrition, which culminated in the 1973 war. Thus, for over seven years the Arab-Israeli conflict was conducted exclusively on the battlefield.

The escalation of the conflict, although it intensified the state of violence and the arms race in the area, stabilized civil–military relations in Israel, but even more so in the Arab countries. The military establishments certainly became gigantic for such small states as Israel, Egypt and Syria, consuming close to forty per cent of their GNP and sapping their people's strength and resources. But praetorianism became more stable in Egypt, Syria and Iraq. The Arab rulers of 1967 (with the exception of Nasser, who died) are still in power—Asad, Sadat, Hussein and the Iraqi Takriti clique. In Israel a score of ambitious 1967 senior retired military politicians moved out of the army into politics.*

In the 1973 and 1977 elections the prominence of former generals in politics was conspicuous—Dayan, Rabin, Allon, Bar-Lev, Sharon, Weizmann, Yadin, Tulkovski, Yariv, Amit, M. Peled, Zorea, and Lahat—all veterans of the 1948, 1967 and 1973 wars. However, the political-civilian authority and structures prevailed. The challenge to stability, order, continuity and legitimacy did not come, as some of the false Israeli and foreign prophets predicted, from the politically ambitious officers, but from the electorate. The collapse of the

*For the full background, see my *Military and Politics in Israel 1948–1967,* to which the present book is a sequel.

Labour Party, the decay of the apparat, the corruption of its second generation elite (Yadlin, Ofer and Rabin), the gap between pioneer values and modern realities, the estrangement between the Labour Party and its historical constituencies—the working classes and the urban and modern middle classes—brought about the decline of authority and legitimacy and the political disaster for the Labour Alignment in the May 1977 elections, which brought to an end the dominance of Labour, whose hegemony and authority had been seriously challenged in the 1973 elections, and finally came to an end after the 1977 elections.

The Israeli senior military since 1967 represents and is an integral part of a new meritocracy. This successor generation is different in quality, composed as it is of retired generals, chiefs of police, active senior bureaucrats and technocrats, and a few university professors, scientists and journalists. The decline of the Labour Party, its authority and political leadership, the fragmentation of political parties, and the party's loss of economic resources, mark a revolutionary turn of events in Israel. Israel today is a society in transition. It seems bound, as before, to have a relatively weak government in the wake of the 1977 elections. In the absence of a cohesive ruling party, no institution is in a position to modify and integrate cleavages and certainly not to eliminate them, as Ben Gurion did in the past. But the Israeli government is highly representative and authoritative. Internal stability still endures. Political systems do not collapse because consensus is no longer prevalent or because public opinion has become polarized, as it has in Israel since 1967, accelerating after 1973. Disruption of consensus characterizes the United States, Sweden, Holland, West Germany and Japan, as well as Israel.

But such companionship should not encourage complacency. Rather, it should demonstrate the critical obligation to ensure the stability of a party system, the integration of cleavage, and the reinstitution of national and political consensus, which are imperative for the preservation of the few precious contemporary democratic political systems.

Israel is not a praetorian state, but a state in transition. Yet the politics of strategy and of national security are the preoccupation of states and people in a permanent state of war—as is true of the United States and Israel, even if the level and scope of open violence which they face are considerably different. Thus, Zahal's high command and its senior officers will remain, as they have been in the last three decades, a prominent group influencing the defence, security, and foreign affairs and politics of Israel.

Meanwhile, the outline of the relationship between the new Begin regime and the military is emerging. Mr Begin is by temperament and conviction a strict legalist and constitutionalist. He once told the author that when, in May 1967, some of the generals approached him with doubts about the efficacy of the then Prime Minister, Mr Eshkol, he urged Ben Gurion and General Dayan to join the government in order to create confidence in civilian leadership, and joined the National Unity government himself for that same purpose.

The indications are that the new government exercises full authority, and the roles of Generals Dayan (Foreign Minister) and Weizmann (Defence Minister) are advisory ones. General Weizmann will restrict himself to military affairs exclusively, in contrast to what would have probably been the case if Mr Peres had succeeded to the premiership. Under Begin there is stricter civilian control, so we are back to the situation of the Ben Gurion era. General Weizmann has remarked to me, 'I only interview divisional commanders—no one else, not even journalists.'

ACKNOWLEDGMENTS

First, once more, to Professor Pinhas Zusmann, Director General, Ministry of Defence, Israel an intellectual and a friend who has never failed to guide me in understanding the military and politics in Israel. To retired General Ariel Sharon for the story of 1973, as he saw it; and to General Adan, as he saw it so differently. To former Generals Tulkovski, Amit, Hod, Beni Peled, the late chief of Staff, David Elazar, and again, Generals Lahat, Yariv, Zeira, Yoffe, Tal and Mati Peled — for their time and explanations on 1967 and 1973, even if I had to take a different road to explain the events than they did. To General Abrasha Tamir for 'strategic' stimulation, Defence Minister Weizmann for constructive debate, and former Prime Minister Rabin for several years of warm (and later, somewhat cooled) friendship. To former Defence Minister Shimon Peres I am grateful for his wisdom, patience, and interpretations. To Foreign Minister Moshe Dayan for our brief but acerbic meetings. To Menachem Begin, the new Prime Minister, a fervent Zionist and a true believer, for pleasant friendship. To Professor Yigael Yadin for his intellectual inspiration, and to former Foreign Minister Yigal Allon and also to my good and warm friend, the present (1977) chief of staff, General Mordechai (Mota) Gur, for two decades of friendship and advice.

Among my academic colleagues: I thank first, Samuel P. Huntington of Harvard, and S.M. Lipset of Stanford for years of friendship and intellectual companionship; William Quandt and Dick Betts of the National Security Council; and Robert Jervis, Murray Feld, Michael Handel, George Quester — all formerly C.F.I.A., Harvard. Thanks for listening. To Professors Yehezkel Dror, Moshe Lissak, Moshe Maoz,

Shlomo Aronson, of the Hebrew University; and to Gabi Ben-Dor of the University of Haifa, a fellow worker in the same field. To Professor Elie Kedourie of London, special thanks, as to Professor John Harsanyi of Berkeley, Roman Kolkowicz of UCLA, and Reinhard Selten of Bielefeld. Last, but not least, to Professor A. Lee Fritschler, Dean of the School of Government and Public Administration, The American University; and to Codelle Rosenberg, for prompt and excellent typing.

To my mother, Berta, I am grateful for her patience and love.

Amos Perlmutter

1977 Cambridge and Washington

CHAPTER I

From the Haganah to Zahal: The Evolution of an Institutionalized Security System: 1909-1949

In the preface to my earlier volume, *Military and Politics in Israel* (1969), I asserted that since 1948 the Israeli Defence Forces have been thrust into national prominence. Army leaders have become politically influential and have gradually assumed high positions in Israeli enterprise—whether bureaucratic, economic public and semipublic, or private. By 1977 the highest positions in the country were occupied by military men. Prime Minister Yitzchak Rabin was Chief of Staff during the 1967 war. The Minister of Commerce, Chaim Bar-Lev, had been Rabin's successor as Chief of Staff, serving from 1968 to 1972. Aaron Yariv, chief of Intelligence, served a brief term as Minister of Information in 1974. Shimon Peres, the Defence Minister, although not a military man is an 'old boy' in the security network, as is the ideologue of the Palmach, Israel Galili. Foreign Minister Yigal Allon was the Palmach's most prominent general in the War of independence. For a time the most brilliant of all Israeli generals, Ariel Sharon, served as Rabin's chief security adviser. General Rehavam Ze'evi was Rabin's adviser on terrorism, and several other generals play a most prominent role in the Defence Ministry and the Foreign Office. Among them is General Chaim Herzog, the Israeli ambassador to the United Nations. The political influence of the present Chief of Staff, General Mordechai Gur, far surpasses that of his predecessors, including Dayan and Rabin, although they too were interventionist officers. Gur enjoys this predominance first, because he is a full member of Israel's chief negotiating team (formed for the talks during the Kissinger peace efforts) and of the cabinet's crisis-management ad hoc committee and second, because he now commands an IDF that, at least officially, has doubled in size since 1973, even though the 1973 Zahal was one of the largest in history.*

Thus, the growing political influence of Zahal and its dominance in the area of national security, to which I pointed in my earlier work, are now undisputed facts. Furthermore, I have been able, to a substantial degree, to retain in this work the theoretical and research criteria and parameters that I adopted for the earlier volume. My major thesis then was that during the 1948-1967 period, civilian dominance over the military had persisted—Zahal as a people's reserve army remained politically and legally the instrument of the government and the regime in power. Happily, this thesis has been fully vindicated. Despite the brilliant victory of 1967, the debilitating War of Attrition between 1969 and 1970, the psychological and strategic debacle that occurred in 1973, and even in the face of Zahal's clear military superiority that subsequently materialized, the Israeli formula of civil-military relations has remained intact.

The complex symbiotic relationship that exists between those who wear uniforms and those who do not has survived. Civilians who lack any military experience and members of the High Command, continue to share power and adhere to the dictum that political responsibility and war-making power remain *exclusively* in the hands of the civilians (principally the Prime Minister and the Defence Minister, although a 'kitchen cabinet' is sometimes formed to assist them). Decisions are made on a functional basis and are not divided along 'military' and 'civilian' lines, although the scope of any particular military confrontation and the informal structure of the Israeli political system (especially of the cabinet) do account, in part, for the way in which decisions are made. Anyone who wishes to divide the civilians and the military into neat and mutually exclusive categories (doves and hawks, for instance) would find the task unfruitful. In Israel, orientations and perceptions do not depend upon the uniform worn but upon the personal conviction of each decision-

*I shall use the terms IDF (Israel Defence Forces) and Zahal (*Tsva Ha'Haganah L'Israel*) interchangeably.

maker, whether he is a professional soldier, an 'amateur' politician who must handle complex security problems, or a defence intellectual.

The inconclusive and psychologically damaging war of 1973 would have been expected to produce more serious challenges to the civilian authority, and did, in fact, lead to mutual recriminations between civilian and military personnel, as well as internal conflicts within the army and the politicians' group. The acrimony was not unlike that produced within the United States by the war in Vietnam, and it is now subsiding in Israel to some degree. In any case, this sort of conflict should not be seen as a sign that there has been any lessening of the country's dedication to the dominance of political, electoral, and democratic processes over the military. Despite the serious crisis of authority that Israel is now enduring, the military elite in Israel has never made a move to form a junta to overthrow the regime. Nor was the regime ever threatened by a 'man on horseback', even though one or two potential praetorians have existed and still do in Israel. Nor was the High Command (or for that matter, any lower echelon) ever involved in planning or executing coups, as so often undertaken by the militaries in Syria, Iraq, Egypt, and Sudan, as well as in the larger 'coup zone' that encompasses many of the countries of the so-called Third World.

Fidelity to political supremacy, democratic ideals, and parliamentary government is the rule in Israel as it is in the United States and in other modern democracies characterised by the predominance of civilian regimes. If my civilian–military formula for Israel is indeed an 'iron law' of Israeli politics, I must insist that three other theoretical propositions have also held true despite the political and military strains the country has endured since 1967, although it has become, of course, a totally garrisoned state.[1]

(1) The high military proportion ratio (MPR), i.e. the proportion of military to civilians within the state, did not turn the state or the army into a praetorian system. (2) The utilization of civilians for military purposes did not change or distort the basic political foundations of Israel. (3) There has been no propensity for the military to intervene politically.

Since 1973 the MPR to the total population is higher than it has been at any time in Israel—or, for that matter, higher than in any other country today—yet the political system has proved resilient. Although there have been challenges to authority since 1973, these are more the result of the political decay of the party-state system and of Labour Zionism, than of challenges to the regime in power posed by the military. The thesis that the Israeli army is highly professional but that highly professional armies can be noninterventionist, has been vindicated.

Professionalization, modernization, and technocratization have created a military elite with enhanced professional and bureaucratic autonomy but without an increased political orientation. In fact, it seems fair to speculate that Zahal in the 1980s will provide fewer officers to high political office than it has in preceding years. In fact, according to Ben Dor, the political aspirations of the officer corps have actually been on the decline since 1967.[2]

Thus, chances for the military's wresting political supremacy from the civilians in 1977 are considerably less than in the pre-1967 period—even if the military is still Israel's most powerful bureaucracy in the national security system. Zahal's nation-in-arms structure follows neither the French nor the German style; among the draftees the old voluntary, pioneer style persists, despite the fact that the spirit of the Palmach as the elite of a people's army is no longer the source of Zahal's inspiration. But Israel is essentially still the nation-in-arms that it was in 1948.

Although the persistence of these conditions meant there was no reason to change my research design, the continuation of limitations on research was a less felicitous continuity in the period during which I was collecting data for this book, and 1966-68 when I was researching the earlier volume. There are basically two problems. First, although material on the early foundations of Zahal is now available, the government will not give scholars access to documentary material on the IDF until the wars between the Arabs and the Jews are ended. Second, the IDF discourages research into its external relations either with the Cabinet or other political bodies; here the files are sealed. Any examination or analysis of its internal structure, evolution, doctrinal development, nature and origins of its officer corps, officer socialization processes, and so on, is officially discouraged by the IDF, but some scholars and perceptive journalists have written with considerable authority on Zahal's internal and doctrinal matters.[3]

Because of these problems, I had once again to depend on the same sources used in my earlier work, despite their drawbacks. I have expanded their range considerably, however, and have consulted numerous friends and acquaintances in Israel, members of the IDF and the High Command, and of the political elites, including cabinet ministers. I have interviewed (although note-taking was not possible) almost every Israeli general who has served since 1967, including three Chiefs of Staff and a great number of senior officers (retired and active); the leading bureaucrats in the Defence Ministry and their representatives, especially those in the United States; and many members of the intelligence community. Although information gathered in this fashion does not make the study authoritative, I can assert my claim that good political judgment is not necessarily dependent on reference to written sources if intellectual honesty is properly applied. I have also enjoyed the invaluable support of a number of Israeli defence insiders. Furthermore, I have read virtually everything that has been published on the IDF in Hebrew, English, and French, no small task, since the subject has attracted numerous writers since 1967.

Although the research design and sources in this work are similar to those in my earlier one, and my major propositions have been vindicated, I owe a summary of the development of the Israeli armed forces to those who might not have read my earlier volume. The army of Israel was mainly conceived by Socialists, who had successfully mobilized human and material resources early in the century for the settlement of *Eretz Israel* (the historical name for the Jewish homeland). The Socialists, however, were in a minority: the most powerful political organization of Zionism and its supreme authority was the World Zionist Organization (WZO) established at the first Zionist Congress in Basel in 1897. Through its department for the resettlement of the Jewish homeland in *Eretz Israel*, the WZO dispensed money and resources and recruited and deployed personnel. Nevertheless, the Socialists eventually took the lead in mobilizing international Jewish capital to buy Arab land and to settle Socialist agriculturalists on the land thus acquired, and it was these groups of farm workers and intellectuals who formed self-defence units.[4]

Contrary to Zionist myth, the land of Israel was neither vacant nor inhabited by welcoming natives. In fact, the assorted Arabs who lived in what was then the Southern Syrian Province of the Ottoman Empire showed distinct hostility toward the Jewish pioneers. Zionism, this century's only colonizing movement, was not appreciably different from its predecessors, and *Eretz Israel* was not settled peacefully. In fact, the Jewish settler faced increasingly open antagonism, organized political opposition, and violence first from the Arabs of Palestine and the neighbouring provinces, and later from those living in the territories given over to Arab domination under the Mandate. If the ideologists and propagandists of the Zionist movement were unwilling to admit the scope and level of Arab antagonism, it was nevertheless very real. No settlement of Jews in Palestine escaped casualties; settlers were killed by bandits and marauders as well as by nascent Palestinian nationalists. Zionist and Socialist Zionist leaders in general chose either to ignore the violence of the Arabs or to hope that their sporadic outbursts did not signify part of a larger movement, and might eventually subside, if a combined policy of goodwill, bribery, and compromise were followed. However, there were some Zionist leaders, especially among the agricultural settlers, who sought to combat the terrorism with force.

The early Nili group of anti-Socialist pioneers, led by Aron and Sarah Aronson, Avshalom Feinberg, and Na'aman Belkind, organized self-defence units like the Bar Giora group. Michael Halperin, a pioneer Zionist, was notorious for his exploits against Arab bandits. So was the courageous defence organization of Zeév Jabotinsky, (who eventually became the leader of Revisionist Zionism and the right Zionist opposition) that fought the Arab rioters in Jerusalem in 1920. The emergence of the forerunner of the Haganah, the Hashomer in 1909, already signified the recognition of both individual pioneers and their leaders that a system of organised defence against the Arabs was necessary. It is true that the Arab nationalist movement, the forerunner of the contemporary Palestinian nationalist movement, did not exist at that time (1880-1920). Even when it began to emerge after 1920, it was not as yet dominant over the Arabs, although it did organize riots against Jews in 1921 and 1929, as well as the 1936-39 Arab revolt.[5]

It is hardly meaningful to describe a collection of Arab peasant bandits as a nationalist movement, but it certainly formed its nucleus. Thus, when the pioneer Zionists, the British Mandate authorities, and the WZO designated the Arabs as rioters, marauders, and bandits (today they would be dignified in some circles as members of a 'national liberation movement'), they were correct in the context of their time. However, the fact that the Arabs were dismissed in this fashion only demonstrated that, with the exception of a few Zionist leaders and pioneers, no one recognized or comprehended the danger that there were Arabs, natives to Palestine, who would never accept the Jews as equals or welcome them as permanent neighbours. Thus, it was not until the mid-1920s that a permanent military organization emerged. But when the Haganah did take shape, it was not totally autonomous, nor did it, for that matter, engage the attention or material support of Zionist and Socialist Zionist leaders, bureaucrats, settlers, and apparatchiks. In 1921, during the first organized Arab revolt against the Jews in Jerusalem, the Haganah was woefully short of resources—money, weapons, and trained personnel.

Organisation of the defence function was, on the whole, treated casually. The Haganah was to be the focus of official interest in the post-riot years but that interest would soon subside and a few dedicated volunteers would be left in control. In neither the WZO nor the Zionist cabinet was there any special department for defence until the 1940s.

Only in the Váad Haléumi (the executive committee of the Jewish community or *Yishuv* in *Eretz Israel*) and the Labour and Revisionist Zionist parties, were there departments and individuals—but only meagre resources—devoted to overseeing security functions.

The volunteer nature of the Haganah was finally changed only some fifty years after the first Zionist immigrants arrived in *Eretz Israel* (1882). Thus, by 1936 the Haganah was formalized and institutionalized. It even acquired a permanent semi-volunteer officer corps. Yet the success of the *Yishuv's* leaders and institutions did not necessarily lie in the attention, time, and resources devoted to Haganah; again these were slight compared to those awarded to immigration, *Hityashvut* (settlement) and Labour. From its inception as a formal organization, the Haganah was established as the supreme military organization of world Zionism, although it was hardly at the political centre of the movement.

A survey of civil–military relations in Israel must focus on the growth of the autonomous professional and political security organization, which began as a series of spontaneous, voluntaristic, task-oriented individuals, groups, and developed into a complex, self-sustaining and highly institutionalized military (1909-1948). This evolution can be analyzed in several parts: (1) the birth of the early security organizations and the rivalries that existed among them; (2) the campaign to dominate and politicize the Haganah; (3) the countereffort to keep the Haganah a purely professional organization; and (4) the transformation of the Haganah's High Command into Zahal's High Command.

1. Most self-defence units were organized to meet the immediate and specific security needs of the Zionist settlers, both farmers and urban dwellers. As each period of Arab violence ended, the security units disbanded, although a few militant army leaders (both left and right) made occasional unsuccessful attempts to politicize the security organization in order to use it as a weapon in the internal struggles of the rival Socialist Zionist groups or in the larger struggle between Socialist and Revisionist Zionists for control of the Jewish community in Israel.

The early defence units, although lacking professionalism, training, financial and organizational resources, and political support from the Yishuv and its ideological protectors—the Socialists—conceived of themselves as a people's militia. Their members were politically and ideologically dedicated and militant, and their embryonic strategic concepts developed, over a period of some forty years, into an elaborate security doctrine.

The first defence units, which were created by the WZO, were the Jewish Legions, the Gdudim. These were three volunteer battalions composed of Americans, English, and Zionists from Palestine who joined the British Allied Army in 1915-1916 and campaigned in Gallipoli as the Zion Mule Corps. (The British command in Cairo did not favour the formation of an independent Jewish field army.) The battalions were disbanded at the end of World War I, with no subsequent military continuity.

The Socialist-Zionists organized security units, which were intended for internal protection rather than external defence. The first was *Hashomer* (The Watchman), a group which former *Poale Zion* pioneers organized in 1909 to defend the early settlements. Members of the *Hashomer* did not conceive its role as restricted to security functions, but considered it a nucleus for a people's politico-military organization. The constitution of *Hashomer* was revolutionary and its aspirations were made quite clear: it sought to gain a monopoly of the defence of the Jewish community in *Eretz Israel.* It failed to control the Socialist-Zionist and pioneer settlements, however, and it was disbanded in 1920, though some of its militants nevertheless continued their conspiratorial activities in an effort to infiltrate the political structures of Socialist Zionism the Histadrut (General Confederation of Labour), and the *Poale Zion* party.

The second defence organization founded by the Socialist-Zionists, a considerable number of whom had served in the Gdudim of World War I, was the *Gdud Ha-avoda* (Labour Legions) organized by *Hechalutz* (The Pioneer), one of the most militant Marxist groups. The Labour Legions were established to protect work teams engaged in construction of roads and pipelines for the chain of pioneer settlements in the Galilee and the valley of Jezrael. Dominated by militant Marxist Zionists and ex-*Hashomer* revolutionaries, the Labour Legions gave birth to the first kibbutz movement, Ha-Kibbutz Ha-Meuchad (United Kibbutz Movement), which eventually played a key role in the development of the Haganah, the Palmach, and Zahal.[6]

2. The creation of these organizations engendered a political struggle to dominate the defence function. The struggle between the different Zionist groups was over the control of the Haganah and the issue of its politicization. The conflict began with the first Socialist-Zionist settlements in *Eretz Israel* (1904-5) and continued without a break thereafter; it became increasingly traumatic after 1932, and climaxed between 1938 and 1949. The struggle was waged in two arenas: between the left-wing revolutionary Marxists and members of the social democratic mainstream within the Socialist-Zionist camp (I prefer to call it the House of Labour (HOL)); and between Socialists and revisionist Zionists.

The struggle for domination within the HOL for domination between the moderate and left Socialists; the Socialists were not only the first group to organize agricultural collective and co-operative settlements and, therefore, defence groups for them, but also (and far more important) were able to display such genius and organizational capacity in securing resources from the WZO.

This struggle was similar to the conflict within the international socialist movement at the same time, with strife between the Marxist followers of Rosa Luxemburg, the Leninists, and the Social Democrats led by Kautsky, Bernstein, and others. In each case the political orientations of the moderates won over the militant, revolutionary and extremist Marxists and anarchists in Europe. In *Eretz Israel* although the pioneer movement faced challenges considerably different from those confronting European socialism, the moderate mainstream leaders of the HOL, including Berl Katznelson, David Ben Gurion, and Eliahu Golomb, the first commander of the Haganah, were equally dedicated to the elimination of Marxist revolutionary militants, especially those in the pre-Haganah security organizations. To this end, they promoted the creation of a special organization for security, the

Haganah. Although it was a department of the Histadrut, the Haganah was supervised by the WZO and *subordinate* to the authority of the Jewish Agency, the political structure in charge of the Jewish *Yishuv* in Palestine under the Mandate.

The Haganah was officially established by the Golomb-Hoz Committee of the Histadrut in 1921, but it did not actually come into existence until 1925. Although Golomb failed to secure WZO funds for the Haganah (the bourgeois Zionists suspected, and rightly so, that the HOL would exercise total domination over the Haganah and the HOL did, in fact, pack the leadership of the Haganah with its own elite), it did become a semi-automonous Histadrut-HOL co-ordinating structure for all security activities. In the 1930s, the Haganah began to be conceived of as the Jewish community's semi-official defence and security co-ordination committee and eventually as the single most significant military structure of the HOL and of the *Yishuv*. Thus, its orientation was no longer influenced by revolutionary Marxists and anarchists, but by the Social Democratic Mapai party and the Histadrut Labour union moderates, whose attitude toward the British authorities was conciliatory (until 1945) and who saw the Haganah as a strictly *defensive* organization against Arab violence.

In 1937, a group of Revisionist Zionists in the Haganah in Jerusalem split off, forming an entity known as Haganah B, because its leaders argued that the Haganah had become totally dominated by HOL and Mapai. This was no simple factional split. Haganah B eventually grew into a political-military structure, the Irgun Zvai Léumi (IZL) (the National Military Organization (NMO)) in 1938, a competitor security organization to the Haganah, led by militant revisionist and bourgeois Zionists. But the NMO, its descendant, founded by Avraham Stern, a brilliant extreme Revisionist and a follower of Zéev Jabotinsky, was established for a single purpose—to overthrow the British Mandate authorities in Palestine by force. Thus, the NMO's goals and perceptions were politically and philosophically opposed to the HOL, the Haganah, and the non-militant Zionists.

The emergence of an activist and fiercely anti-British force among Jewish youth after the 1936-39 Arab revolt, especially in the big cities of Tel Aviv, Jerusalem and Haifa, represented a grave challenge to the Haganah, the *Yishuv*, and world Zionism. It also exacerbated the conflict between the two irreconcilable adversaries, the Labour and Revisionist Zionists, as to who would exert the greatest influence on the youth and youth movements, which formed the major source of Haganah's and NMO's recruits. The struggle for the youth lasted for almost a decade and was part of the larger struggle between the Haganah and the NMO. This struggle was not simply, as some authors have suggested, between 'left' and 'right' Zionist ideologies, but involved a battle for the domination of the security structures of the *Yishuv* and eventually the *Yishuv* itself. It led to a minor civil war, which ended with the destruction of the *Altalena*, a NMO weapons ship, on the orders of Israel's first Prime Minister and defence Minister, David Ben Gurion, in 1948. The end result was the annihilation of the NMO as a military organization.

3. To understand the evolution of the Haganah as a professional military organization, however, one must first retrace its steps. The Arab revolt of 1936-39 provided the catalyst for the Haganah's expansion from a Histadrut department for co-ordinating security measures to a full-time general staff in embryo, because the revolt was correctly perceived as a forerunner of future Arab opposition Zionism. The Haganah continued to defend the Jewish settlements, but its major function became the organization of the *Bricha*, the brilliant large-scale clandestine immigration of Jews to *Eretz Israel.* (The NMO also engaged in such activities but on a smaller scale.) Although the Haganah's activities were greatly expanded, however, concern for the professionalism of the High Command, provided the impetus for a fierce debate lest its automony should encourage 'Bonapartism' (to use the language of the Socialists, who were influenced by traditional Russian fears). To ensure that the Haganah remained totally subordinate to the authority of the Jewish Agency, the Agency assumed control of the two politically 'suspect' departments of the High Command, namely, intelligence-gathering and weapons procurement.[7]

The evolution of the High Command was distinguished by the creation of a special office to serve as a nucleus for special operations. This eventually became the Palmach, or shock troops, the Haganah's elite corps and training ground for the first professional officers of the Haganah and Zahal. From its inception, the Palmach was designed as an elite professional corps, largely as a result of the influence of one of the Haganah's and Zahal's most remarkable and innovative commanders, Yitzchak Sadeh. Sadeh was in charge of the High Command's special office for operations and as such, he personally picked and trained Israel's most illustrious future officers (among them Generals Dayan, Allon, Bar-Lev, Elazar, and Rabin; these men dominated Zahal's senior command between 1953 and 1973). The leaders of the Palmach, despite being the Haganah's professional officer corps, were involved in internal HOL politics, but nevertheless still remained dedicated to military professionalism. The Palmach trainees were influenced by the United Kibbutz Movement (UKM) ideology and the Ahdut Ha'avoda left-leaning party. Its ideologues, Yitzchak Tabenkin, Yitzchak Sadeh, and Israel Galili attempted to exert political and ideological influence on the Palmach.

The professional growth of the High Command was also enhanced by a short honeymoon period that relaxed tensions between the *Yishuv* and the British Mandate authorities in Palestine. Between 1936 and 1938 the first priority of the British army in Palestine was to suppress the Arab revolt and, in this effort, co-operation from the Jewish community was welcomed. Thus, the British now made it their policy to furnish arms and training to the Jews and the semi-legal Haganah. Special Haganah units were organized, led and trained, by British officers. The most distinguished of these were Captain Charles Orde Wingate's Special Night Squads (SNS) which enjoyed great success in their mission to destroy centres of Arab terrorism and guerrilla activities. Wingate played a key role in influencing the new Palmach and Haganah officers, including men of such different political persuasions as Dayan and Allon. The era of good feelings between the British and the Jews was short-lived, however, and by 1939 the British government had reversed its policy.

British attempts to appease the Arabs, Wingate's departure from Palestine, the abolition of the SNS, and the new effort to disarm the Zionists, represented a trend culminating in the 1939 White Paper, which restricted Jewish immigration and land purchase in Palestine. The British, however, failed to perceive the reality in that their authority over Palestine was now seriously challenged. Both militant Zionists and Arabs called for the overthrow of the British Mandate and the new activism expressed itself in renewed violence against the British. This movement was interrupted by the beginning of World War II, and once more, the WZO, the Jewish Agency, and the Haganah collaborated with Britain in a common effort against the Jews' most dangerous enemy, the Nazis. A small group of zealots led by Avraham Stern, of the NMO, and its splinter, the Lehi (Freedom Fighters) considered the overthrow of the British in Palestine as an immediate goal and, to achieve Jewish independence, they even sought to collaborate with fascist and Nazi authorities in Vichy Syria and in the Axis Balkan states.

The war enhanced the growth of professionalization and the recruiting of the High Command and the Palmach; the Jewish Brigade (founded by the Jewish Agency in co-operation with the British Government in 1944) added new, well-trained military men. Characteristically the Jewish Brigade made *little* impact on the growth of the Haganah. The Haganah became autonomous and the Jewish Agency bestowed upon it the legitimacy of the single and most authoritative military instrument of the *Yishuv*. The Jewish Brigade was a pure creation of the Agency. The Haganah, and NMO organizations continued to exist as separate entities within the Jewish Brigade. For example, although the Brigade was under the authority of the Eighth Army, the Haganah instructed the British whom they should choose for officer training. Thus, although the Jewish Brigade was composed of 30,000 men and the Palmach had less than 5,000 men, the Brigade left little or no imprint on the traditions of Zahal; the Haganah and Palmach alone shaped the army —High Command, officers, and men.

The issue of professionalism could not be resolved, however, until the power struggle between the Haganah-Palmach and the NMO-Lehi had ended. Ben Gurion advocated the exile and elimination of the NMO and in 1944 transmitted a list of its leaders to the British, thus collaborating with them in eradicating the 'private' armies of Revisionist Zionism. Most Palmach commanders, including Sadeh and Allon, opposed Ben Gurion. However, the Jewish Agency, dominated by Mapai moderates, organized the *Sezon*, a full-scale witch hunt, and informed the Mandate authorities on the *Porshim* (renegades) from the NMO and Lehi. The Haganah actually arrested and tortured NMO soldiers. Meanwhile Haganah leaders Golomb and Galili, in opposition to Ben Gurion, were making efforts to negotiate with the NMO-Lehi and, for a while, even achieved joint co-operation in military operations (1944). Nevertheless, Ben Gurion, Mosh Shertok (Sharett) and the Mapai leaders never ceased to fight the *Porshim* and to the end co-operated with the British in eliminating them.

4. The story of the evolution of the Israeli military did not end with the destruction of the NMO, however. The fundamental relationship between the military and the civilian power in any country relates to three issues: authority, responsibility, and performance. In modern industrial political systems, the question of authority unquestionably has been resolved in favour of the subordination of the military to political authority.[8] The story of the evolution of Zahal's High Command from its Histadrut-dominated beginnings through the eras of control by the Zionists and the *Yishuv* is a record of continuing struggle to ensure political supremacy for the civil authority.[9] As I have noted earlier, however, although the effort to ensure that the Haganah and Zahal remained in a subordinate position was not without its strains and tensions, the Haganah did become essentially an arm of the political authority.

The question of responsibility proved more difficult, however, and its ultimate resolution had much to do with the structure of Socialist Zionism and the nature of the concepts of the state and political voluntarism in the *Yishuv*. The challenge to civilian authority did not come from the military, but from the two competing camps of Zionism—the Socialists and the Revisionists (including most of the non-Socialist members of the Yishuv). These *Ezrahim* (citizens) were not organized politically, but they espoused the doctrines of bourgeois and, on the whole, moderate Zionism. As Socialists and Revisionists struggled to dominate the Zionist movement, patronage over the Haganah became a bone of contention. The Revisionists rightly claimed that the Haganah was more than an instrument of the HOL, which wanted the patronage and control of the Haganah and thus, desired the responsibility for it transferred from the Histadrut to the Jewish Agency so as to maintain the High Command's political neutrality. The Revisionists, however, argued that the Socialists had undue influence in the Jewish Agency and WZO. The Socialists eventually succeeded in transferring the responsibility for the Haganah to the Jewish Agency, where they were in the majority. Thus, a difference does emerge between political responsibility and civilian control: the Socialists fashioned the Haganah into an instrument of the Zionist movement as a whole. It was not the tool of any political party or movement of left or right, but an instrument of the state-in-the-making of the society-in-the-making.

Pa'il clearly distinguishes four phases in the High Command's evolution, each relating to the relationship between authority, responsibility, and performance.[10] His most perceptive observation is that the relationship between professionalism (i.e. performance) and politicization are inverse. In terms of Huntington's subjective-objective control models,[11] Pa'il demonstrates that in the era of Histadrut domination (subjective control), the professionalism of the Haganah was low while its political orientations were high. Performance in general increased (1) when the Haganah became an instrument of world Zionism under the direct control of the Jewish Agency, then dominated by David Ben Gurion and (2) when the Arab revolt served as a catalyst. By 1937 the first professional High Command and general staff had taken shape and two national forces, the *Notrim* (roving police force) and the Palmach, the shock troops, had been created. Political interventionism gradually declined, and state-making instruments enhanced the professionalization of the Haganah and the institutionalization of the high command, the progenitor of Zahal's General Staff.

David Ben Gurion, the architect of the state of Israel, was the mastermind behind the depoliticization of the Haganah and Zahal, its professionalization, and the institutionalization of authority relationships between the Jewish Agency, its defence department, the Haganah's High Command, and the General Staff. Ben Gurion tailored civil-military relations in *Eretz Israel* as well as in the state of Israel to fit his concept of the Jewish state, which was that of an independent Zionist democratic republic. An unrelenting foe of Zionist extremism, whether of the left or right, Ben Gurion took steps to eliminate real and imaginary political opposition. In the realm of security, convinced, as he was, that Zahal would be the mailed fist of Jewish independence, he never compromised. As a result of his ruthless efforts to eradicate opposition on all fronts, Ben Gurion, during the War of Independence (1947-49), destroyed the NMO and dissolved the independent Palmach headquarters headed by Yigal Allon, the Southern Front's commander. From 1947 to 1963, Ben Gurion alone shaped the nature and structure of Zahal and laid down the formula of Israeli civil-military relations.

Chapter II begins with the first war that Israel faced without Ben Gurion at the helm. His doctrine of civil-military relations, however, is an enduring legacy, as the following pages will demonstrate.

NOTES

1. Let me reiterate that when I speak of garrisoned Israel, I refer to its special situation. It is surrounded by implacable and well-armed foes dedicated to its destruction. Over 40 per cent of the national budget is devoted to defence and it has an elaborate and permanent reserve system which provides that the individual citizen must spend considerable time in the army. No analogy, however remote, is intended between Israel and Harold Lasswell's crude concept of the Garrison State.
2. Gabriel Ben Dor and Shevach Weiss. 'The Israeli Military Elite in Mufti: Senior Officers in Politics.' Unpublished paper, The University of Haifa, Israel. May 1973. 23pp.
3. For Zahal's internal structure, see the short studies made by Professor Moshe Lissak for the Department of Sociology, Hebrew University in Jerusalem, 1970-1972.
   The evolution of the IDF's military doctrines could be assessed by closely following its publications, especially *Macarachot*. The scant and very incomplete studies of Zahal's doctrines are found in Michael Handel, *Israel's Political-Military Doctrine*, CFIA, Harvard, No. 30, July 1973, p. 94; and Dan Horowitz and Edward Luttwak, *The Israeli Army*,

Harper's, New York, 1974. Little use has been made of these sources for this volume.

4. Neither the Socialist Zionists nor the pioneers (not all pioneers were Socialists) had the honour of forming the first Jewish self-defence groups; such groups existed in the Eastern European diaspora. In fact, they were not even the first self-defence organizations in *Eretz Israel.* The first defence units were formed by members of the Moshavot, born in Palestine.
5. The most comprehensive and reliable source on the emergence of Palestinian nationalism is Yoram Porath, *The Emergence of the Palestinian-Arab National Movement, 1918-1929*, Frank Cass, London, 1974.
6. For a full analysis of Ha-Kibbutz, Ha-Meuchad, and the Palmach, see *Military and Politics in Israel*, 1948-67, pp. 35-40.
7. See Meir Pa'il, 'The Evolution of High Command from Haganah to Zahal.' M.A. Thesis, The University of Tel-Aviv, 1950; and *Sepher Ha-Haganah*.
8. *Ibid.*
9. *Ibid.*
10. *Ibid.*
11. S.P. Huntington, *The Soldier and the State*. Harvard University Press, Cambridge, 1957, pp. 81-93, Vol. III. Parts 1 and 2.

CHAPTER II

Escalation into the Six Day War

The Six Day War was not planned. Not until the last ten days of May 1967, did Egypt or Israel even think of war. After May 22, both were poised for such a possibility. But neither perceived nor was prepared, psychologically or indeed in any other way, for its ultimate dimensions. The great tragedy lay in the fact that the period of escalation was also a period filled with opportunities to avoid war. And yet, while the conditions leading to war had existed for two decades, they gave no hint of its terrible consequences.

What chiefly characterized this period of crisis was its uncanny mismanagement: the United Nation's abrupt dissolution of its Emergency Force, British and French apathy and apprehension, the lack of preparedness and general misperception of the growing crisis by the whole international community.

Arab-Israeli relations can be summarized as follows:

1. An unequal intransigence on the part of both, with no chance of reconciliation.

2. Lack of political, economic, social or cultural cooperation on any significant level.

3. A permanent state of warfare existing on two levels: the short, swift major wars, and the continuing minor skirmishes between.

4. A protracted state of Arab internecine warfare.

5. Use and abuse of the Palestinians by both Arabs and Israelis.

6. No effort by the international powers, except those governed by their own immediate interests, to modify conditions in the Middle East. (We can discount diplomatic pressures on Israel and Egypt by the Kennedy and Johnson administrations, since no commensurate military or fiscal pressures were ever applied.)

We start with the United States, its response to the crisis, its reliance on an impotent United Nations Secretary-General, and the host of unrealistic military solutions it proposed. Creative diplomacy was an art unknown to Washington's Middle Eastern experts. At every stage in the process of escalation, diplomacy and crisis management were forced to give way to military solutions for the countries directly involved.

Although the Soviets helped precipitate the rise in tension during May, American vacillation cleared the way for it. The Sinai settlement of 1957 had produced an aide-memoire signed by Dulles, with the tacit co-operation of Hammarskjold, a worthless document reflecting America's please-everyone approach to the problem. A paper that was politically unacceptable, imposed on Egypt only by the combined pressure of the US and the UN, could scarcely be expected to withstand the weight of Arab–Israeli conflict, or the instability of the Middle Eastern regimes.

At the end of the October 1956 war (Operation *Kadesh*) Israel occupied the Sinai desert, the Gulf of Aqaba and the Straits of Tiran. Israel declared that any of the following alternatives would be sufficient to guarantee the removal of Israeli troops from Egyptian territory: (1) a guarantee from any major power that an Egyptian blockade of Aqaba would not be tolerated; (2) the stationing of the UNEF force at Sharm-el-Sheikh to insure freedom of passage; or (3) an agreement among the nations bordering the Gulf (including Egypt) which would permit the free passage of ships of all nations.

On February 11, 1957, the US offered a plan through Secretary Dulles by which Israeli forces would be withdrawn from the Gulf of Aqaba and the Gaza Strip, the US would use all of its influence to establish the Straits of Tiran as an international waterway with free passage of all nations; Israeli troops would be replaced by UNEF soldiers in the Gaza Strip; and the Strip would be placed under a de facto UN trusteeship.

To assure Israel of the above, an aide-memoire was handed by Secretary Dulles to Israel's Ambassador to the UN, Abba Eban, on February 11, stating *that Israel accepted the principle of*

American assurances on Israeli security, through the UN, to prevent Egyptian raids from Gaza, and which would support the principle of free navigation in the Gulf of Aqaba. Accordingly, on February 28, 1957, Abba Eban informed the US of Israel's decision to withdraw its troops from both Gaza and the Gulf of Aqaba area. Egypt's Foreign Minister Mahmoud Fawzi immediately denounced American efforts to secure Israel's withdrawal from the above areas. On March 1, Foreign Minister Golda Meir said that the withdrawal decision was based on the assumption that free navigation would continue, and that Gaza be administered by the UNEF until a peaceful settlement on the future of the territory was reached. On the same day Secretary Dulles assured the representation of nine Arab States that Israel had obtained no promises or concessions *whatsoever* from the US in return for the withdrawal and the stories about a secret undertaking between the US and Israel were 'Communist propaganda'. In fact, the aide-memoire (published as late as 1965 as an Appendix to Eisenhower's *Waging Peace*, Doubleday, New York, 1965, pp. 684-5) specifically stated that 'With respect to [Israeli withdrawal from Sharm-el-Shaikh] the Gulf of Aqaba and access thereto—the United States believes that the Gulf comprehends international waters and that no nation has the right to prevent free and innocent passage in the Gulf through the Straits giving access thereto.'

On March 1, Mrs Meir told the General Assembly that *any interference with Israel shipping in the Gulf of Aqaba or the Straits of Tiran would be regarded as an act of war.* On March 11, Egypt appointed a governor for Gaza, violating the UN—US—Israel agreement. Washington was 'shocked' and surprised by Egypt's act. Next on March 15, Egypt and Saudi Arabia described the Gulf as an absolute Arab territory and Egypt announced that Israel would not be allowed to use the Suez Canal.

The erosion of the agreement began when the US abandoned the UN as an international instrument; when Egyptian forces were permitted to deploy in Gaza after the Israeli withdrawal; when Dulles admitted to a conference of Arab diplomats that the UNEF was not intended as an anti-Arab instrument. Thus America oscillated between globalism and

Arabism, between 'muddling through' and 'benign neglect'. Because the US failed to back the 1957 Sinai settlement, it was gradually abandoned, with the blessing of the UN Secretary-General and the Afro-Asian bloc. Egypt's hopes that it could finally annihilate the settlement were rewarded. By May of 1967, the Sinai settlement was in fact a dead letter.

American diplomacy failed in 1967 for several reasons: a policy of globalism which was never clearly explained to Middle Eastern clients by its diplomats, except in terms of military alliances; refusal by the Arabs to adopt a pro-American, anti-Soviet posture (which did not of course please Washington); and the American policy of 'even-handedness', which was hardly 'even' at all. For this last reason, Israel did not trust America's Arab experts; they never succeeded in convincing Tel Aviv that modifying the Sinai settlement would ameliorate the conflict. Nor were Arabs convinced of the American half-hearted turnabout.

In an address to the UN on October 31, 1956, President Eisenhower clearly said: 'We have considered it a basic matter of the United States policy to support the new state of Israel and—at the same time—to strengthen our bonds with Israel and with the Arab countries'. (In R. Branyana and Larsen eds. *The Eisenhower Administration 1953-1961, A Documentary History*, Random House, New York, p. 698).

Israel was now left with two options: to accept the final undoing of the settlement, or to go to war to prevent it.

And what of the USSR? The military presence of the Soviets, their exploitation of Arab nationalism were no more effective in 1967 than they were in 1958. The Soviets no more succeeded in forming an Arab radical neutralist bloc than they had during the peak of Egyptian-Syrian-Soviet cooperation between 1955 and 1959. By 1967 neither Egypt, Syria nor Iraq had become the model of a 'national-democratic revolution' the Soviets had hoped for. Nor did the Arab regimes become 'progressive', or successful in toppling 'reactionary' regimes in South Arabia. The Egyptian debacle in Yemen showed the limits of Nasser's 'progressivism', if the UAR experiment had not already done so.

There are those who consider Soviet moves to defend its southern frontiers legitimate; there are those who say the

USSR did not act in the Middle East in the responsible manner expected of a great power. Both sides agree, however, on the role of the Soviets in that turbulent month. Russian support of Syria and Egypt, given without demanding political or military commitments in return, tied its hands, kept it from acting in its own interests, and also threatened its hold over the Middle East. Egypt has claimed that the Soviets did support an autonomous action in Sinai but this claim was proved false during the 1967-1968 trial of the Egyptian officers 'responsible' for the 1967 defeat. Certainly no Soviet pressure could force Syria and Egypt to forego what they saw as their own best course: to provoke a controlled international incident in Sinai and so help reverse the gains made by Israel in 1957.

The Soviets may have pushed the Syrians into mobilizing by incorrectly reporting the presence of Israeli troops on its borders. But neither the Syrians nor the Egyptians would have risked military action without a signed guarantee by the Soviets of immediate support in a crunch. The opposite is true. Egypt responded to a Syrian war scare and an 'imminent' attack by the Israelis *because Nasser was convinced of the fragility of the 1957 settlement*, not because of Soviet guarantees of support. Nasser gambled on the assumption that with the big power apparently tilted toward Egypt, he could wipe out Israel's Sinai gains, establish Egypt's political influence in Syria, and possibly even establish its dominion over Jordan.

The war was, in short, the unpredictable outcome of the conflicting aspirations of the local states. It was the most brutal, as well as the greatest in scale and speed, of all the Arab-Israeli wars of the first two decades of conflict. It was, however, a war between Arabs and Israelis, not between the great powers. Its analysis begins, therefore, with Syria, Israel, Egypt and Jordan. We will deal later with those less directly involved: the US, the UN, the USSR, and the international community as a whole. The interaction between these casts of characters explains the escalation into war.

Syria: Organizing for a War of Liberation

Between 1949 and 1967 Syria had, with considerable

turbulence, moved from a restricted parliamentarianism to a militarist rule, which called for a war against Israel. The period was kaleidoscopic. There were more than a dozen dazzling military coups and counter-coups. There was the unexpected and hurried marriage with Egypt, followed by their violent separation, between 1958 and 1961. A bitter rivalry between two radical nationalist parties, the Partie Populaire Syrienne (PPS) and the Ba'th was brutally resolved in favour of the Ba'th.

The most unexpected change came in February of 1966, when the Druze-Alawi officers rose to power on a platform of popular war. The Druze-Alawi was a coalition of the military and the Ba'th, an amalgam of Islamic sects and socially deprived ethnic groups representing about 20 per cent of the population. In 1967 it took over Damascus, and what had once been the centre of a great Muslim Empire was now in the hands of a social and political 'proletariat'.

The Druze-Alawi cabal immediately broke with Nasser, both to assert its independence from Eygptian ambitions, and to focus once again on Palestine as the spearhead of a popular Arab war. A contingent of Syrian-dominated, semi-autonomous Palestine fedayeen, trained and equipped in Syria, were poised for terrorist activities against Israel. Militants were mobilized into the Fatah; members of the Palestinian diaspora, both in the Arab world and elsewhere, were brought together to march under the Syrian banner for a popular war of liberation against Israel.

The concept of a 'Popular war' goes a long way toward explaining the struggle against Israel. Major General Ahmed Suwaydani, the Syrian Army's commander-in-chief, who was to be executed after the 1967 war, wrote:

> I believe that Israel is not a state, but serves as a military base for the Imperialist camp. By means of this base we confront directly the forces of Western Imperialism. The question is: Can we hope to overcome these forces, on the ground, at sea and in the air? Certainly not. This leads to a second question: What is the purpose of equipping our forces at the expense of the development of our country? We have bought arms . . . and not used them . . . Can we

ensure for ourselves military superiority over the US, or Britain or Western Germany?

We must not, therefore, take the line of conventional warfare, using conventional weapons. We must take the line of Popular Liberation War, which is founded on the individual and his belief in his cause, and on the rifle rather than on heavy weapons.

If we regard Palestine . . . as part of the Arab homeland which has been occupied by Imperialism, just as Imperialism has occupied part of Vietnam, we shall see that the situation in Palestine is indeed similar to that in Vietnam now, or in Algeria in the past.

Should Israel react to the Popular Liberation War by conventional warfare, the Arab armies under progressive command must be ready to enter the battle, even if it is a defensive battle only, in order to safeguard the bases of the fedayeen who are the basic element of Popular warfare.

Arab unity is a necessity. . . . We believe that unity born in battle is the unity we long for; therefore we must increase the tension of the struggle to a maximum. We believe that Palestine is the proper place for this. . . . He who liberates Palestine will be the one to lead the Arab nation forward to comprehensive unity. He who ignites the fire of Popular Liberation War can throw all the reactionary regimes into the sea.

This is why we believe that Popular Liberation War is the road not only towards the liberation of Palestine but also towards the liberation of the Arab homeland and towards its unification. The sons of Jordan, Saudi Arabia and other reactionary countries will overthrow the Kings and traitors and join the liberation march.[1]

The programme called for a two-phase war: one phase popular, the other conventional. The second phase was to follow on the success of the first.

Neither the Syrians nor their Arab antagonists recognized the Pandora's box that was being opened in their midst.

The first to be pressured by Syria's radical new leaders was King Hussein of Jordan, whose overthrow they coveted. Since Jordan was to join Syria as a launching pad for the popular war, Hussein was pressured into obstructing the Israel-Jordan Valley water project, so that the Palestinian guerillas could use his northeastern territory as a base.

Syria's next move was to involve Nasser in its popular war by destroying the relatively tranquil truce established between Israel and Egypt after 1956. To do this, Syria increased its pressure on Egypt to heat up the front, and thus destroy the UNEF, that paper tiger 'protecting' the Sinai settlement.

Egypt: Praetorians vs. 'Progressives'

The period from 1962 to 1967 in Egypt was marked by two inter-related events: the exhausting Egyptian war in Yemen (which we may call Egypt's Vietnam), and the struggle between Nasser and key military and Intelligence personnel in the High Command for control of the new political party, the Arab Socialist Union (ASU).

The struggle for power over the new party created a series of crises in the military,[2] which had, along with the bureaucrats, governed Egypt since 1954. Nasser at this point exercised patrimonial control over the military, the government and the ASU. He served as chief and final arbiter over all three power structures, and he tolerated no cabal. He did, however, allow the ASU and its cadres considerable autonomy.

Nasser's concepts of rule and political organization found adherents in both the government and the military. The army, a strongly political body, was run ostensibly on behalf of Nasser by Marshal Abdul al-Hakim Amer. A devout Muslim traditionalist, son of a prominent village sheikh, Amer was related to Farouq's former Chief of Staff, General Muhammad Khaider Pasha, Egypt's Minister of War in 1948. He served, paternalistic and sultan-like, in two capacities: as 'Father-in-Chief' of the army, in charge of the personal welfare of the officers, and as spy-in-chief over the political behaviour of the officers' corps. His official function was to discourage a political falling-away from Nasserism.

There was reason for such vigilance.

The unsettled UAR and Yemeni affairs had left the army

professionals without political *Lebensraum*, apart from Israel. Further, their power was being challenged by an army of civilians, a new generation of 'progressive' bureaucrats, technicians, diplomats and party secret service men. Though clustered mainly first in the Arab National Union and now in the ASU and in the National Assembly, these bright newcomers were to be found as well in the cabinet, the senior civil service, and even in the Presidential Office. Thus, 'for both military and political reasons, Nasser decided there must be changes in the high command and the officer corps and that the political and military control of the army should be separate.'[3]

The aim was to draw a line between the professional and the political soldiers. Nasser hoped to achieve two things: to integrate the army into the Presidential Council, a patrimonial super-organization expected to oversee both the military and the bureaucracy; and to challenge Amer, whose influence, especially among senior officers and the intelligence community, was considerable.

In both efforts, he failed. He still held control over the military, however, through the Free Officers, a network of loyal veterans.[4] Therefore, to conserve his power base, Nasser dissolved the Presidential Council, now challenging his own authority, and permitted a compromise designed to avoid a split in the military. In 1964, 'political control over the army became divided in practice between the "general political control" exercised by the President and the government as a whole and the "special political control" exercised by Amer and his staff.'[5]

Late in 1966, the military faction, led by Marshal Amer, Defence Minister Shams ad-Din Badran and Intelligence chief Salah Nasser, and supported by Anwar es-Sadat, began, at first secretly and later with the tacit support of Nasser, to prepare for an eventual showdown with Israel. The hope was that a well-armoured Egyptian army could at least hold its own against the Israelis. If the battle ended in a draw, the military and the *Rais* (chief) could claim, at the very least, that Israel had not won. Curiously enough, Nasser's last battle was organized without his inspiration, although it had his full blessing.

Israel: The Defence Gap Crisis and the Modernization of the IDF

After 1956 the Israelis made considerable progress in military research and development, and achieved a degree of self-sufficiency, at least in small weapons. More importantly, after 1958, under Shimon Peres, Deputy Defence Minister from 1958 to 1965, the Ministry of Defence increased its efforts in the nuclear field. Its first success was the Dimona reactor and nuclear complex.

By 1966, we recall, Israel's state of economic crisis and psychological and political exhaustion was leading to a considerable 'brain drain'. In that year, a brutal struggle took place between David Ben Gurion and the leaders of Israel's ruling party, the Mapai. When it was over, Ben Gurion, the man who had founded the Mapai-Histadrut, who had ruled it since 1935, who had been Prime Minister and Defence Minister for all but two years from 1947 to 1963—Ben Gurion—was gone. In 1965 he had organized a faction of the Mapai into the Rafi party, taking with him his disciples, Moshe Dayan and Shimon Peres, and some of the younger retired officers and bureaucrats from both the Mapai and the Ministry of Defence. Rafi's aim was to put pressure on Prime Minister Levi Eshkol's government to pursue a policy of aggressive military procurement and modernization. This would call for rapid and large-scale research and development, new means of warfare and nuclear preparedness.

Borrowing a phrase from John F. Kennedy, Rafi accused the government of allowing a 'defence gap', citing especially Eshkol's 'failure' to develop an effective military and nuclear deterrent.

The government accepted Rafi's challenge. Under Chief of Staff Yitzchak Rabin, Zahal underwent a complete modernization and expansion. Its military doctrine was overhauled. From a collection of small units, predominantly infantry, whose chief tactic was the raid, it developed into an army geared for large-scale war. It spent much of its time in desert manoeuvres, training for swiftness and mobility. It became an army of steel, speed and firepower, with the emphasis on large divisions of armoured troops, paratroopers, and above all, air power. The government, in fact, worked as closely with the

IDF as had Ben Gurion. And because Eshkol was inexperienced in military strategy, General Rabin became surrogate Defence Minister.

Jordan: Between the Hammer and the Anvil

In 1923, Abdullah, second son of Sharif Hussein and brother of Faisal of Iraq, formed the Emirate of Trans-Jordan, in alliance with the British, from a geographic area known as Sharqi al-urdun (the lands east of the Jordan). Abdullah, a skilled politician, persuaded the British to carve the new country out of their Palestine Mandate as a base for the Hashemites whom France had driven from Syria. By the end of the first decade, Abdullah had gained full control through his able exploitation of Bedouin rivalries and with the aid of the Arab Legion. The Legion, now the Jordanian Army, was trained by the British; most of its officers were also British. It was then, as it is now, the most powerful group in Jordan after the royal family.

The notables, the second most powerful group, were a mixed bag. They included the Bedouin proper, the semi-nomadic peoples; natives of the cities east of the Trans-Jordan, now Jordan, families who had come chiefly from Palestine, and to a lesser extent, from Syria and the Hejaz; and finally, those thousands who had come to Trans-Jordan between 1921 and 1949, to run the administrative and economic life of the Emirate. Although Jordan's inhabitants are Sunni Moslems, two minority groups have been prominent among both the Hashemite military and the notables: the Circassians, who are Sunni Moslems originating in Caucasia, and the Christian natives of Trans-Jordan, who have migrated from Palestine.[6] Thus, the dynasty depends on conservative political, ethnic political and military forces.

The army became the Hashemites' praetorian guard. From a group of desert patrols it evolved into a small but capable elite corps which fought respectably in the 1948 Arab-Israeli War. Between 1948 and 1956, it further transformed itself into a national military establishment. It adopted universal conscription, established armoured and air units, and built up an engineering and technical services force.

The base of Hashemite power, the army, has also been a source of danger to it. In 1955, 1956 and 1959, three abortive coups were mounted by disgruntled Jordanian officers, each time with the support of Nasser. Nationalist feeling flared, and on March 3, 1956, the government expelled Britain's Glubb Pasha from Jordan. Three months later the remainder of the British officer corps left. New officers from among the young, educated, urban members of the army took over, but their attempt to replace the Circassian and Bedouin officers was unsuccessful, ending in an abortive coup in the same year. The coup, though brief, threatened the new King Hussein, Abdullah's grandson (1953); it took British support in 1956 and, later, the American intervention in Lebanon in 1958 to save him.

Pressures from the army on one hand were matched by pressures from another source. The most significant act in Jordanian history was Abdullah's formal annexation of western Palestine after the 1948 Arab–Israel War. Jordanian-occupied Palestine contained a population larger and more sophisticated than Abdullah's Bedouins. The Palestinian Arabs, better educated, more modern, more volatile, were responsible for Jordan's most turbulent years.

In 1956 and 1957, Hussein was forced to accept a leftist government headed by the Palestinian Arab Sulemann Nabulsi. The Palestinian Popular Front (PPF) was an anti-Hashemite, urban, radical regime with leanings toward the Syrian Ba'th. In spite of its strength, however, Hussein and the military succeeded in neutralizing the Front and in integrating many of the Palestinians into the administration. The notables, thanks to their resiliency, the support of the King, and the protection of a loyal army, managed to override both the nationalists and the Palestinians.

For some years, relations remained good between the regime and the political elites. In 1966, inspired by the Syrian cry for a popular war, the Palestinians began once again to pressure the monarchy. Forced to seek support from Nasser against Syrian–Palestinian radicalism, Hussein found himself, in the last days of May 1967, caught indeed between the hammer and the anvil.

These, then, were the belligerents, Syria, Israel, Egypt, and Jordan. But what of those less directly involved: the US, the UN, the USSR, and international community? The US, anxious to preserve the status quo, swinging from Arabism to globalism to pacification, totally mismanaged its role as conciliator.

The U.S.A.: Vacillation between Arabism and Globalism

Twenty-five years of American activity in the Middle East can be characterized by two opposing influences. The first was Arabism, a commitment to progressive Arab nationalism, which imposed a limit to progressive Arab commitment to the reactionary oil regimes in the hope of protecting the status quo. The second was globalism, the desire to safeguard the Middle East from Soviet aggression, as illustrated in America's active role in the creation of the Baghdad Pact and the CENTO Treaty.

American behaviour during May and June thus can only be described as a pendulum swing between the nineteenth century, represented by missionary Arabism, and the twentieth, represented by cold war globalism.

Arabism has governed America's attitudes in the Middle East for over a century, under the guidance, since 1900 particularly, of an integrated elite within the Near East Division of the State Department. From the start, the aims of the pro-Arabist elite reflected the backgrounds of its members. Its antecedents were a close-knit group of Protestant missionaries,[7] whose children were teachers and graduate scholars in Islamic language and culture from both the United States and the American University in Beirut. Today the State Department Arabists have political ties with the oil executives who, of course, support the Arab cause and its oil interests. There are others who, while not part of the missionary-teacher or oil networks, are nonetheless champions of the Arab cause. These are the career officers. Like most foreign service career officers, they have become attached to their clients and have undergone a pro-Arab conversion, some while studying in American Middle East institutes, where Arabism has always been the fashion.

The Arabist elite has determined American policy in the Middle East by virtue of its cohesion, the effectiveness of its network, and its intimate association with the architects of the cold war.

In general, the Arabists believe that American political, economic and Protestant religious interests in the Middle East will result in the 'Enlightenment of the Degenerate',[8] that is, the Christianization of pagans and Moslems. Trade and oil will, in short, bring the blessings of liberalism to the peoples of the Near East. Furthermore, a cautious and proper American attitude can assist the growth of democratic and 'reasonable' regimes, and an even-handed policy help to develop their political maturity.

The State Department Arabists hope that an Arab world, united under the banner of progressive nationalism, will bring about internal reform and produce a rational foreign policy among the independent states. Led by the 'enlightened, anti-communist' military, the new middle class will create favourable conditions (that is, maintain the status quo) for the exchange of those key trade items, missionary good will, democratic-liberal regimes, and oil. Freed from the yoke of colonialism (only the British, French and Soviets are colonialist, never the Americans) the sovereign Arab states will become pro-western and anti-communist. And as such, these progressive, independent and united Arabs will form a tier of states against communism in the Middle East.

It should surprise no one, then, that the Arabists in the State Department consider Israel a liability to America's real national interests in the Middle East.

The Global Orientation

The influence of globalism on the Middle East can be discerned in two separate periods: one from 1952 to 1961, the other from 1961 to 1967.

Between 1952 and 1961 Arabism and globalism were indistinguishable. To quote a former Ambassador to Egypt, John S. Badeau, an Arabist:

> Obviously their [the Arabs'] strategic location makes the communications facilities of the Middle East an international concern. With the Mediterranean Sea, the Red Sea,

> and the Persian Gulf penetrating the Eurasian land mass, the land, air, and sea routes linking the hemispheres cross here. The Middle East has thus long been the vestibule of East-West communication, particularly for any power having interests or bearing responsibilities in Asia and Africa.
>
> Of comparable importance is the interest in access to the petroleum supplies of the area. Middle Eastern petroleum is a principal source of power for the Western European economy . . . and a basic resource in global defence.[9]

This Wilsonian idealism and cold war pragmatism met under a single banner with a single purpose: to create an Arab world united against communism.

The second era began when John F. Kennedy became President. He was the first to distinguish between the cold war and narrower Arabist interests. The distinction could not become policy, however, as long as the Arabists continued to treat the two as one. Meanwhile, the Soviets were increasing their political intervention (in Egypt after 1955, in Syria after 1958, in Iraq after 1963). In addition, Soviet military aid was being used for political leverage in the radical Arab states. Both factors led to a re-examination of America's attitude toward the Middle East.

In response to the Soviet penetration of the Middle East, the Kennedy administration decided to make a radical change in its policy toward Israel. The US, Israel's banker and powerful moral ally, also became its chief source of arms. Because strategic supplies from France and Germany were not sufficient to counter the new Soviet equipment entering the area, the US now decided to supply Israel with America's most up-to-date aircraft. The decision was not taken lightly; the first Phantom jets equipped with electronic equipment arrived in Israel only *after* the Six Day War.

In 1965 Governor Averell Harriman, on a special mission to Israel, negotiated the first of these deliveries of strategic weapons, and a new era opened in American–Israeli relations. Yet overall policy in the Middle East was still dominated by the Department of State which, in turn, was dominated by its Arabists. In April and May of 1967, therefore, the US found itself torn by two contradictory attitudes, and this split decisively influenced its actions during those crucial months.

Crisis Mismanagement

This chapter must not be taken as an indictment of America's Middle East policy. In the end only the Arabs and the Israelis are responsible for their actions. Certain facts, however, must be noted. An impotent UN, dominated by forces hostile to one of its own charter members—Israel—could not have been expected to act differently in that angry month of May. Nor could one blame the Soviets for taking advantage of a situation they hoped would offer considerable political opportunity with minimal risk. The US was the only power with any chance of containing a Middle East crisis. And it might have succeeded had its goals been less ambiguous.

Unfortunately, in 1967 America was in no position to alter the pattern of a policy which it had followed since 1957. It failed to perceive the consequences of its neglect of the 1957 Sinai settlement; it failed to see that Egypt would make the most of that neglect.

Egypt's Sinai mobilization was based on the belief that the 1957 settlement could be undone by quick, shrewd and careful manoeuvres. How it managed this can be traced from day to day as the crisis grew. *Phase One* lasted from May 14 to May 22, when Egypt was examining the validity of the Sinai settlement. In *Phase Two* (May 22 to 28) Egypt realized that a show of political determination, which would be followed by international panic, would effectively nullify the Sinai settlement. During *Phase Three*, from May 28 to June 5, Israel awoke to the fact that the settlement was being abandoned. During *Phase Four* (June 5 to 6) the US tried to rescue parts of the settlement. It hoped to persuade Israel to make some compromise and thus avoid an international incident. It failed, not least because it missed a vital fact: Israel was being victimized by Egypt.

Instead of rehearsing the events of May and June 1967, we will analyze each phase of the escalation in terms of its setting, and of the perceptions (or misperceptions) of the actors during the crisis.

Egyptian Mobilization and UNEF Withdrawal

The crisis opened on May 14. On that day, Field Marshal Amer issued Battle order No. 1 (secret at the time)*, calling for mobilization in reaction to Israel's air strike against Syria. On May 17, the Chief of Staff, General Fawzi, demanded the evacuation of the UNEF troops concentrated along Egypt's eastern borders, and the crisis became international. The dealings a decade before, between Dag Hammarskjold and Nasser, had made one thing clear. Between November 1956 and February 1957, Egypt had agreed to permit the UNEF on its borders only reluctantly, had avoided publicizing the arrangement, and was ready to abandon the UNEF whenever it would contravene Egyptian national interests. Hammarskjold's purpose had been to solve problems on a practical level without raising questions of principle on which it would be impossible to obtain general agreement.[10] By evading such thorny matters, the UN left Egypt free to interpret 'principle' as it wished.

Nasser's removal of the UNEF was a political act, not a military one. I tend to accept the arguments of Anthony Nutting, a British Arabist and a former Minister of State for Foreign Affairs in the British Foreign Office, who is also an apologist for Nasser, and those of Robert Stephens, a Nasser sympathizer who was foreign editor of the London *Observer* and a responsible correspondent.[11] Stephens points out that Nasser did not request the dismissal of *all* the UNEF forces. He did not remove those in Gaza or Sharm al-Sheik. He did not request removal of those in the Gulf; the closing of the Gulf would have constituted a *casus belli* for Israel, as indeed it did later. Nasser removed only those forces in Sinai, in order to give Egypt the chance to re-negotiate the settlement, or at least to compromise the arrangements to its own advantage.

Secretary-General U Thant has been criticized on the one hand by the Americans for 'succumbing' to Nasser, and on the other by the Israelis for being 'pro-Arab'. Neither charge is wholly accurate, even though it is true that U Thant's

*S. Shamir, 'The Middle East Crisis: On the Brink of War', *Middle East Record 1967*, Vol. 3, Israel Universities Press, 1971, p. 185.

clientele were the Afro-Asians, who supported Egypt. The fact is, the 1957 settlement was so fragile that Nasser could safely predict a UN surrender. He knew the UNEF was powerless; the speed with which U Thant dismantled it proved him right. Secretary of State Dulles had at first seemed enthusiastic over the concept of an Emergency Force. As Urquhart (Hammarskjold's biographer) notes, the 'UNEF was an important innovation in the technique of crisis management by the United Nations'. Once the US cooled to the idea, however, the UNEF was at the mercy of Nasser and the General Assembly. Its termination removed the last barrier between Egypt and Israel.

Washington: An Ambiguous Reaction

American diplomats did not react to the crisis admirably. They should have moved with vigour, and forced Nasser to revoke his orders on the basis of the Hammarskjold-Dulles-Eban aide-memoire. But they hesitated. A task force headed by Eugene W. Rostow, Under Secretary of State for Political Affairs, substituted for diplomacy a semi-military solution designed to salve, not solve, the problem. Instead of pressuring Egypt to return to the status quo ante, they made empty promises to Israel. An 'armada', they said, a 'flotilla' of the maritime nations would at once be sent to safeguard the Straits of Tiran.[12]

By the end of May, the US had lost its credibility in Tel Aviv, particularly among the army and the Intelligence community. Ever since 1961, Israel had hoped that globalism would replace Arabism in American policy. The 'armada' killed that hope. To Tel Aviv, it was yet another in the long chain of paper promises and hollow guarantees emanating from Washington. The American initiative was lost, and misunderstandings between America and Israel increased.

The reaction in Cairo was quite different. Nasser capitalized on America's indecisiveness; he never took the 'armada' seriously. He interpreted America's failure to rescue the UNEF as a cautious political move stopping very far short of war. The suggestion by the US and Britain on May 24 that the UNEF be stationed on both sides of the Israeli-Egyptian

frontier was regarded by Nasser as a Western accommodation, a step toward rescinding the Sinai settlement.

His next logical step was Phase Two: close the Gulf, abolish the settlement completely, and so achieve his political goal. By May 27 Nasser moved to clinch the diplomatic demarche by accepting new American initiatives. For a vigorous, two-pronged American diplomatic effort had at last begun. But it was aimed at coming to terms with Cairo.

The new effort was carried out by an experienced diplomat and Arabist, Charles Yost, who was sent to Cairo on May 28[13] by Johnson to achieve two things. He was to find out whether 'the Israeli tiger [was] unleashed'. He was also to persuade Nasser to open the Gulf and lift the blockade.[14] Nutting, who is not a reliable source on the whole, claims the Egyptians rejected Johnson's suggestion to 'simply cancel the blockade and allow the UNEF to return to all their former positions', [15] and that Yost and Mahmoud Riad, Egypt's Foreign Minister, asked themselves instead 'how the operation of the blockade could be modified to enable both sides to *live* (italics mine) with it.'[16] Riad suggested that the 'American Battle Act', once used in China, should now be applied to Israel—that is, that Israel be permitted to move only non-strategic goods through the Gulf.[17]

According to Nutting, Yost left Cairo after two full days of discussion. It was agreed that Nasser's deputy, Zakariyyah Muhiyaddin, would go to Washington on June 2[18] to negotiate ways to lift the blockade. (Nutting fails to mention that Vice President Humphrey would be going, too.) According to Stephens, to my mind a more reliable source, Nasser informed Johnson on June 2 that he would be sending Muhiyaddin to Washington, but did not specify a date.[19]

Tel Aviv: Escalation and the IDF

During Phase One, Israeli leaders adopted a wait-and-see attitude. While Eshkol assured the Cabinet of the importance of the American Sixth Fleet as a deterrent, the military began its preparations, accelerating its mobilization, concentration and deployment of forces. Political controversy, cabinet tension, and public pressure all mounted during the Eban missions to France and England which failed (see below), and the reluctance to help of these two countries, together with American procrastination, were interpreted by Israel as an accommodation to Nasser.

Two incidents finally convinced Israel that it should take fate into its own hands. The first was a vague statement by President Johnson on May 23 concerning the 'independence and territorial integrity of all nations in the area'. The second was his warning to Moscow that same day to stay out. Both were interpreted by Israel as an effort by America to extricate itself from the 1957 settlement and from its commitments to Israel. Furthermore, the Intelligence experts, led by Chief of Intelligence, Meir Amit, who had just returned from his fact-finding mission to the Defence Department, the CIA and the Pentagon, argued that the US would take no serious military steps and that the diplomacy of the 'armada' was designed to restrain, not Egypt, but Israel itself.

The bitter controversy between members of the Cabinet, and more so within the High Command, raged over the interpretation of Egyptian motives, American commitments and the credibility of West European intervention on behalf of Israel with Nasser.

On May 22, in a speech on the Sinai front, President Nasser ordered the closure of the Gulf of Aqaba to ships bearing Israeli flags and those carrying strategic material to Israel. Prime Minister Eshkol, on the same day, reiterated in an address to Israeli Knesset that interference with Israeli ships violated the Meir statement of March 1, 1957 to the General Assembly, and entitled Israel to exercise its right of self defence under Article 51 of the UN Charter, while President Johnson stated on May 23 that his government regarded the Gulf of Aqaba as an international waterway and that a blockade of Israeli shipping in the Gulf was 'illegal and potentially dangerous to peace'. The Cabinet, and more particularly the High Command, doubted a firm American stand behind the utterance of this principle.

As soon as Nasser announced the closure of the Straits of Tiran Prime Minister Eshkol moved into a high gear of diplomatic action. Stating that Nasser had committed 'an act of aggression against Israel', he sent Foreign Minister

Eban to Paris, London and Washington. On May 24, Eban met General de Gaulle, who warned Israel not to start a shooting war. In the afternoon, he met Prime Minister Wilson of Great Britain who assured Eban that Britain would co-operate with the US in promoting international action to uphold the right of free passage in the Gulf of Aqaba. On May 25, Eban conferred with both Rusk and McNamara and met the President only the next day—May 26—seeking assurances for the fulfilment of the American commitment made in the aide-memoire of February 11, 1957.

Eban was armed with all the 1957 documents when he met President Johnson and the State Department officials. In fact, President Johnson, unaware of the 1957 aide-memoire, called for the State Department, who did not possess a copy of it. A call was made to Princeton and the document was found in the Dulles' papers. Thus, the full document was only published as an appendix to President Eisenhower's *Waging the Peace*, mentioned earlier. Johnson reiterated to Eban his opposition to the Egyptian blockade and said that the US was considering an Anglo-American 'flotilla' to demonstrate free passage through the Straits. The Eban mission became part of the cabinet-military controversy. The Israeli political and military leaders felt that the blockade was not as dangerous to Israeli's security as the continued Egyptian troop deployment in the Sinai. Eban had failed to convey the nature of this threat to Israel to the international community, the High Command felt, and instead had dwelt excessively on the blockade issue rather than on Egyptian preparation for war in Sinai. Instead of mobilizing support for Israel, the mission revealed Israel's lack of determination, thus inviting diplomatic international pressure, de Gaulle style. The mission was ill-conceived and faultily executed, Evan's critics maintained. Eban's defenders, however, insisted that the Eban mission fulfilled an important Israeli purpose—to exert strong American and international support for free passage, and above all, to demonstrate that Israel had exhausted all possible diplomatic means to avert war, thus enabling Israel later to capitalize on the IDF's victory.

The Israeli attitude during Phase Three is best summarized by Stephens. 'Given the way American and British policy seemed to be drifting, the neutral attitude of France, and the hostility of Russia, a negotiation with Nasser would doubtless have seemed to the Israeli leaders bound to end in a political defeat for them.' Now the debate, conducted in both the military and in the cabinet, turned to the reaction of the USSR and the line the United States would take if the Arabs were defeated. These were the unknowns, the unpredictable factors, and they created havoc among Israel's political leaders. The public panicked, and the cabinet deliberations grew fuzzy and complex. But there was no such confusion among the High Command. While they disagreed on many aspects of the operation, they were unanimous on one point: there would be a military confrontation, and it would end in the total defeat of the Arabs.[20]

The thinking of the IDF High Command, and the workings of the IDF system, are of great significance here. General Rabin, as Chief of Staff, had been de facto defence Minister in Eshkol's cabinet, which, with the assistance of the military leaders, had determined Israel's strategy before 1967. After Ben Gurion's retirement, the IDF, with no objection from Eshkol, took over the sole conduct of military strategy[21], even if the decision to resort to the use of force was a Cabinet prerogative. The role played by Chief of Staff Rabin and his colleagues, in the absence of a decisive and commanding Ben Gurion, was crucial in 1967. Further, the character of the military mobilization of May 1967 clearly predicted Israel's military behaviour. These insights into Israel's political and defence system eluded American diplomats, who managed to ignore the dynamics of civil–military relations in Israel. Their oversight, I submit, was the achievement of the State Department's Arabists, whose traditional anti-Zionism is modified only slightly by political pressures from America's Jews.

'Even-handedness' kept American policy-makers from looking too closely at Israeli military or political behaviour—except of course for its consequences. The Intelligence and military communities, however, were fairly up-to-date on Israel's military stance, and for this reason achieved greater influence in the last days of May. These groups are said to have given the President a reasonable assessment of Israel's military strength, actions and options.

The IDF's High Command had studied Nasser's military moves carefully during Phase One (May 14 to May 22). Egypt, they thought, had no more than three defensive divisions in the Sinai. As the generals debated on when to move against Egypt, Israel's military planning proceeded ahead of political developments. The High Command had little faith in Eban's chances of diplomatic success, or for that matter, in the possibility of America's intervening on behalf of Israel. General Dayan, then outside the senior military and political councils, was already arguing on May 18 that war with Egypt was inevitable. Until May 30, the High Command still considered Egypt's now seven Sinai divisions as defensive. Altogether there is no doubt that the IDF was poised for war by the end of May. On June 2, under pressure from both public opinion and the opposition parties, a coalition government was established and General Moshe Dayan was appointed Defence Minister. The political leadership now joined the IDF in its determination to go to war. They accepted the IDF strategy, which was to pre-empt and destroy Egyptian forces in Sinai before they could switch to the offensive. For both the High Command and the political leadership, victory was to be achieved by frustrating Arab strategy, with as little loss of Israeli life as possible.

Once mobilized and ready for offensive action, the IDF could begin its strategy of pre-emption. On May 28, with the seven Egyptian divisions still in Sinai, Israel decided to move a large army to the border, to be ready in case no satisfactory political settlement was achieved. Israel was not prepared to accept the Egyptian challenge, either psychologically or economically, and an Egyptian entrenchment in Sinai would have entailed a far greater loss of Israeli lives in the long run. These factors were ignored (were, in fact, not even perceived) by American diplomats, or by the task force at the State Department. Yost's mission to Egypt was, in effect, a post-mortem diplomatic move. Once Israel came close to total mobilization, the die was cast. The army had to be ready to move swiftly and effectively against Arab forces before the UN, America, or the international community could come to Egypt's political defence or revivify the dead letter of 1957.

Israel's military strategy, wrote Moshe Dayan in his diary of Sinai (1959), was dictated by its political isolation and the narrowness of the area it had to defend. It could only win by striking into enemy territory, and those strikes had to be lightning fast. Israel had to demoralize Egypt's cumbersome military forces, disperse them, and conquer enemy territory before external political forces could intervene. In 1967 Israel acted to correct its failure of 1957. Its military leadership and its political elite were not about to repeat the mistakes of the previous decade.

NOTES

1. *Middle East Record.* Vol Three (1967), p. 159.
2. For the most informative analysis of the 1962 army crises, see Robert Stephens, *Nasser* (New York: Simon Schuster, 1971), pp. 358-362. For a full analysis of the army-ASU conflict, see Amos Perlmutter, *Egypt, the Praetorian State* (Brunswick, N.J., Transaction, 1974), pp. 167-199.
3. Stephens, *Nasser*. p. 359.
4. *Ibid., p. 360:* Perlmutter, *Egypt, the Praetorian State*, Chapter 6, pp. 175-188.
5. Stephens, *Nasser*. p. 361.
6. See Uriel Dann, 'Regime and Public in Jordan since 1949,' unpublished paper, Van Leer Foundations, Jerusalem, Israel, February, 1971.
7. Missionaries could be found on the frontier of US cultural internationalism, in the Turkish Empire, for about a century before Wilson became President. They have always operated much as the American missionaries did in China, who identified Protestant morality, politics, and purpose, with American foreign policy.
8. For the extraordinary role played by missionaries in the Near East, see Joseph L. Grabill, *Protestant Diplomacy and the Near East* (Minneapolis, University of Minnesota, 1971); Clifton J. Phillips, *Protestant America and the Pagan World* (Harvard, East Asia Ms., 1958); John De Novo, *American Interest and Policies in the Middle East*, 1900-1939 (Minneapolis, University of Minnesota Press, 1970).
9. John S. Badeau, *The American Approach to the Arab World* (New York, Harper and Row, 1968), p. 21.
10. See Brian Urquhart, *Hammarskjold* (New York, Knopf, 1972), pp. 195-230.
11. Stephens, *Nasser*. p. 485.
12. Two years of research and interviews with key Johnson officials and with a member of the 'task force' have convinced me that the 'armada' had no basis in reality. It was a futile and dishonest idea, to be used as dust thrown into Israeli eyes by bewildered and tired officials of NSC and the State Department.

13. I rely here on interviews mentioned earlier and on both Nutting's and Stephens' accounts of the role of Ambassador Yost in Cairo, May 30–June 3.
14. Nutting, *Nasser*, p. 413.
15. There is no evidence that the demand was ever made by Johnson, either in writing or through channels. Nor was any such demand corroborated by my numerous interviews with key US officials at the time.
16. Nutting, *Nasser*. p. 412. (Emphasis added)
17. *Ibid.*
18. *Ibid.*
19. Stephens, *Nasser*, p. 490.
20. *Ibid.*, p. 489.
21. Based on interviews with five of the eighteen members of the IDF's High Command during the Six Day War: Generals Weizmann, Sharon, Hod, Yariv, and Chief of Staff Rabin. This was also the view taken by Generals Peled and Gavish, and of several colonels who were interviewed.
22. See Amos Perlmutter, 'The Institutionalization of Civil Military Relations in Israel', *Middle East Journal*, Vol 19, no. 2 (1968), pp. 434-60.

CHAPTER III

The War of Attrition and the Ceasefire

The divisions were deep and the debate was rending. But once the decision was made to go to war, Israel found itself ready for one of the most decisive military victories in modern times. The diplomatic manoeuvring had taken three weeks, and those three weeks had given the army strategic advantages. They had also demonstrated the excellent staff work of the Eshkol-Rabin team. The mobilization was complete by the end of May. The army was ready on all fronts. Above all, the air force, magnificently trained under General Ezer Weizmann, was set to launch one of the most brilliant pre-emptive strikes in modern military history.

By the end of May, the High Command was impatient to spring its surprise. It was ready for a blitz, and a blitz it delivered. In three hours, the Arab air forces were destroyed on the ground. In two days the Egyptian front was broken, its army nearly annihilated, and the remnants struggled in confusion to cross the canal in their retreat to Egypt. The Jordanian army was broken. By the fourth day, although Dayan hesitated for fear of Soviet intervention, the IDF went on to storm the heights of the Golan and defeat the Syrian army, most of whom retreated into Damascus.

The IDF now dominated the Golan Heights, the Jordan River, and the Suez Canal, which was to remain inoperative for the next eight years. The Nasser regime almost collapsed; Hussein had lost over two-thirds of his territory; Syria was driven back. The blitz was complete. But the military victory was no greater than the political and psychological shock to the Arab world. On June 10, 1967, Israel could have marched into all three Arab capitals, Cairo, Damascus and Amman, with little or no resistance.

The aftermath of the Six Day War, however, showed that

defeat had not altered the Egyptian outlook. Egypt believed then, and believes now, that what has been lost by war and violence can be regained by international extortion, diplomacy, and pressure on Israel.

Egypt now entered upon a phased escalation and attrition which was analyzed by General Taha al-Magdub, head of Zionist and Palestinian Studies in the Presidential Office (that is to say, Nasser's Cabinet). Egypt was to chart a strategy of attrition that would end in brinkmanship, a phase that would tip over into war. The first stage of escalation was political–diplomatic. The second used violence to escalate the arms race and overcome Israel's superiority in military hardware. Both steps were designed to force the enemy to retreat. Escalation, as Egypt planned it, was composed of three elements: the 'struggle of the will', a cold war to mobilize resources and build the strength needed for resistance; the 'war of attrition', which included political, economic, military and propaganda activities to weaken the material and psychological power of the enemy; and finally, brinkmanship.[1]

Speaking on Cairo radio on November 23, 1967, Nasser gave a preview of the Egyptian strategy: 'We shall choose the opportune moment. First and foremost we need time to complete our military preparations so that when a time of operation comes, we shall not be on the defensive . . . we shall attack to cleanse our land which the enemy is occupying.' The overall aim was for hostilities to be resumed against Israel and the status quo ante 1967 restored.[2]

It is not surprising, then, that Nasser officially declared a War of Attrition against Israel. It was the kind of offensive that suited the Arabs best. A 'War of Attrition' means exactly what it says: to weaken and exhaust the enemy by constant harrassment.

The strategic concept is simple, based as it is on the facts of life in the Middle East. In principle, it states that time is on the side of those countries with the resources of energy and manpower; when united, they will create a formidable block. Essentially, it is a war of the many against the few, of quantity versus quality. It is a war of those states which have plenty of manpower and which regard life as cheap, against states in which every person counts. It is a war between those leaders who consider the lives of their peasants expendable against those who have no souls to spare in the drive to fulfil their nation's dreams.

The Khartoum Conference

The War of Attrition was adopted as Arab policy shortly after June 10, 1967. Between August 29 and September 1, the Arab nations met at Khartoum, Egypt, in an extraordinary summit conference. They enunciated Arab aspirations clearly. There was to be no peace with Israel. There were to be no negotiations with Israel, no recognition of Israel, and no free navigation for Israeli fleets. The conference agenda called for the discussion of three points: increasing efforts 'to eradicate the traces of aggression' of 1967; examination of the 'possibility of a new war in the near future'; and the drafting of 'a comprehensive, long-term plan for the realization of Arab aims by military, economic, and political means'. These were the political and strategic aims. 'Eradication of the traces of aggression' was a euphemism for the military preparedness required to carry them out.

In retrospect, the Khartoum Conference appeared to have drawn up the following plan of action:

(1) The Arabs were to exploit the political and military aspirations of the Great Powers in the Middle East.

(2) They were to maintain a permanent stage of belligerency through joint Arab action.

(3) They were to build and train a new Egyptian-Syrian military machine with the advice, assistance and support of the USSR.

(4) They were to raise fears in the United States and throughout Western Europe that the Middle East was becoming an international powder keg.

(5) They were to encourage, support and provide sanctuary for the Palestinian guerrillas.

(6) They were to put the onus of responsibility for belligerency on Israel, through an international propaganda campaign.

(7) They were, finally to persuade the liberal public opinion of the West, and the regimes of the Third World, that Israel was an imperialistic, aggressive and ruthless colonial power.

The Arabs made a token search for a political solution. But it was never more than that: a tactical ploy that gave them time to rebuild their armies. Until they were ready for regular military action, they relied on Palestinian irregulars. The resolutions of the Khartoum Conference proclaimed that 'the conference has affirmed the unity of Arab ranks, the unity of joint action, and the need for co-ordination and elimination of all differences.' The conferees agreed on 'a need to consolidate their efforts and eliminate the effects of aggression on the basis that the occupied lands are Arab lands and that the burden of regaining these lands falls on all the Arab states.' * In effect, the Arab heads of state agreed to unite their political efforts at the international and diplomatic level. But their expectation, their ultimate intention, was war.

The Security Council Resolution

On November 22, 1967, Resolution 242 of the Security Council of the UN became the international formula for disentangling Arab-Israeli hostilities. And it happened not because Israel welcomed the paper, or because Egyptian hearts were in it, but because the great powers, chiefly the Soviet Union and the US, adopted it as their programme for peace. The Resolution was a British proposal amended by India, Canada, Denmark, and a number of Latin-American countries. Its major clause read:

> The Security Council affirms that the fulfilment of Charter principles requires the establishment of a just and lasting peace in the Middle East which should include the application of both the following principles:
> (i) Withdrawal of Israeli armed forces from territories occupied in the recent conflict.
> (ii) Termination of all claims or states of belligerency and respect for and acknowledgement of the sovereignty, territorial integrity, and political independence of every state in the area and their right to live in peace with secure and recognized boundaries free from threats or acts of force;[3]

*Resolution quoted in the *Middle East Record 1967, Ibid*, p. 264.

The Resolution requested the Secretary-General to send a special representative to the Middle East, to establish and maintain contact with the states concerned, promote agreement, and assist efforts to achieve a settlement in accordance with the provisions of the Resolution. The mandate was given to Gunnar Jarring, then Swedish Ambassador to Moscow. The Jarring mission was doomed to failure from its inception. It was doomed because Egypt and Israel differed in their interpretations of the Resolution.

To Egypt, Resolution 242 required the withdrawal of all Israeli armed forces from all the occupied territories as the pre-condition for negotiation. Israel interpreted the second part of the Resolution as a recognition of its right to exist within 'secure and recognized boundaries free from threats or acts of force', and saw this as a pre-condition to any Israeli withdrawal.

The Arabs, though bound by the Khartoum Conference not to stop short of war, preferred to obtain their objectives until ready for war again through a political solution, if possible. To the Israelis, however, the four 'No's' of Khartoum precluded any serious discussion of troop withdrawals. For a time, Israel refused to accept the UN representative and demanded negotiations with the Arabs; only direct negotiations, they felt, could overcome the Khartoum diktat.

Earlier, on August 14, Israel had made it clear that it considered the Armistice Agreements of 1949 to be void. New borders, it said, would have to emerge through negotiation with the Arabs. Despite differences as to what those borders should be, responsible Israelis were united in their determination not to withdraw without acceptable guarantees of 'secure and recognized boundaries'.

For Israel no question arose as to what should be done with Jerusalem. Jerusalem was unique, and to protect its historic identity, Israel annexed it. Toward the occupied territories, Defence Minister Dayan adopted a policy of non-interference. Israel recognized the status quo in Jordan, but specifically discouraged independent political activity. At the same time, it proclaimed an 'open bridges' policy over the Jordan River. Arabs in the occupied territories were to have a right to move freely into other Arab countries, bound, however, by strict security measures.

What was to be done with the occupied territories? Public opinion in Israel has run the gamut of ideas. Throughout 1969 and 1970, a variety of 'Palestinian' entities was proposed by government ministers, as well as by the public at large. In the end, though, Dayan's policy prevailed. The West Bank was to be semi-autonomous, and yet politically dependent on Israel. It would maintain its economic ties with Jordan, and would be required to establish economic relations with Israel as well.

Dayan's position on the Suez Canal was simple: both Israel and Egypt were to use it, or neither country would. Sinai, the historic battleground, could be returned only on the condition that it be demilitarized.

The War of Attrition, Phase I: August 1967 to August 1970

It began with skirmishes over the Suez Canal as early as August 1967, and culminated in a mini-war between November, 1968 and August 1970. From the cease-fire violation in August 1967 until December, 1968, Egypt's major effort was simply to cross the Canal. And it was this effort that gave the Soviets their excuse for greater involvement in the Middle East. By May, 1970, after Nasser had failed several times to cross the Canal, and after the Israelis had successfully raided Egypt's Western desert, the Soviets, by Egyptian invitation, became deeply involved with Egypt.

Soviet intervention took three forms.

First came indirect intervention. The USSR supplied logistical aid, airlifts, and strategic weapons to the Egyptian Army, which adopted Soviet military theory under the guidance of Soviet instructors. The number of Russian instructors in Egypt reached 5,000 by the middle of May, 1970.[4]

The Soviets next progressed to direct military involvement. They provided Egypt with the latest interceptors, as part of an anti-aircraft missile defence system. It was the most expensive system available, and it gave the Egyptians 130 Sam sites, as well as Sam II and Sam III launchers manned and protected by Russian troops.[5] During this period Egypt also acquired over 500 combat aircraft, among them 200 MIG's, and over 2,000 tanks, as well as 100 T-62 Snapper and Frog anti-tank missiles. To deliver all this hardware, the Soviets set up steady airlift operations and a supply system.

By the end of 1970, the USSR was to make its third contribution; an autonomous air system. For six months, from February to August, 1970, Israeli planes had bombarded Egypt's side of the Suez, in response to Egyptian artillery shelling of the Israeli side. As the Israeli pilots penetrated Egypt, threatening Cairo, Alexandria, and Aswan, the Soviets became directly involved for the first time. Ten squadrons of MIG-21 fighters, manned by Soviet pilots, began flying as part of the Egyptian air defence screen.[6]

Early in August 1970, Defence Minister Dayan openly accepted the Soviet challenge: 'Let's hope the Soviets do not intend to do what they have in mind, and let's hope the Americans will not do what they have in mind, and let us not believe that the Arabs will receive what they do not want.'[7]

Dayan announced that the IDF would fight any military force, regardless of its tag or identifications, to protect Israel's front line on the Canal. Furthermore, 'We shall not allow the establishment of a Soviet missile defence system within fifty kilometres of the Canal.'[8] Dayan made it clear that Soviet pilots who flew for Egypt would confront Israeli pilots.

General Chaim Bar-Lev, now Chief of Staff replacing General Rabin, said: 'The road deep into Egypt is open to our air force.' Later: 'Israeli deeds and American deeds and misdeeds could restrain or encourage Soviet intervention.' And: 'We shall fight against *all* enemies.'[9]

By early August, 1970, Egypt had lost over 5,000 men, and its civilians had been severely harassed by Israeli air raids. But the strains on Israel were greater. After sixteen months of particularly heavy fighting, 513 Israelis had died in the mini-war with Egypt, Syria and the guerrillas, and over 700 had been wounded. Israel had lost the equivalent of 60 per cent of its total losses during the Six Day War, a significant proportion, if one considers the loss of 850 men in 1967.

In addition, the Soviets were now involved, though in a limited way, and the Israeli military and cabinet were engaged in a serious debate over the wisdom of the deep-penetration raids into Egypt. Economically, the country was under severe strain: its sophisticated aircraft and electronic systems were causing a phenomenal drain on the military budget.

On August 7, the Americans moved in and successfully negotiated a ceasefire between Israel and Egypt. All in all, while the Egyptians had managed to create the powder-keg atmosphere they sought, the War of Attrition was in fact won by neither side.

The Bar-Lev Line

Israel, during this period, was undergoing a spell of military soul-searching. The skirmishes over the Canal, the forays into the Nile Valley, and the army's positions on the Canal's East Bank called for a re-thinking of strategy for the first time since the 1967 War. The new approach was to propel the Army into a semi-defensive posture along a line of fortifications known as the Bar-Lev Line, after its originator, Chief of Staff Bar-Lev.

General Avraham Adan (Bren) had been appointed to head an inter-service task force to create a new defence system in Sinai, based on a fortification line along the East Bank of the Canal.

General Adan's first recommendation was to establish a forward alert warning system—a position defence system —ten kilometres from the Canal, buttressed by small observation points on the Canal itself. He was opposed by two powerful senior officers, General Israel Tal (then attached to the Ministry of Defence) and General Ariel (Arik) Sharon (then Chief of Military Training). The plan, they argued, failed to provide the flexibility the army needed i.e. mobile defence. Instead, Tal-Sharon proposed to keep the observation points on the Canal, maintain armed divisions as roving forces around the Canal, and add armoured forces to patrol directly on the Canal. Rather than a defensive system of large-scale fortifications, they preferred a flexible and open posture.

General Adan clearly argued that the plan (hence the Bar-Lev Line) was both a political and strategic concept. Politically the IDF had to make sure that the Egyptians would not be able to cross the canal with a considerable force. There were at least two options, Adan suggested. One position was defensive i.e. fortified observation points separated about ten kilometres from each other. Ten kilometres behind these fortified observation points a military road designed for tank warfare would be established so that Egyptian penetration squads could be annihilated once they managed to penetrate space between the observation points. A special electronic detection system was also to be erected beyond the tank road patrolled by IDF armour. Ambush groups would be set on the hills some twenty kilometres from the canal so that no serious Egyptian force could hope to penetrate.* Sharon-Tal's argument was that the Adan plan was expensive in men and resources. The former suggested leaving the Canal open, so that Egyptian troops could cross the Canal where the IDF forces would annihilate the penetration forces.** Adan replied, 'So what? If the Egyptian army decides to stay a few kilometres behind the Canal, would it be an Egyptian political victory or an Egyptian strategic advantage?' The Sharon reply was that Israeli penetration into the Egyptian side would be made tactically possible and static observation posts would make excellent Egyptian targets. Sharon dismissed Adan's claim that the Egyptian forces could really establish themselves in Sinai once they had crossed the Canal. 'We would have made mince meat of the latter' was his reply to Adan's challenge.

Chief of Staff Bar-Lev decided in favour of a fortified line around the Canal. Adan was appointed to oversee the fortifications. The work was ready by the time Nasser chose to open another round in the War of Attrition in March 1969. Between then and August 1970, the Bar-Lev line withstood both artillery barrages and Egyptian commando raids. and no Egyptian flag rose on the east bank of Suez.[10]

After the August 7 ceasefire, the IDF started a crash programme, not only to rehabilitate the war-torn Bar-Lev line, but to bolster the strategy which underlay the concept of fortification. The programme was supported by Dayan and

*Interview with General Adan in Washington, May 1976.

**Several interviews with General Sharon in Tel-Aviv, 1973, 1974, 1975 and 1976.

Bar-Lev; once again, fortification per se was opposed by Israel Tal, now Deputy Chief of Staff, and Ariel Sharon, newly appointed commander of the Southern Eygptian Front.

A compromise was finally arranged. General Bar-Lev stepped down in 1971 and General David Elazar took over as Chief of Staff, and it was decided that the line would serve two purposes: one as a warning system, the other as a defensive line. Israel's stance was clear. To counter the War of Attrition, it was committed to its defensive lines, it would insist upon territorial integrity, but would avoid extra-territorial conquest.

By the end of its first phase (the cease-fire of August 7), the War of Attrition had forced Israel into a relatively static posture, thereby completely changing the strategy of the IDF. Israel was plunged into a ferocious debate, not in the defence establishment, but in the pages of the dailies, *Ma'ariv* and *Haaretz*. Ex-generals, professors, intellectuals, and journalists all tore into the country's handling of the War of Attrition. The fiercest debate raged, naturally, around the plans adopted to counter it. Bar-Lev was the chief spokesman for government policy. 'We had the courage,' he said, 'to advance the peace and Israeli security [in the War of Attrition] and we did not expand the territory of the State [beyond the 1967 lines] nor did we succumb to dreams about secure borders.'[1]

Dayan added that Israeli policy was necessarily defensive. 'From a strategic point of view we are fighting a defensive war—we are permanently deployed in lines [Bar-Lev]; we fortify and strengthen our lines. But to change policy . . ., that is, not accept the lines [ceasefire borders] as permanent but by-pass them, for new targets, moving on to Cairo, Damascus, Amman, or southern Lebanon—the answer is *no*.'[12]

Ezer Weizmann and Matitiyahu (Mati) Peled, two retired 1967 generals, disagreed, but for different reasons. They both believed that Israel had lost the War of Attrition. They both opposed any dependence on permanent lines; like Sharon and Tal, they opposed the creation of the Bar-Lev line. They advocated dynamic defence and a firm grip on the offensive. But while Weizmann advocated crossing the ceasefire lines of 1967, Peled wanted Israel to give up most of the territories.

They differed, too, in their suggestions for preserving the army's integrity, mobility, and effective lines of supply, and in their reasons for opposing static warfare and the sort of Maginot Line mentality that accompanies it.[13]

The clearest defence of Israel's response to the War of Attrition came, again, from Defence Minister Dayan: 'The question, if a new war erupts, is whether it will be an Israeli preventive war. The answer is no. We have no intention of opening a preventive war and we are not operating on such assumptions. We do not [intend] to declare a widening of the war, nor are we responsible for its escalation . . . we shall do our best to restrain the enemy and forestall him from organizing for a new one . . . we are not planning on fulfilling a policy of preventive war.'[14]

The War of Attrition, Phase II: The Standstill That Would Not Stand Still. 1970-1972

The War of Attrition ended officially on August 8. In the small hours of the night before, Prime Minister Golda Meir had announced Israel's consent to the American proposal for a standstill on the Suez front. No one in Israel, no one in Egypt believed that either country had lowered its sights, or that diplomacy or politics could modify the rigid stance each had adopted. The ceasefire for the belligerents was simply a respite. Both were tired of war.

Muhammad Hasanyan Haykal, chief editor of the regime-dominated paper, *Al-Ahram*, explained his country's reasons for accepting the standstill. The Israeli enemy, wrote Haykal, had become demoralized, and was labouring under a heavy psychological burden. Israel had awakened to the futility of the 1967 victory. Now, in August 1970, it found itself in a political quandary, just as it had in May 1967. The state was on the verge of a coup d'etat. Since Dayan, Peres, and Begin, the militant Zionists, had entered the government of June 2, 1967, Israel had followed a militant and even fanatical course—bombing Egypt, raiding the Western desert, fighting frantically over the Canal. Israel was doing all it could to convince the US that it was the only power in the area upon which America could depend. The USSR was unable to play a decisive role in the political and military struggle. And Washington had finally come to realize that the Middle East was a powder-keg that could bring about a great-power confrontation.

Thus, wrote Haykal, on May 1, 1970 President Nasser had appealed to President Nixon, requesting that Israel withdraw from the occupied territories and that the US halt its military aid to Israel. The American response had come in the form of an 'American initiative', a letter from Secretary of State William P. Rogers to Foreign Minister Mahmoud Riad. The note requested the political resurrection of UN Resolution 242, and suggested that Ambassador Jarring help in implementing it. Egypt had accepted the request, convinced that it would help split the militant coalition which included Israel's Rafi and *Gahal* parties. And Egyptian forecasts had proved correct. Menachem Begin, and the militants of the *Gahal*, the hard-line party opposed to withdrawal, had resigned from the National Unity government.

'Do I, Haykal, believe that the standstill ceasefire will work? I hope so, but I am pessimistic. The only hope is to persuade the United States to keep up the momentum, to pressure Israel and make it compromise now that it is in its darkest hour. But Israel is liable to do crazy things. Therefore, let's keep up our vigilance and not let go for a second of our military capability to confront the enemy.'[15]

Israel saw Egypt's acceptance of the ceasefire very differently. Dayan, lecturing before IDF commanders, argued that it showed Arab failure in many directions. (1) The inter-Arab military organization had failed to establish an eastern front to buttress the Suez front. (2) Operational military policy had failed. (3) Soviet advisers and equipment had failed to drive the Israelis back from the current ceasefire lines. (4) Above all, Egypt had failed to touch off the powder-keg. The Egyptians, according to Dayan, had failed to involve the Americans in the conflict; they had failed to get America to pressure Israel into relieving it from its Middle East involvement. On the other hand, Israel, said Dayan, had achieved its goal in the War of Attrition. 'We have succeeded in holding to the lines. We have carried our policy through. We have deterred further escalation of the war and we have demonstrated the length of our arm. We can reach them everywhere.'[16]

The American view of its initiative was explained at a special briefing given at San Clemente, the Western White House, on August 24, 1970, by the senior American adviser, Henry Kissinger, his staff, and members of the State Department headed by Assistant Secretary of State for Middle Eastern Affairs, Joseph Sisco.[17] The war in the Middle East was, in the long run, essentially a search for peace. In view of this, the US had to concentrate on (1) the question of withdrawal of forces, (2) the refugee question (a euphemism for the Palestine question) and (3) concrete arrangements for security of the entire area. These imperatives had 'inspired' the American initiative of June 1970. The most significant aspect of the initiative, Kissinger felt, was that it represented 'the first time that Israel recognized the principle of withdrawal,' even if the gap between Israeli and Egyptian interpretations of the word was wide. The Middle East was an area of potential great-power conflict, in view of the presence there of both the US and the USSR. The two powers had to endeavour to find ways of resolving conflicts within a general political framework. Kissinger, however, stressed this point: 'Above all we must depend on all the means at the disposal of Israel for the essential fulfilment of the present military balance.' The military balance would be 'fulfilled' by a proper arms supply and by efforts to provide the atmosphere that would enhance a political settlement.

Moscow did not alter its strategy of escalation after the 1970 ceasefire. While America was putting out preliminary feelers toward its initiative, the Soviets had indicated an apparent support for their efforts. Later Soviet actions belied that appearance. Despite the prohibition against any military build-up in a thirty-mile-wide zone west of the Canal, the Soviets and Egyptians installed new anti-aircraft missiles there. This was an open violation of the ceasefire agreement as understood by both the US and Israel.[18]

On August 19, Brigadier General Aharon Yariv, IDF Chief of Intelligence, demonstrated with the aid of aerial maps and satellite reconnaissance that the Egyptians had violated the neutral zone by advancing some forty new missile sites to a point just west of the Canal. For three weeks the United States refused to acknowledge the validity of General Yariv's claims. A crisis of confidence, as the *New York Times* preferred to call it, occurred between the United States and Israel. 'The immediate point at issue centred in the realm of sophisticated intelligence gathering. Israeli public charges of an Egyptian and Soviet build-up of missile air defence in violation of the August 7 ceasefire agreement were initially greeted by official silence, and private annoyance, in the United States.'[19]

To quote Foreign Minister Eban: 'This is really too much. On the one hand our adversaries endanger our security, on the other our friends impugn our accuracy and sincerity.'[20] Washington, of course, did not wish to undermine the delicate American initiative. It appeared to Tel Aviv, that Washington was turning its back on Israel. The analysis of the *New York Times* correspondent, Peter Grose, was prophetic. 'This [the movement of the missiles] is significant for the future defence of Israeli positions on the Sinai banks, for without air superiority over the Canal, the Israelis would be hard-pressed to prevent an amphibious crossing by Egyptian units and the establishment of a bridge-head on the Sinai.'[21]

The Soviets had helped establish, on the Canal, the densest and most comprehensive missile defence system in the world outside the USSR. It had not, of course, been conceived as a defensive system. Its chief purpose was to give Egypt the opportunity to begin a new war once its armed forces and its political leaders decided the time was right.

The violation of the cease-fire was the turning point in the Egyptian–Israeli military confrontation over the Canal. Egypt had now taken the first step toward resumption of hostilities. Although the Israelis were well aware of this, Dayan and the IDF chiefs were confident—over-confident, as it turned out—that the events which took place after the cease-fire would not change the status quo. They therefore continued to support the Bar-Lev line as the chief strategy of defence.

Between 1970 and the first day of the Yom Kippur War (October 6, 1973), Dayan insisted repeatedly that the Israeli army could meet all challenges, including the new Soviet–Egyptian strategic deployment west of the Canal. He was, of course, very wrong. Dayan wrote in *Ma'ariv*: 'The Egyptians torpedoed the American initiative. They think that when they violated the standstill ceasefire they "gained" a missile system stationed on the west side of the Canal.'[22] It is significant that 'gained' is in quotes. Dayan was apparently largely convinced that the Israeli air force could succeed in penetrating and destroying Egypt's defensive system. But another theory advanced at the time proved him wrong: 'The Egyptians were prepared to accept opposition to the truce in the Arab world as a small price to pay for the *tactical freedom* afforded by the standstill ceasefire.'[23]

The War of Attrition was a continuing phenomenon. It did not cease after 1967, nor again after 1970. On the contrary, Arab and Israeli confrontations became more frequent. The Soviet-Egyptian political alliance continued at the expense of a half-hearted moral (but not political or military) American commitment to Israel.

The War of Attrition, Phase III: The Twilight: Drumming for Fifth Round.

The movement of missiles toward the western bank was enormously significant. It marked the end of the 1968-1970 War of Attrition, and opened the first phase of the War of 1973. It was overshadowed, however, by an event of great significance, which seriously delayed the Arabs' strategy. On September 28, 1970, the Egyptian dictator, President Gamal Abdel Nasser, died. What followed was a period of relative stability on the Suez front contrasting sharply with the series of coups and countercoups inside Egypt.

When the upheaval was over, Anwar Sadat had eliminated all opposition and had become master of Egypt. He ordered a purge of intelligence and senior military officers including the left-wing ASU leader Ali Sabri, the right-wing Nasserites Sharawi Gouma'sh and Sami Sharaf, and Army Chief of Staff General Muhammad Fawzi. With Nasser's supporters gone he began concentrating on developing a professional rather than a political army.[24]

He also set about, shrewdly, to 'prolong' the ceasefire. The Egyptians had decided that if Israel did not begin withdrawal by November 1970, they would annul the ceasefire, but Sadat kept postponing the deadline. His promises that 1971, and then 1972, would be the 'Year of Decision' aroused ridicule in his own country and contempt in Israel.

Unmoved, Sadat continued to improve and modernize his armed forces. On May 27, 1971, Egypt and the USSR signed a fifteen-year treaty of friendship and mutual aid, and Soviet support to Egypt accelerated. But the Israelis continued to believe that 'unlike Nasser, Sadat could not endanger his position by inviting defeat: he would have to pay a price for defeat.'[25] Despite his often-heard threats that he would go to war when he was forced to conclude that there was no hope for a favourable political option for Egypt, the Israelis and the West, and possibly even the USSR, were convinced that Sadat was not the man to go to war—certainly not in the '70s.

On July 18, 1972, less than fourteen months after the treaty of friendship was signed, Sadat called for the expulsion of the Soviet advisers. They had, he claimed, failed to equip the Egyptian army with the latest models from the Soviet arsenal of electronic missiles. This was a deceptive move. In fact the Israelis now felt that the 'Year of Decision' had probably been postponed for a considerable period. The IDF Monthly Report for June 1973 proclaimed: 'Israel is now freer than ever to dictate political action in the Middle East.'[26] And yet on May 23, 1972, William Beecher and Drew Middleton, writing in the *New York Times*, had warned that American experts believed Soviet military activity might well be aimed at challenging and destroying much of the IDF air force. NATO sources, said the *Times*, were reporting that the military balance had shifted in favour of the Arabs. 'The character of the fighting has changed to the point where Israel's capacity to defend all her frontiers must be seriously questioned' the NATO analysts concluded.

Egypt, in fact, was ending its dependence on diplomatic and political weapons; the time was approaching for a military solution. In the search for allies, Sadat's options were clear. He could continue to depend on military and political support from the USSR: or he could build political and financial support among the Arabian oil potentates. He decided to disassociate himself politically from the USSR in order to isolate the radical states, Libya, Iraq and Algeria, and was determined, instead, to forge a new Arab political front based on an alliance with the kings, potentates and oil sheikhs of the Arabian peninsula. The decision was based not on the value of oil as a weapon, but because he felt these states were politically more stable and could modify American commitments to Israel. Faisal of Saudi Arabia became the cornerstone of his new policy.

Having disposed of left-leaning radicals and friends of the Soviets at home, and having isolated, with Faisal's help, the radical Arab states abroad, Sadat next turned to Syria.

Although a radical state itself, Syria was nonetheless, like Egypt and Jordan, a victim of the 1967 war and its aftermath. Sadat knew that an Egyptian military option would be possible only if the Israeli eastern front could be activated. Neither the Arab guerrillas nor Jordan could be counted on as fighting partners. The guerrillas had undermined their position in Jordan when the extremists among them began hi-jacking international airliners, and threatening the Hashemite regime. Hussein had ousted them in September of 1970. Syria was now his only natural ally. With its militant Pan-Arabist Ba'th Party, Syria, the torch-bearer of radical Arab nationalism, part of whose territory, the Golan Heights, was still occupied by Israel, could be persuaded to join Sadat's military venture. In 1972, Sadat and General Hafez Asad of Syria began to build a military alliance that would be ready to strike when the time was right. It was to be a single-phase operation: a joint Egyptian-Syrian mobilization and surprise attack with a complex political purpose.

NOTES

1. Taha al-Magdub, 'The Egyptian Strategy of Escalation', *Al-Ahram*, August 6, 1969.
2. 'From September onwards, Arab commentators intended increasingly to stress that the Arabs had accepted the principle of political solution only for tactical reasons.' *Middle East Record, 1967*, p. 269.
3. *New York Times*, November 23 , 1967, p. 17.
4. Edward Kolcum, 'Soviets Accelerating the Middle East Drive,' *Aviation Week and Space Technology*, June 1, 1970.
5. *Ibid.* See also *The Military Balance, 1970* (London, International Institute of Strategic Studies, 1970).

6. John Erickson, *Soviet Military Power* (London, Royal United Services Institute, 1971), p. 61.
7. Moshe Dayan, 'Accepting the Russian Glove,' *Ma'ariv*, August 5, 1974, p. 17.
8. *Ibid.*
9. 'Interview with General Chaim Bar-Lev', *Ma'ariv*, June 5, 1970.
10. Chaim Herzog, *The Atonement War* (Heb.) Idanim, Jerusalem, 1975; pp. 14-15.
11. 'Interview with General Bar-Lev,' *Ma'ariv*, op. cit. p. 20.
12. Uri Dann, 'Interview with Dayan,' *Ma'ariv*, September 12, 1969, p. 11.
13. See Ezer Weizmann, 'Why Does Dayan Retreat?' *Ma'ariv*, May 14, 1971: Mati Peled, 'The Russians Are Coming,' *Ma'ariv*, May 8, 1970.
14. 'Dayan Lectures Before Students,' *Ma'ariv*, February 20, 1970.
15. Haykal, 'Why Did Egypt Accept The Rogers Proposal?' *Al-Ahram*, August 15, 1970. My paraphrase.
16. General Moshe Dayan, 'Assessment of the Situation,' *Bamachane* (IDF Army Weekly), September 9, 1971, pp. 4-8. (quotation from p. 8).
17. *New York Times*, August 25, 1970.
18. See *Ma'ariv*, October 27, 1970, p. 9; *Time*, November 2, 1970; 'Week in Review,' *New York Times*, September 6, 1970, p.1; 'Week in Review,' *New York Times*, August 23, 1970, p. 1.
19. *New York Times*, September 6, 1970.
20. *Ibid.*
21. 'Review of the Week,' *New York Times*, August 23, 1970.
22. Moshe Dayan, 'The 1970 Ceasefire,' *Ma'ariv*, November 8, 1970, p. 10.
23. Robert Semple, Jr., 'The Week in Review,' *New York Times*, September 6, 1970. Emphasis added.
24. On the anti-Sadat coup of 1971, see Amos Perlmutter, *Egypt: The Praetorian State* (New Brunswick, N.J., Transaction, 1974), pp. 188-199.
25. *IDF Monthly Report*, June 1973.
26. *Ibid.*

CHAPTER IV

Political and Military Misperceptions: Israel's Fourth War, October 1973

The October War has left Israel more vulnerable than at any time since its founding. It is not that the battle was lost. On the contrary, despite a bad start, the Israeli soldiers so brilliantly redeemed themselves that they carried the day militarily. But the nation's limited territorial gains were concomitantly rendered all but meaningless by the rise in Arab political fortunes. As a result the tiny, geographically isolated nation has found itself cut off politically, deserted by former friends.

Much of Israel's plight can be laid to factors beyond the control of the nation's leaders. Israel was hurt by deepening American isolationism, the oil crisis and Russian-American reapproachment, and Israeli leaders were certainly not responsible for these events. But they have only themselves to blame for failure accurately to interpret these changes and act on them accordingly. Their misjudgments and the subsequent strategic and tactical conduct of the war will be the focus of this analysis.

To fully understand what went wrong it is necessary to examine the actions and policies of the national security inner circle.

Until 1973, Israel's political system was highly institutionalized and understandably dominated by cohesive ruling groups which also controlled the dominant group in the governmental coalition—the Labour Party. Executive power was held in the hands of the few who ruled the cabinet, the Labour Alignment government and the national security 'kitchen cabinet.' The individuals and groups that made national security policy and managed the war can therefore be identified more readily than in most societies.*

The National Security Inner Circle [1]

Israel, a garrisoned state, has existed as an independent entity since 1948. Israel has fought four major wars, and has one of the highest military outlays in the world (close to 25 per cent of the GNP by 1973). Yet the state has no formal, legal-institutional structure for the making of national security policy. Between 1947 and 1973, national security was conceived and implemented by a small, informal, and clandestine body known first as Ben Gurion's inner circle and later as Golda Meir's Kitchen Cabinet.[2] Only under Eshkol's reign (1963-1969) did the cabinet play a more significant role in the making of national security policy.

Between 1967 and 1973, a small informal group within the Labour-Alignment's 'Kitchen' Cabinet—the inner circle—conceived, designed, and formulated Israel's national security and military policies.

No other single institution in Israel has had the information, the machinery or the instruments for the design, conception, and implementation of Israel's national security. This arrangement is due partly to the Ben Gurion legacy, whereby the Minister of Defence as supreme commander deals with grand strategy and national security, while the High Command executes military policy. The problem with this tradition is that the lines of demarcation between defence policy and implementation of military strategy by the High Command, especially between the Chief of Staff and the Defence Minister, have never been clearly drawn.[3]

Between 1967 and 1974, the national security inner circle was composed of three layers. At the top, national security was the business of the triumvirate: Meir, Dayan, and Galili. Deputy Prime Minister Yigal Allon (former commander of

*Let me caution the reader that this chapter is designed only to raise a number of interesting points, and relevant observations. Based on some inside information and critical core of analysis, it is still only an opening statement in, and a contribution to, a scholarly debate. I certainly do not have and nor have others sufficient information to provide a summation of Israeli misjudgment, nor the perspective for a creative evaluation of men, actions and consequences. Nevertheless, this is intended to open the debate.

the Palmach) and Minister of Justice Yaacov S. Shapira played a key role in the kitchen cabinet. In defence policy however, Dayan was pre-eminent and Mrs. Meir left Dayan to conduct defence policy and policy over the occupied territories. In 1971 when Chief of Staff General Chaim Bar-Lev retired and entered politics to become Minister of Commerce, he also joined this group. On the strategic level the input of the military was considerable, particularly that of General Bar-Lev (until 1971), General David Elazar (1971-1974) and General Aharon Yariv, Chief of Intelligence from 1961 to 1972 and a close associate of Golda Meir who also served as Special Adviser to Combat Terrorism (1972-1973). Thus, national security policy and military strategy were divided between the political and military inner circle that governs Israel. This inner circle became a powerful instrument over and beyond its constitutional role. The upper trio ruled supreme since the formation of the Labour Alignment in 1969, when the latter became the most powerful political structure in Israel. The union, in 1969, of the three splinters of the Socialist–Zionist parties (Rafi, Ahdut-Haavoda and Mapai) into the Labour Party, and a governmental coalition—the Labour Alignment, together with the leftist Mapam—disproportionately strengthened the power of the Labour Alignment oligarchy and consequently of the national security inner circle. The division of Labour among the Labour Alignment trio over national security was as follows: Golda Meir was Foreign Minister in all but name, assisted by Ambassador Rabin in Washington, and General Yariv for formulating policy against terrorism, while Foreign Minister Abba Eban handled less significant Israeli policy outside the US. Moshe Dayan, the Defence Minister, became the architect of Israeli policy toward the Arab countries. Between 1967 and 1973, Dayan gave pre-eminent consideration to the occupied territories and was the author of the successful 'Open Bridges' policy with the Arab world via the Jordan River. Since January 1973, Dayan also acted as chief negotiator and was the only authority other than Mrs Meir (and her aid Ambassador Dinitz) to deal with Henry Kissinger. The power of Galili, Minister without Portfolio, lies in the fact that until the 1973 war he was Golda Meir's *eminence grise* and adviser. Before the October 1973 war, opposition to the defence trio in the Labour Alignment was meekly led by finance Minister Pinhas Sapir, otherwise Golda's most loyal party-government ally, and until his resignation (1974), Israel's economic czar. The opposition of Sapir and Eban was not significant enough to change the national security elite's orientations and actions. Ambivalent hawk-dove policy orientation and rivalry with Dayan complicated a concise analysis of his contribution to the trio's defence policy. The opposition of Mapam, the Labour government's ally, was nil. The power of the trio (who were known as bitter rivals before 1969, like Meir-Dayan) was consummated during the 1973 campaign when, in August 1973, the party platform (better known as the Galili Document) was modified in favour of policies advocated by Dayan since 1969: encouragement of Israeli settlement and gradual annexation of the occupied territories, and an affirmation of the policy of status quo, i.e. military support from the US and a militant stance on territories and terrorism.

The members of the inner circle were also the leading politicians of the Labour Alignment government. Golda Meir, Shapira and Galili had worked together for over two decades. A cohesive, if not coherent, group, despite the enormous difference in personality and party factional affiliation, they worked generally apart from Israel's formal (and impotent) political structures. Although the Party pressured the inner circle (as demonstrated by the politiical struggle over the 'oral doctrine', i.e. a non-commitment on the part of Israel to present a withdrawal map before direct negotiations with the Arabs commenced), the struggle over territorial annexation was finally resolved in the vague Galili Document, a modified annexation platform. The inner circle operated outside the framework of other socio-economic elites and the Histadrut (General Confederation of Labour) as well.

With the passage of time, national security functions became institutionally and personally characterized by cohesiveness and conspiracy (common will to action). The inner circle exhibited such qualities as clandestineness, decision-making in relative isolation (even if debated within the cabinet, the party, and in public), self-righteousness, and self-assurance in taking the right course of action at critical moments, intimacy, collegiality, and political 'covering up.'

In general, the inner circle has shunned advice offered by defence intellectuals, or by security experts who have not been socialized or politicized by the inner circle. Instead, this group has consistently turned to its own, to the High Command, particularly the Chiefs of Staff and the Intelligence, for advice on strategic and intelligence matters. Recruitment policies have been informal, but these too have been characterized by a fierce sense of group exclusivity and collegiality. Actual membership has been determined by seniority within the party (Meir, Shapira, Galili) and in defence matters (Dayan, Galili, Allon, and Bar-Lev). It is hard to argue that the inner circle's single quality was loyalty but its paramount power was that *it* dictated defence policy, whatever the differences in personality, age, and orientations of its members. The inner circle shared what Janis calls 'Group Think',[4] namely the group's high priority for getting along together. Erwin Hargrove says that 'group think' demonstrates, inter alia, 'excessive risk-taking based on a shared illusion of invulnerability;' that it blocks negative information; has a stereotyped view of the enemy, and above all, a 'shared illusion of unanimity'.[5]

*Misperceptions**

The term 'perception' has been defined as 'those cognitive

---

*The literature on misperception has been dominated by social psychologists. Only recently have a few students of international politics developed a conceptual framework for the study of perceptions and misperceptions.[7] In view of the fact that literature on social psychology is burgeoning in the field of perceptions, cognitive processes, etc., I have no intention to test here a conceptual framework on misperceptions or the relationships between perceptions, cognitions and misperceptions and cognitive dissonance. I shall restrict myself to an hypothesis, i.e. a suspected relationship between variables that *can be* tested (but not necessarily tested here) empirically. At best I shall rely on Jervis's pioneer effort to relate the concept of misperception to international political theory. Thus the relationship between the social-psychological concepts of misperception policies and the actions of the inner circle and the High Command in 1973 will only be approximated. The reader should be as suspicious as I am that the relationships between variables in a rigorous empirical sense are mechanical. Nevertheless I dare to tread on virgin soil only to illuminate and better explain my case studies presented here.

processes that refer to events occuring and objects present in the immediate environment.'[6] Thus, defined simply, the term means a cognitive process attempting to represent the current state of the environment. The cognitive process itself includes the various aspects of knowing—perceiving, judging, reasoning, and remembering. The relationship that exists between perception and conception (an 'idea' or 'notion', a psychological thing that pre-supposes understanding) is extremely close.[8] Perception either stimulates or 'involves' a conceptual activity such as a proposition, a theory, a thesis. Thus, it is from the persistence of perceptions and the process of integrating existing cognitions that concepts flow and a conceptual framework is established.

Decision-makers misperceive events when they try to fit incoming information into their existing theories and images, particularly when the latter play a large part in determining what is expected. Under these circumstances, reality is 'screened' and an actor perceives what he expects.[9] Thus most misperceptions, though *not all*, may be defined as instances of cognitive dissonance. 'Two cognitions are said to be dissonant when they are either logically inconsistent or incompatible with the person's past experience.'[10] Dissonance of cognition takes place, according to Leon Festinger, when behaviour is incompatible with a person's values.[11] Under these circumstances misperception becomes a cognitive process 'misrepresenting' the current state of affairs and one of moulding events according to personal cognition. Reality is misrepresented in order to adapt these events to the actor's cognitive map.

A post-decisional analysis of Israeli misjudgments is not difficult for several reasons. First, the personal predictions, cognitions, and policy orientations of the inner circle were persistent and stable, and therefore easy to identify. Next, despite some fundamental differences, the process of cognitive integration within the group was collective. And finally, that process correlated with the members' highly integrated perception of Israel's national security and military strategy.

The inner circle used the terms 'security', 'defence', and 'strategy' interchangeably to denote the posture of Israel's national security. They used 'military' to refer to tactical military perceptions, intelligence, and military actions. Their inter-changeable terms will be used in this analysis. Political misjudgments, to be discussed first, will refer to decisions made on the national security level resulting from the perceptions of the politically dominant echelon of the inner circle, and their allies. Then, military errors and the military consequences of security misjudgments will be discussed in terms of errors made primarily by the IDF's high command.

The aim, above all, is to spell out the relationship between political and military misperceptions and find their source, thus exploring the 'relationship between mind and the objective world'.[12]

NATIONAL SECURITY PERCEPTIONS AND POLITICAL MISJUDGMENTS

There were at least four major misjudgments. On these perceptions was built the foundation of Israel's political and military strategy between 1967 and 1973.

Misperception Number 1:
The Failure to Transfer War into Enemy Territory

By deterrence we mean 'working on the psychology of the enemy so that he will not decide to attack,'[13] and that the cost of attack may outweigh the damage inflicted on the adversary. This policy was intertwined with the strategic concept of territorial defence which entails blunting the enemy attack and minimizing its effects on oneself. Thus two strategies became mixed—defence and deterrence. The misperception in 1973 was that territorial defence, now in enemy-occupied territory, provided the necessary deterrence for Israel. The concept of territorial defence, a product of several decades of Haganah-IDF strategic thinking, blunted the decision-makers' understanding of the real nature of deterrence. If we mean by deterrence an effective Israeli military doctrine, i.e. the defence of the territories under Israeli domination, then this was the perception of the inner circle. But what was misperceived is the real property of deterrence, i.e. creating conditions in which the enemy will find it costly or irrational to attack. Domination over territory did not deter the enemy. What could have deterred the enemy was a strategy that would make the enemy's highest aspirations so costly that he would have been deterred from attacking Israel once more. The political posture of Dayan, viz. that the post-1967 borders were ideal and that the deployment of military equipment and forces on the Suez and Golan Heights should be minimal, provided an invitation, as subsequently proved, for a combined Egyptian-Syrian military mass effort to achieve restricted military successes in order to gain far more valuable political advantages. In that sense, the inner circle misperceived its ability to deter and, actually, the policy of minimum military deployment on the border and accepting the 1967 lines as 'ideal' proved to be not costly to the enemy. On the contrary, rather than using psychology to convince the enemy to decide against an attack, the so-called Israeli deterrence strategy invited him to attack. Thus Israeli deterrent strategy proved faulty mainly because of Dayan's misperception of the price the enemy was willing and is able to pay in order to overcome the Israeli deterrent factor. Several political analysts in Israel and abroad are convinced that deterrence has never, in fact, worked for Israel (see 1967, 1973). This is probably true.

Israeli deterrence policy, despite its claims to the contrary (see later), appears never to have worked, for both in 1967 and 1973 the Israelis found that the Arabs were ready to go to war, that they were not psychologically deterred from attacking. In 1974 the Israeli deterrence may be working in the sense that periodic mobilization, frantic preparedness, and continuous pressure on the Syrian front, may yet deter the enemy. In fact the mini-crisis of November 15-17, 1974 on the Syrian border demonstrates that Israel can secure the price of deterring the enemy if the Israeli arrow is permanently set ready in its bow, as has been the case since 1973. Thus, the misperception concerning deterrence seriously damaged Israeli ability to deter and immediately inflict on the enemy a blow that would have deprived him of the minimum military achievement in the first two days of the war.

Israel's incredibly narrow geographical configuration prior to 1967 had always dictated her concept of deterrence. Basically, that concept was embodied in a political-military doctrine which advocated (a) deployment of forces on the enemy's borders, (b) if necessary, temporary acquisition of Arab territory as a bargaining leverage, and (c) keeping the enemy far removed from Israel's urban areas. It was finally institutionalized as a policy of deterrence by David Ben Gurion in 1949. The military imperative of this policy was that any future campaign must be waged on Arab territory,[14] which does not imply annexation.

General Yigal Yadin, Chief of Staff from 1949 to 1952, had formally stated the IDF's purpose as one of 'transferring the war into enemy territory.'[15] Toward that end he completely reorganized the structure and composition of IDF. In 1953, Moshe Dayan, Yadin's successor, was assigned the task of preparing the IDF for its role in saving Israel from territorial strangulation. A series of successful border raids and crossings by paratrooper-commando units made it clear Dayan had accomplished his task. The IDF was ready to take the offensive.[16] Deterrence worked in 1956. For eleven years the Egyptian front was silent.

David Ben Gurion's policy was not carried out during the 1967 war. Deterrence was cancelled once Israel pre-empted, and Israel's territorial deficiencies were remedied. In the war's aftermath, Israel was surrounded by the Jordan River on the east, the Golan Heights in the north, and on the west by the Suez Canal, 'the best ditch in the world',[17] as Moshe Dayan called it. The new borders, he said, were 'ideal'. With Galili, another key member of the inner circle, Dayan betrayed Ben Gurion's policy by initiating a 'status quo' policy, and substituting 'ideal borders' for the strategy of carrying the war into enemy territory, i.e. beyond the Canal and into Syria.

In one other important respect, Dayan and his Chief of Staff, Chaim Bar-Lev, modified Ben Gurion's basic theory of deterrence. Convinced now that Israel's new borders were 'secure', they constructed the Bar-Lev line, an elaborate defensive line on the East bank of the Suez Canal, which was an important modification of Israel's previous offensive concept of deterrence. The entire structure of the IDF was reoriented along defensive lines, with deterrence relying heavily on the IDF's Intelligence and thus not rendering an Arab attack on Israel psychologically impossible.

The IDF's targets were no longer Egyptian and Syrian territories. The new strategic stance, however, was clearly based on the consensus within the inner circle that because Russia was supporting Egypt, Israel could no longer risk an offensive along these frontiers or seek to penetrate too deeply into enemy territory. Anyway, such actions were deemed unnecessary, given the post-1967 'ideal' borders, and there was American pressure against it. Thus, except in a case of extreme provocation, Israel could no longer use the pre-emptive strategy, its favourite political deterrent. Deterrence was now completely dependent on the IDF's Intelligence warning. Adopting this strategy was a gross misperception of what might deter the Arabs from launching an attack.

The fact of Soviet involvement was generally known since the 1969-1970 War of Attrition, certainly at least to the inner circle. Yet they failed to devise a political strategy geared to that fact or to deploy the IDF accordingly. Israel's misperception was a dissonance between two logically incompatible cognitions: between the dynamic concept of an immediate transfer of war into enemy territory and the static concept of adapting the IDF after 1967 to the new 'ideal' Bar-Lev Maginot line.

When Israel's inner circle chose to adopt the tough Meir-Dayan-Galili stance as expressed in the Galili document of August 1973, it set forth a policy of partial settlement and annexation of occupied territory.[18] The course was one which was bound to provoke the Arabs, and having chosen it, Israel should have pursued a strategy which kept most of the Israeli army on its borders, strengthening its meagre forces on the Suez and Golan fronts. The Israeli army should have been kept on a permanent alert—in a constant state of vigil. A comprehensive deployment system should have been devised. Despite the high cost of maintaining a large army on the borders, internal lines should have been extended all over, reaching the Canal and the Golan Heights, which would have given the enemy a sense of psychological insecurity to discourage contemplating a successful attack.

Alternatively, the inner circle should have opted for another concept of deterrence, i.e. withdrawing from the occupied Arab territories in Sinai and from the populated Palestinian–Jordanian West Bank and the Gaza Strip—that is, returning to slightly modified post-1967 borders with a thin IDF deployment on the borders of the Negev-Sinai and on the Jordan River, thereby lowering Arab aspirations to go to war. Instead, no effective deterrence was really employed. This was a gross misperception.

As Michael Handel has written, Israel's strategy was offensive while her tactics were defensive. The inner circle had failed to resolve two conflicting cognitions and, with it, their implications for policy, strategy, and troop deployment.[19] The inner circle's policy of deterrence was a misperception because it involved a commitment to territory in preference to real security. The inner circle wavered between two cognitions: (1) the war must be transferred into enemy territory, and (2) such a move was no longer politically feasible. In October 1973 the war was not transferred to enemy territory. Instead, the IDF waited for Arab forces to take the offensive. And they did. The Israeli strategic concept of deterrence and military deployment did not convey to the enemy the purpose for which it was intended—'don't go to war as we can defeat you under any circumstances.'

Misperception Number 2. International Detente as a Defence

Within the slippery arena of international politics, events are easily misread. Israel's misinterpretation of the political consequences of international detente—as being advantageous to Israel—had larger implications, however, because it reinforced the inner circle's misperceptions surrounding the political policy of deterrence. Incorrectly, they ascribed to a US–USSR accommodation a decrease in the Arab insurance policy i.e. a diminishing likelihood of Soviet intervention on behalf of the Arabs; with no Soviet guarantee to intervene on their behalf, the Arab armies could be annihilated by IDF.

David Ben Gurion's disciples in the inner circle were convinced that an Arab–Israeli rapprochement was impossible as long as great power rivalry existed in the Middle East. The Arabs, they felt, had consistently exploited great power tension, supporting East against West, always for the purpose of their own political and strategic advantage. Only with the lessening of rivalry between the superpowers, their reasoning was, would the rivalry between Arabs and Israelis subside. Accordingly, when the great powers ushered in the era of detente, in the area of US intervention to end the War of Attrition, the inner circle moved somewhat away from a policy of status quo toward negotiations, and, in 1970, Dayan offered minor Israeli withdrawal. The withdrawal of Russian troops from Egypt in August 1973 reinforced the inner circle's conviction that their status quo policy during the War of Attrition provided a good political trump card for future negotiations with the Arabs. For no Israeli government has *ever* foreclosed the need to negotiate. Furthermore, in the absence of superpower rivalry, there was a general consensus among the inner circle that Soviet aspirations in the Middle East would be lowered. The situation, they thought, would frustrate Arab political ambitions and induce them (particularly Egypt and Jordan) to come to terms with Israel on terms advantageous to the latter.

This point of view was supported by Yitzchak Rabin, former Ambassador to the US, and by Simcha Dinitz, the present (1975) Ambassador. Both were convinced that the Nixon Administration was treating Israel as a political and military ally.[20] To them, the Nixon attitude seemed 'perfectly' tailored to Israel's needs.[21] In countless interviews between 1970 and 1972, Ambassador Rabin impressed upon me that he saw an unwritten Israeli–American strategic alliance emerging, whose origins he dated back to the Soviet violation of the ceasefire in August 1970. It had been reinforced, he felt, during the Jordanian civil war, when the United States expressed political and military support for Israel.

With Rabin's assistance, Israel not only misread Soviet ambitions in the Middle East but also Soviet military and political fidelity to detente. The inner circle also erred in the assumption that the Nixon policy suited Israel's needs;[22] they believed that with detente blossoming, an Israeli–American entente cordiale would serve as a pillar to uphold the concept of deterrence. That such an arrangement would ipso facto deter the Arabs was a misperception par excellence, one which converged neatly, almost dogmatically, with the inner circle's misperceptions concerning 'ideal borders', and low level of troop deployment.

Misperception Number 3. Misreading Arab Intentions

Israel's misreading of Arab intentions, a misperception laden with layers of cognitive dissonance, is the foundation stone of the Arab–Israeli conflict in its present form.[23] Both antagonists suffer from political paranoia and harbour deep animosity towards each other which has intensified with the institutionalization of the conflict over the years.

The seriousness of Israel's failure to read Arab intentions correctly can only be grasped if it is seen not as an excusable error but as a cognitive failure directly traceable to the inner circle.[24] Some have argued that had the Israeli inner circle, unlike the American Intelligence network at the time of the Pearl Harbour attack, correctly interpreted enemy intentions, the 1973 war could have been averted, or at least been won decisively in a short time by Israel. The analogy is only partially true. As was the case with Pearl Harbour, sufficient information concerning enemy mobilization was passed on to higher authorities but the response was inadequate.[25] The Pearl Harbour analogy, however, fails to focus attention upon the more important aspect of Israel's failure, which consisted not so much of using bad judgment in one incident, as misperceiving Arab intentions over a longer period of time.

Israel's grave misperception consisted of several conflicting cognitions.

First, Israel refused to recognize the Arab commitment to settle the conflict in 1973, preferably by military means, and not diplomatically or politically although there were vague signals in this direction.

Second, Israel failed to see the war hidden under the fog of peace. It presumed that its conception of deterrence, detente, and an efficient IDF would cancel Arab aspirations to move against Israel by military means.

Third, Israel believed that its military superiority would destroy any Arab will to wage war in the foreseeable future; that the Arabs would not fail to take note of Israeli military might and so would be reluctant to launch a surprise attack which would expose them to military defeat. Even the 'irrational' Arabs (an Israeli perception), Israel reasoned, would not be so suicidal as to begin a war which would be completely disadvantageous to them.

Fourth, the 'solutions' devised by the hawks and doves among Israel's inner circle and other Labour Alignment power elites, and the intellectuals, were all convenient to Israel but irrelevant to Arab aspirations. The doves were convinced that under certain conditions (a) a policy of moderation, oriented toward a modification of territorial annexation (but annexation nonetheless), (b) negotiations from a position of strength, and (c) the formation of a moderate Palestinian state would persuade the Arabs to negotiate and give up the military option as the only solution to the conflict. The hawks and all inner circle members, without exception, believed that a policy designed to frustrate the Arabs politically, militarily, and psychologically would precipitate them into adopting a more reasonable stance. In the words of Mrs Meir, 'For every year of no peace you pay interest in a piece of territory.'* Accordingly, Dayan threatened to settle Jews in Arab lands and employed a tacit but constant policy of creeping annexation. These policies were designed to 'break the stubborn Arab back'. Yet, within the inner circle both hawks and the new doveish members were convinced that (1) the most moderate of Arab aspirations was the elimination of Israel's political independence, and the most extreme was its physical annihilation; (2) the conflict was of a permanent nature and only the frequency of wars had been advanced; and (3) regardless of Israel's policy orientation—moderate or militant—in the long run, the Arabs intended that the nation would be isolated, divided, impoverished, and eliminated; and (4) coming to terms with the Arabs would be a long and protracted process (in Dayan's view). And yet the inner circle policy failed to reflect these perceptions.

Fifth, Israel's inner circle was fooled by the Arab strategy that evolved following the Khartoum Conference of August

*Israeli Television appearance in 1973.

1967. The Arabs portrayed Israel as an occupier, an aggressor, a racist, ruthless Prussia, while presenting themselves as the victims, the oppressed, the colonized people, the weak. Meanwhile, they prepared carefully and diligently for the next war, which would be justified in the eyes of the international community as a war of liberation from Israeli colonialism.[26]

But Israel saw the world through Israeli eyes. It failed to sense the Arabs' mood and gauge their aspirations, their dedication to regaining their territory, their 'honour' and 'pride' about which they had been talking and writing incessantly for years. Nor did Israel strongly sense a changing mood in the international community. It did not ask itself seriously what 'anti-colonialism', 'racism', the pusillanimity of Western Europe and Japan, and the change of mood in post-Vietnam America would entail for Israel.

Hopelessly misperceiving the Arab mood and the international climate, the Israelis screened their perceptions in such a way as to deny any contradictions with their basic beliefs and national security-political concepts. The inner circle's erroneous conclusion on October 4 that the Arab mobilization was just another war exercise stemmed from conflicting cognitions. The 'fact' of Arab military preparation did not 'conform' with the inner circle's values and perceptions, which were characterized by a conviction that the Arabs could not, therefore would not, opt for a military solution and that the IDF's Intelligence warning system was an infallible safeguard of the republic.

Arab rationality, however, was oriented toward going to war. Sensing that the necessary political and international conditions were advantageous (detente and the energy crisis), the Arabs successfully forged the Saudi–Egyptian–Syrian coalition in September 1973. Whereas Israel was thinking in terms of its own military superiority and the lack of Arab will to wage war at an unpropitious time, the Arabs had decided the moment was ripe to achieve the 'liberation' of their territories by military means.

Misperception Number 4. The Normalization of Israel

Ever since 1948, Israel has sought peace and security. Her

need for peace has been genuine. Whether or not Israel's efforts to attain it have been equally genuine, and whether it has chosen the right road or the wrong, have been controversial topics since 1948 and will remain the subject of scholarly debate for some time. These matters, however, are not relevant to this analysis. The concern here is with how the inner circle perceived Israel's role after the 1967 war.

They were convinced that either the 1967 war was the final Arab–Israeli war or that it had dealt the Arabs a blow decisive enough to deter them from further aggression for the next decade.[27] They held to a belief that time was working in Israel's favour. After all, immigration rates were high, the nation's industry and technology were coming into their own, urbanization was moving ahead, and Israel's GNP was elevating its standard of living to that of a small European state. In the IDF the inner circle sought the republic's invincible shield; its air superiority, increased supplies, sophistication of weapons and manpower training, was seen as sufficient means to guarantee Israel's readiness to dismantle its garrisons. There was to be an end to the Masada complex. After all, the frontiers were 'ideal'. The concept of deterrence also created a mood of confidence which obviously stemmed from the dazzling 1967 victory. A sense of security pervaded the nation, and even if it did not altogether delude the members of the inner circle, their perception of deterrence was served by their confidence in the military superiority of the IDF.

Accordingly, the concept of degarrisonization or normalization of Israel became a political and security sine qua non between June 11, 1967 and October 5, 1973. As perceived by the inner circle, normalization was a purely military, as opposed to a political, process. Budget allotments for nonmilitary purposes increased accordingly. This misperception was one for which Israel was to pay dearly.

Israel's progressive politicians had hoped that a post-1967 respite from warfare would give the country a chance to focus attention on many other problems—political nepotism and centralism, wage and salary structures, education, medical services, unequal tax structure, church–state relations, and general questions relating to the quality of life. But the inner circle did not modify the defence budget. Security matters still predominated. Certain concessions were made (for example, the length of compulsory military service was reduced, fewer mobilization exercises were held, and attempts were made to economize in the defence industries), but whether those decisions stemmed from societal pressures or from the inner circle's own conviction that the Arabs were unwilling to go to war is difficult to know.

What is important is that the inner circle's commitment to degarrisonization and the measures they took meant that henceforth they could handle the Arab–Israeli conflict principally in military terms. Diplomacy as a means to reach the Arabs was, on the whole, ignored, even though reality required the recognition that strictly military approaches could not resolve security problems. Reality required that normalization be pursued by political and diplomatic, not military, means. The inner circle's misperception of this matter was political and resulted from the asymmetrical relationship between Israel and her antagonists in regard to the military establishment. The latter's total effort was military aggrandizement, while Israel's military effort and deployment was based on a tenuous conception—that the IDF's Intelligence system was the major military signal to predict an Arab attack.

Somewhere along the line Moshe Dayan lost sight of Arab strategy: viz that what you lose by war and violence, you try to gain by diplomacy and political extortion, and when you fail to fulfil your aims by political extortion and diplomacy, you try again by war and violence. Taking Arab actions in the War of Attrition as a model, Dayan assumed that the Arabs would seek political solutions with concerted military initiatives, although as late as July 1973 he was quoted as saying that he felt that, given the low value they placed on political solutions, the Arabs would opt for a military conflict.[28]

The Arab War of Attrition against Israel was really a *permanent*, ongoing war, against which the inner circle's policy was unrealistic (although Dayan was always cognizant of the real Arab military intentions). Forever escalating (since 1925), it had been a war of the many against the few, of quantity versus quality, of lives regarded as expendable versus lives considered valuable, of Islamic fundamentalists against progressive, Zionist non-fundamentalists. For the Arabs the War of Attrition was buttressed by the belief that at any time they had more international leverage than Israel and that there would always be one Machiavellian great power whose aspirations converged with theirs. In the past it had been Britain and France. Now, it was Russia. In the future it might be America or China. Possessing abundant resources of men and oil, the Arabs hoped to convert quantity into quality, imposing upon Israel the final solution, its political and physical annihilation.

In 1973 the Arabs shook Israel's complacent belief that its armed forces could deter any Arab force at any time or any place. Had the members of Israel's inner circle not allowed themselves to be lulled into a spirit of normalization, had they confronted their environment, mobilizing twelve times a year if necessary, and made greater efforts in diplomatic concessions —had they perceived reality—they would not have been surprised by the successful Egyptian crossing of the Canal. Normalization and military mobilization were antithetical. The achievement of normalization (as perceived by the inner circle) had been dependent upon military factors, that, is, Israel's military success in the 1967 war. From this military success came Israel's post-1967 military solution—minimal security vigilance on the Bar-Lev line and the Golan Heights. Normalization and reliance on purely military solutions, however, changed dormant hostility into active conflict: the Arabs opened a total and general war on October 6, 1973.[29]

Misperception Number 5.
Israel can Pre-empt a Military Coalition of Arab States

Ever since the turn of the century, when the Zionist *Yishuv*, the Jewish community in Palestine, was established, the Zionists have viewed the Arabs as a feudal, backward, and pre-nationalistic people. This view was expounded by major Zionist leaders, including Dr Chaim Weizmann, president of the World Zionist Organization and Israel's first president, and Zéev Jabotinsky, the founder of Revisionist

Radical Zionism. Although others expressed hope that upon maturing the Arab national movement would become a progressive one, Socialist–Zionist leaders agreed in general that for the time being the Arabs qualified not as a nation with a legitimate national movement but as a coterie of notables, Muslim autocrats, and fellahin. Hence their conviction that only the establishment of a Jewish state would modernize the Middle East.

Progressive Zionists foresaw the possibility of an alliance with the Arab national movement in a common struggle against colonialism and in efforts to promote new, socialist nation states in the Middle East.[30] The Arab revolt of 1936-1939, however, convinced most Socialist Zionists—David Ben Gurion, in particular—that the Arabs were a bitterly divided people and that unity among them was hopeless as long as there was competition between the Arab regimes. From 1919 to 1945, Arab differences widened as factions became increasingly antagonistic. The Fertile Crescent was set against Egyptianhood; the 'greater Syria' concept of Arab unity clashed with all others; there was competition between northern and southern Arabs, and between Hashemite and Wahhabi dynasties. Arab divisiveness was deemed inevitable, and his view was held firmly by David Ben Gurion and his successors.

While the post-Ben Gurion inner circle believed that Arab nationalism was awakening, they were equally convinced that the political modernization taking place was only contributing to Arab divisiveness. The differences within the post-1952 Arab world were seen as far more irreconcilable than the traditional, territorial, and dynastic antagonisms of the pre-1945 years. Deeper divisions were emerging: between radical and monarchical, praetorian and conservative regimes, between Ba'thism and Nasserism, and between neo-Marxists and Arab radical nationalists. The inner circle's view that an Arab political coalition was impossible was only reinforced by a series of Arab military debacles and the hopeless divisiveness among the Palestinians. No Arab military coalition was considered feasible, even with Russian assistance. Past Arab military failures against Israel were convincing enough evidence. Further, it was believed that the

Arab armed forces lacked the institutionalized military structures necessary to sustain a united command.

In a closed session on the fourth day of the 1973 war, Moshe Dayan spoke with the editors-in-chief of the Israeli press. He revealed then the extent of the inner circle's commitment to this view of the impossibility of coalition. More important, he stressed that even periodic attempts to unify politically, such as the abortive Egyptian and Syrian efforts between 1954 and 1967, *were of no military and political significance.* 'Since the days of Ben Gurion,' he said, 'we have proclaimed we could withstand the combined Arab military forces if they decided to attack us. I believed this with all sincerity—and this was not a mystical belief. Ben Gurion possibly had mystical beliefs—but I was raised on tanks and planes and I believed *that we could stand against the combined Arab countries.*'[31]

Dayan went on to admit that the 1973 war was a shock for him and his government. 'I had a theory that we had the capacity to stop the Egyptian build-up across the Canal, that the Egyptians would need no less than a whole night to build bridges [over the Canal] and that we could prevent them from doing this. . . . What emerged during the days of October 5 and 6 was that the idea that an Israeli armoured war of attrition would keep the Egyptians from crossing the Canal was too simple and it is costing us very dearly. It makes no sense to approach [the Canal] with tanks and prevent the Egyptian bridge build-up. Beforehand, we thought one way; afterwards [when the Egyptians had crossed the Canal] we learned otherwise. Israel's struggle against a co-ordinated two-front campaign has made it apparent to the whole world that we are no longer stronger than the Egyptians. Our reputation and advantages, political and military, over the Arabs have been dissipated. The theory that when they would wage war we could annihilate them has not been proven here [in Sinai]. . . . We must live with the truth, with our public, the American public and the world public and with the Arabs. To disgrace the truth will serve us badly.'[32]

Although Dayan's statement is significant for its reinforcement of the inner circle's perceptions that no Arab coalition, political or military, was possible,[33] its real importance lies in its revelation that because the members of the group were committed to this view, they failed to perceive the significant political advantages that might be gained by the Arabs from even a temporary military alliance and limited success. Nowhere in his statements did Dayan even allude to this as a possibility. Instead he said: 'I think that if Sadat does not reach the Sinai Passes in this offensive, not only will he fail to conquer Sinai, or to liberate Palestine or the occupied Arab territories, after six years of intensive preparation for this war: he will not even reach his limited goal—20 kilometres east of the Canal. I don't think this (5-7 kilometres) will be a great personal achievement for Sadat.'[34]

At least during the first few days of the war, Dayan misperceived Sadat's goal, which was essentially political and not military: that of establishing a symbolic and real Egyptian stronghold on the east bank of the Canal. Dayan's failure in this respect stemmed from not absorbing the Egyptian message during the War of Attrition, a war waged for political purposes using military means. This again is linked with the Israeli concept of deterrence which relied on the military's power to deter an Arab attack. The Israelis' confidence in their belief that not even a temporary Arab political or military unity was possible was reinforced by the doctrine which declared the 1967 lines 'ideal'. In that sense the Israeli military prowess was deemed to be impregnable. The misperception here was a reliance on military deterrence which would cancel out the political ambitions of the adversary and his psychological orientations.

TACTICAL–MILITARY MISPERCEPTIONS

Misperception Number 1. Failure of Timing, Surprise, and Deterrence

The combined strategic doctrines of the IDF, (timing, surprise, and deterrence) failed to be deployed on the critical first two days of the war (October 5 and 6). Since 1948, the IDF's military strategic concepts have been composed of those three elements and not one of those vital concepts was applied to the 1973 war.

The Hourglass Concept. As Chief of Staff (from 1953 to 1957), General Moshe Dayan had defined clearly what was meant by timing, which he chose to call the 'Hourglass Concept.' Israeli military victories needed to flow rapidly and decisively from beginning to end, or from top to bottom, as with sand in an hourglass, he said, or they might be cancelled out by Arab political and diplomatic advantages, Israel, a non-allied nation—isolated on the whole—needed rapid victory to deny the Arab world time to mobilize the international community and the UN, which was heavily disposed in its favour. But in 1973 the hourglass concept was abandoned. The concept of deterrence failed. In 1967 deterrence failed but the elements of time and surprise brought victory to the superior army. In 1973 a superior army was deprived of the elements of surprise and time. Accordingly, after seventeen days of war, the Arabs' political power increased disproportionately to their military position, the danger of superpower intervention arose, and Israel found itself politically isolated and subjected to combined Soviet and American political pressure to end the war as it undoubtedly could—decisively.

The surprise factor. Between 1948 and 1967, Israeli military strategy required the immediate transfer of war into the enemy's territory and the use of a mailed fist against its forces. In effect, these tactics were devised to 'erase' enemy forces by inflicting upon *them* a war of annihilation and surprise. Two convergent actions were required: (1) pre-emption, and (2) rapid mobilization of reserves. Neither was achieved in the 1973 war. The IDF was not mobilized the moment the Intelligence reports reached the inner council. Intelligence reported a low probability of an Arab attack. The IDF, dependent on its alarm intelligence, 'erred'. It was not an error but was based on a political misperception concerning the deterrent effectiveness of the IDF. No serious attempt to deploy the armoured mailed fist was made even though military plans for Sinai required no less than 300 tanks to be deployed in order to deter the aggressor. It was not until the fourth day of the war that the IDF launched its major thrust. The only surprise occurred when Israel's General Ariel Sharon, on the evening of October 15, crossed west of the Canal—ten full days after the outbreak of the war. The delay in fully mobilizing the IDF's reserves and the failure to transfer the war immediately to enemy territory, led to monumental tactical errors: loss of time, of surprise, and of the ability to wage mailed-fist warfare, as the IDF strategy required.

The military element of deterrence. Two separate but closely related factors contributed to the breakdown of the IDF's military strategic concept concerning deterrence. The first, which had to do with the IDF's Intelligence unit, may have been a structural problem. Although certain Intelligence personnel took the Egyptian–Syrian war preparations seriously, the evaluation department of the IDF's Intelligence Services reported a 'low probability of war in the Canal'. The error was structural since the functions of the research division and the evaluation department had never been clearly differentiated in terms of information-gathering and its interpretation. In October, the evaluation department must have prevailed, but in so doing it failed to impress upon the head of Intelligence and the Chief of Staff the exact condition of the Arab forces and their intentions. The second factor was the inner circle's failure to interpret the Egyptian–Syrian mobilization of early October as an act of war. This failure can be laid to a misperception of enemy's intentions and of Israeli deterrence capability.[36]

Misperception Number 2. Mobilization, Lines of Supply, and Military Capability

Israel's major military error, according to retired General Matityahu Peled,[37] was its abandonment of the IDF's two leading military–security doctrines: the transfer of war into enemy territory, and the imperative that until a decisive victory has been achieved the IDF must fight on one front only. Equally disastrous was Dayan's 'betrayal' of the pre-1967 concept of 'inner' or short lines of supply for which he had substituted a doctrine of strategic or territorial depth that became, according to Peled, the basis for Israel's acquisition of territory as a security guarantee.* Dayan's new concept led

*I seriously disagree with General Peled's ideological interpretation of what actually was a political misperception.

to the Bar–Lev military doctrine, embodied in the Bar–Lev line—thin lines of defence constructed along the Suez and in the Golan area, with occupation of Sinai representing 'strategic depth,'[38]—that the strategy designed to meet the War of Attrition was also conceived as a deterrent strategy in the post-1970 years.

What Dayan and others within the inner circle failed to realize, argues Peled, was that territorial acquisition only *lengthened* the IDF's lines of supply and rendered the meagre forces on the Canal and in the Golan area prey to the invading Syrian and Egyptian forces. General Peled vehemently criticized the High Command for its tactical failure in not foreseeing that this revolutionary change in doctrine, one which advocated a *defensive* Maginot line concept of deployment, would be ruinous and catastrophic for the IDF's offensive operations. From my point of view, these should not be seen as Peled views them as tactical, strategic–military errors—but as deeply rooted in the inner circle's political misperceptions and not in IDF doctrine. After all, the new doctrine, which had been promoted by a few (Bar-Lev, Elazar) was adopted by all the members of the inner circle after 1967 because it conformed to their national security perceptions. Again, it was not a change of military doctrine so much as a political misperception of the IDF's strategic capability to deter the enemy.

Post-1967 doctrine relied almost entirely upon Israeli air superiority and Intelligence warnings which were to buttress Dayan's concept of strategic depth. The inner circle believed that air superiority would permit the IDF, once it was properly mobilized, to annihilate the Arabs. To this end, a complex alert system was devised around the Bar-Lev line. The system consisted of three separate lines: the first was composed of about thirty heavily fortified but thinly manned fortresses, behind which was a second line, less well fortified but more heavily manned. These two lines were to alert a third line composed of Israel's armoured brigades. The assumption was that a combination of Israel's first and second lines of defence would hold the Arab forces and give Israel the time needed to mobilize its armoured brigades and to ready them for a thrust beyond the Golan borders and across the Suez.

The inner circle's depth strategy, the idea that Israel could hold the line militarily with very few people, proved unworkable. Not only did Israel's air superiority fail to deter, in face of the Soviet-supplied, Egyptian-manned missiles, but failure to mobilize rapidly (upon which the Bar-Lev doctrine so heavily relied) deprived the first and second lines of defence of adequate manpower and denied the armoured divisions the time they needed to reach the Canal for a crossing. Although in November, General Bar-Lev readily admitted Israel's failure to mobilize—'the success of the enemy forces stemmed from the fact that in the critical hour of the campaign, the defensive line of IDF was not in its full mobilization strength'—he clearly missed the deeper political and military aspects of Israel's failure. 'The results of the war demonstrate the validity of the operational concepts of the IDF, that is, defence and strategic depth as surrogates for permanent mobilization. . . . What happened in the first phase of the war does not demonstrate organizational errors of the IDF or a fundamental weakness in the IDF's post-1967 concepts, nor a failure to assess either Israeli or enemy forces. The failures are the result of the unfortunate conditions which prevailed in the hour of fate on October 6.'[39]

General Bar-Lev was further quoted as saying: 'I must emphasize that it was not the absence of reliable information which led us to this condition [being caught by surprise]. The IDF possessed *all* the information on the strength of the enemy, his conditions, and the new weapons (the anti-tank, anti-aircraft, modern Soviet missiles). The mistake was in the assessment of the Intelligence information. Exact and reliable Intelligence information was available.'[40]

If we are to believe the General's contention that the Intelligence information was complete, then surely the failure to evaluate its political purpose was not the consequence of Intelligence errors but of political misperception.

Misperception Number 3. Failure to Identify the Arab Enemy's Integration of Modern Soviet Weapons

Both General Sharon and General Peled are convinced that in 1973 the concept of strategic depth proved catastrophic for the IDF: that it denied Zahal the initiative, mobility, surprise, and ability necessary to assure the offensive, i.e. deterrence.[41]

Equally important, according to Peled, was the effect this concept had on Israel's assessment of the Arabs' potential to integrate modern Soviet weaponry into their forces.[42] The IDF was unprepared for the new type of Egyptian–Soviet warfare which confronted Israel in 1973. The Russians, it turned out, had substituted technological superiority for manpower. They made compensation for Egyptian and Russian pilot inferiority, for instance, by giving Egypt sensitive strategic weapons: Sam-6 anti-aircraft missiles and RPG 7 anti-tank missiles. The availability of these weapons to the Egyptians in 1973 meant that Israel was deprived of superiority in the skies. In turn, Israel's armoured divisions were prevented from destroying the enemy's forces as they had done in 1967. This problem was compounded by the reliance of the Dayan–Bar-Lev defensive strategy on combined infantry and armoured divisions rather than on the skills of the innovative and brilliant IDF infantry and commando men. (Those skills were amply proven in the successful Suez Canal crossing.) Nor did the inner circle's defensive strategy provide in any way for means to destroy the new Soviet–Egyptian defences—their weapons on the ground.

General Sharon's crossing of the Suez Canal proved the invalidity of the Bar-Lev doctrine. Sharon successfully employed the pre-1967 concept of the offensive, which called for (1) penetration behind enemy lines by a combination of commando and armoured divisions (an armoured commando of sorts); (2) the destruction on the ground of enemy defensive missile systems; and (3) the annihilation of enemy infantry and artillery. Israeli paratrooper-armoured forces cracked the Egyptian armoured divisions that protected their artillery infantry, and which simultaneously served as a shield for the Egyptian anti-missile carriers. It was because Sharon employed these pre-1967 concepts that the Suez crossing was successful. Again, to quote General Peled: 'The new security doctrine, the doctrine of long lines, the territorial doctrine has failed. This defensive doctrine has been an utter catastrophe both on the Golan Heights and in the battle of Sinai. This failure has been demonstrated by the success of General Sharon's contrary strategy.'[43]

Clearly, the inner circle had not absorbed the lessons of the 1969-1970 War of Attrition, when for the first time it was obvious that Russia was providing Egypt with defensive strategic weapons in order to strengthen its offensive capability. During the final days of that war, the Soviet missile system shot down close to nine Israeli Phantom jets. The message should have been clear to Israel: air superiority could only be maintained by the destruction of Egypt's defensive missile system on the ground. Had the Israelis taken seriously the Russian missile system and made use of the Intelligence that was available to the IDF after 1970 on the endless simulated Canal crossings by the Egyptians, they would have been aware of the extent to which the Soviet factor was altering Egypt's offensive inferiority. This again was an error of misperception concerning the deterrent capability of the IDF.

Israel's military strategists should have taken more seriously the effectiveness of the RPG 7 (anti-tank missile) deployed by the Egyptian infantry divisions. This might have led to a change in military strategy, returning Israel's infantry to its pre-1967 role, which would have allowed it to annihilate Egypt's infantry before the latter could inflict serious damage. Furthermore, the war of 'squares', that is, of armoured weapons, tanks, and air force, should have been combined flexibly and proportionately with the paratrooper-infantry. The failure to use the paratrooper-infantry to support and enhance Israel's air and armoured power was one of the IDF's greatest strategic errors in the Sinai campaign of 1973.

In a strategic sense, then, the reason Egypt was not deterred in 1973 was that it must have realized Israel was unprepared for the type of assault intended to be launched. By a strange twist of fate, Israel, whose deterrence had failed and had given the Arabs a chance to open hostilities in 1967, was denied an opportunity to assess the kind of campaign the Arabs would wage—again under Russian auspices and training—in 1973.

The Institutionalization of the High Command Under Dayan and its Consequences for the War.

This problem is not one of misperception but a factor that

contributed to the failure of a serious debate on deterrence strategy between 1967 and 1973, and was unsuccessfully resolved by Dayan and the Chief of Staff.

Junior, middle-level, and particularly senior officers in field positions did, on the whole, a highly professional job in 1973. In some cases, performance was superior to that of 1967. It was at the highest levels of command, and in the areas of logistics, intelligence, and planning, as well as in the Southern Command, that failures occurred.

On the whole, Chief of Staff Elazar's rigid insistence on a rapid turnover of senior IDF officers and his emphasis on the rapid rise of young commander-leaders was an important institutional contribution to the professionalization, modernization and rejuvenation of the 1967 IDF. Dayan had introduced and institutionalized this policy in the early 1950s. His point had been to avoid the creation of the type of professional-corporate establishment which was prevalent in Western armies. He did not want such conservatism, slow turnover of officers and seniority rules for succession, and instead, Dayan oriented IDF policy toward a constant rejuvenation of the army and the High Command. Accordingly, provisions were made for the rapid promotion of junior officers and successive changes of senior officers.[44]

Many changes occurred in the High Command itself between 1967 and 1973. In line with Dayan's policy, a substantial number of the distinguished team of 1967 were retired.[45] In 1973 the new team was composed of 1967 divisional and brigade commanders and a few joined the High Command in senior command positions, as in the crucial Southern Command. Many of these men, however, lacked the administrative experience necessary to run an army command, particularly on the front. This shortcoming became glaringly apparent within the first few days of the 1973 war. It was at this point—on the second day of the war—that Chief of Staff Elazar reappointed to key positions the old 1967 war heroes—retired Chief of Staff General Bar-Lev and such reservists as Generals Sharon, Eytan, Adan, Lenner, Hod and others. This action provided balance to the structure of the IDF's command, especially in view of the fact that the 1973 war was the most brutal of all and required the talent and resources of some of the most distinguished war heroes of the 1967 campaign. Their contribution was considerable. On the Southern front it was decisive, especially the contributions of Generals Bar-Lev and Sharon.

Their success in holding command positions and in assisting new officers was proof of their worth and usefulness. It was this group, the 1956 to 1967 generation of senior officers, that helped check the catastrophe in 1973 and turned the tide against the Egyptian and Syrian offensives. By their performance they did not disprove the logic underlying Dayan's rigid concept concerning the rapid turnover of officers. What it had lacked was the balance between experience and youth. Perhaps the best illustration of this was the performance of General Sharon, who at the age of forty-six was Israel's most brilliant field commander, often referred to as a 'general's general'. (In his case however, there had been reason, other than Dayan's iron law, for his retirement in July 1973.)

What was principally lacking in General Elazar's High Command was a healthy debate over strategy. An adversary system, such as existed under Ben Gurion, should have been established within the High Command as a challenge to its institutional behaviour. Ben Gurion's High Command had been characterized by endless struggles between different groups over interpretations of the most suitable military strategy for Israel. Under him, the office of the Chief of Staff always contained at least one spokesman for opposing doctrines. Each Chief of Staff was given a deputy (appointed by Ben Gurion) whose doctrines, personality, and style were opposed to his own.[46] Contending strategies were tested against one another and their strengths and weaknesses revealed. After 1967, however, only Generals Tal, Sharon, Weizmann and Peled remained to challenge, when necessary, the concepts of the High Command and the latter two were soon retired. Sharon, however, retired in July 1973, only three months before the beginning of the war.

Dayan's discouragement of intervention in the Chief of Staff's decisions and his failure to encourage debate (the anti-Bar-Lev line advocates Tal and Sharon) contributed to the stagnation of the High Command. Within its ranks a 'crony system' was already being promoted by Elazar; some officers were appointed to the High Command not because they had distinguished careers, but because they were close friends or old Palmach chums.[47] This sort of policy had a critical effect on Israel's army. Those who were responsible should be held accountable. Israel, after all, depends for its political *survival* upon the ingenuity of those who command its army. Israel can afford to have nothing less than its most brilliant and distinguished men as senior officers in the High Command.

Dayan's Chief of Staff, David Elazar, demonstrated a lack of political vision. His routinization and professionalization of the IDF command did not include keeping the minds of his officers sharp both militarily and politically, and Dayan failed to press upon his Chief the need to re-examine strategic policy. Had Dayan been more firm he would have encouraged the Chief of Staff to see reality not only in terms of the perceptions of others but through their own understanding. But again, Dayan misperceived Arab capability to cancel out the IDF's strategy.

Last, but not least, Dayan's friendship with Chief-of-Staff Elazar was not intimate. In fact, it was Dayan who opposed the appointment of Elazar in 1971, the latter being groomed by Bar-Lev and strongly recommended by Allon, Galili and Golda Meir. On the whole, Dayan, while he was Defence Minister, did not interfere with the Chief-of-Staff. However, the events between the 6 and 8 of October created a deep estrangement between the two. The failure of the IDF to halt the Egyptian crossing, the confusion in the Southern Front, and the overconfidence of General Elazar caused Dayan to strongly mistrust the IDF's senior officers, and his relationship with Elazar bordered on suspicion. Dayan was terribly disappointed in the IDF after 6–8 October 1973 and, consequently, this influenced his attitude toward the Chief-of-Staff.*

Still in 1973 (despite the political and strategic debacle of

*I am basing this judgment on reading some of the unpublished Agranat Report documents, and on claims of some senior commanders on the Southern Front I have interviewed, and on interviews with many senior and middle-ranking officers in the Southern Command. In his autobiography, (Hebrew edition), Dayan indirectly and cynically describes his attitude towards Chief-of-Staff Elazar. (See Moshe Dayan, *Avney Derekh*, Adanim, Jerusalem, 1976, pp. 599-612.)

the first two days), the IDF proceeded to demonstrate resilience of the first magnitude. The aggressor was halted and an inferior defensive position was converted to a superior offensive position. The IDF achieved what few armies in history have done: the reversal of a military collapse followed by a seizure of the initiative, within two days and in the midst of the campaign. Neither the British nor the French accomplished a similar feat in the two world wars. In Vietnam, the American army spent ten years gaining the initiative. General Sharon's crossing of the Canal will surely enter the annals of history as one of the greatest campaigns in modern times.

Given adverse conditions, such as the loss of initiative, Israel's 1973 victory was superior to that of 1967 from a strictly military point of view. But the military victory was not consummated, and the sands of the political hourglass ran out for Israel. Within days, its isolation from Europe and Africa, the development of the Arab oil weapon and the energy crisis, and a Soviet–American confrontation all converged to endanger Israel's very survival. Israel emerged from the war with little political advantage aside from a direct American involvement in mediation. Israel's loss of 3,000 men dealt it a sharp blow. The war marred its golden record—seven successful years. Faced with psychological and economic hardships Israel was forced to retrench. Fear of Soviet intervention was no less real. So, too, was concern over the type of peace the United States would secure for Israel. The Geneva Conference concept was viewed with suspicion. The Suez agreement of January 15, 1974, and the Golan agreement of May 30 were regarded not as diplomatic or political breakthroughs, but as having achieved a more stable ceasefire at the expense of a partial and unilateral Israeli withdrawal. The next Israeli cabinet, headed by General Rabin, refused to make further territorial concessions in 1974 unless the Arabs would make commensurate political concessions. An American–Arab rapprochement increased Soviet intervention. To outbid Kissinger the USSR sent the largest and most sophisticated weapons shipments to both Egypt and, especially, to Syria.

On the whole, in October 1973, the Arab world demonstrated unprecedented political and military unity. The co-ordination between Egypt and Syria was well synchronized. But would the relationship survive the Geneva Conference? By mid-1974 the coalition of Syria and Egypt had already been disrupted. Asad torpedoed Sadat's moderate stand in the Rabat November 1974 Conference. Two new camps appeared to be emerging after Rabat: (1) a radical camp led by Syria, Iraq, Libya, and the Palestinians, and (2) a pragmatic camp led by Egypt, Saudi Arabia, and the Gulf Emirates. The prospect for pacification if not modification of the conflict appeared dim. Only an imaginative Israeli foreign policy could to keep them divided and ready for compromise with Israel. An imaginative American policy could impose upon the Soviets a real detente orientation if the latter were to guarantee the US that they would not intervene if and when an Arab state pre-empted war again.

Conclusions

In an article in *World Politics*, Robert Jervis has proposed four 'safeguards' to assist decision-makers in avoiding misperception.

1. Decision makers 'should know that what may appear to them as self-evident and unambiguous inference often seems so only because of their pre-existing beliefs.'
2. Decision makers 'should see if their attitudes contain consistent or supporting beliefs that are not logically linked.'
3. Decision makers 'should make sure their assumptions, beliefs and predictions are as explicit and consistent as possible.'
4. Decision makers 'should try to prevent individuals and organizations from letting their main task, political future, and identity become tied to specific theories and images of other actors.'[48]

Clearly, Israel's inner circle violated safeguard number 1 by believing only what they wanted to believe. Thus, neither General Dayan nor any member of the High Command had foreseen Egypt's ability to wage the type of war that it did in 1973. Dayan had thought only several days would be required to defeat the Arabs. Later he admitted, 'The war was more difficult than I had thought.'[49] Golda Meir relied on

Dayan's theory and refused to take General Elazar's advice to pre-empt and to mobilize at least five divisions. Undoubtedly, she feared the world would accuse Israel of militancy and expansion if she heeded Elazar. But this explanation is not in conformity with the policy that was constantly pursued by the inner circle, viz. if necessary, go it alone, or as Ben Gurion is alleged to have said, 'What matters is what we Jews of Israel do, not what the gentile nations say.' What had become 'self-evident' to the inner circle was the invincibility of Israel's deterrent power.

Interviews with five generals in the high command (including the chief of staff) in July 1973 revealed that the inner circle took little account of safeguard number 2—that of making sure their assumptions were logically linked. They were overwhelmingly optimistic concerning Israel's chances in the next war. Not only were they convinced that a decisive victory was possible, but that it was inevitable. Dayan's admission in December 1973 that 'at the outbreak of fighting on October 6, the Arabs operated with more and better equipment than had been anticipated and they handled it better than it had been thought they would,'[50] shows the extent to which Israeli optimism was not logically linked to Intelligence information. The experience of the failure of Israeli deterrence in 1967 could not support such optimism. Under the fog of peace they preferred to ignore the Arab tenacity and dedication to go to war. Despite overt and covert Arab aggressive actions (War of Attrition, the principles of Khartoum), the inner circle deluded themselves that the logical consequence of Israeli occupation would lead the Arabs to negotiate with Israel.

Nor did the inner circle heed Jervis's third proposal, that of making sure their assumptions were consistent. Rather their beliefs and predictions concerning the role the occupied territories played in the post-1967 strategic and military doctrines were unclear—even contradictory. Some advocated territorial annexation for purely military defensive purposes or as a security measure. Others perceived annexation as a legitimate and reasonable act of Zionism: 'Settlement is Israel's best weapon.' Allon and most of the High Command regarded territorial annexation in the former sense and as a potentially useful political bargaining card. To Galili, it was the latter—a raison d'etre of Zionism. Dayan and Peres vacillated between the two interpretations, although their inclination was to lean toward Galili's view. And for Golda Meir, the occupied territories invoked a mixture of Zionism, security, and a tough bargaining stance toward the Arabs. There was no explicit military strategy, and deterrence was never made consistent. Did deterrence mean territorial Lebensraum? Was it the Bar-Lev line? The Intelligence warning system? The Arab inability to pay the cost? The efficiency of the IDF's mobilization and deployment? Rapid and guaranteed American supplies? There was no clear political and strategic concept of deterrence, and it certainly never became an explicit or a consistent policy. Despite the knowledge gained in 1967 about the loss of deterrence and of Israel's power to surprise, the inner circle did not re-evaluate their own failures and successes in the light of 1967 in order to establish whether the enemy also learned from his 1967 errors.

Not one member of the Israeli elite, hawk or dove, inside or outside the inner circle, was explicit concerning the nature of the peace that Israel sought. Over the years, as the conflict grew increasingly bitter and institutionalized, any concept of peace became increasingly vague and unrealistic. The continuum between ceasefire standstill and a final peace conference was never filled. Beyond the first post-ceasefire step and a final peace conference the inner circle had no blueprint. Harkabi's pessimistic view on the asymmetry between Israeli and Arab aspirations was concurrent although not convergent with that of the inner circle. Dayan always spoke of an Arab-Israeli rapprochement as a process, but as the Arabs believed that diplomatic measures had only marginal value, diplomacy ranked low in the hierarchy of aspirations of Israel's political and security elites. As a result of this perception, the inner circle had predicted war and not negotiations. Yet, in their forecast of war, they simultaneously predicted immediate success and total victory and missed the scope and nature of the next Arab round. The IDF's High Command and Intelligence violated Jervis's fourth safeguard. As individuals and as a formal organization, the High Command identified specific theories (some carelessly examined) and images of the inner circle as their own and provided little challenge and certainly no institutional adversity to the inner circle. Many of the 1973 misperceptions were tied to the Israeli image of what the Arabs want, can, and will do. Was the purpose of maintaining the occupied territories seen as a strategic bargaining card in future negotiations with Arabs, or as fulfilling the pioneer Zionist concept of settling the 'empty deserts?'

Would a different inner circle and a different High Command have suffered fewer misperceptions and made fewer mistakes? Or did Israel's pre-1973 inner circle and High Command represent the perception and orientation of alternative political elites as well? After all, perceptions, it could be argued, are also bound to the environment. The climate of the conflict and the aspirations of Israel and of Israel's adversaries contributed greatly to Israeli misperceptions.

The lessons of 1973, however, should serve to produce different strategies in the future. If not, new perceptions will only feed old images—particularly if there is no change in the hostile environment.

NOTES

1. For the position and attitudinal behaviour of some of the national security inner circle, see Michael Brecher, *The Foreign Policy of Israel*, Yale, 1972. Also Shabtai Teveth, *Moshe Dayan*, Houghton Mifflin, Boston, 1973; Yuval Elizur and Eliahu Salpeter, *The Establishment* (Hebrew), Levin-Epstein, Tel-Aviv, 1973. For Dayan's Military doctrine, see Michael Handel, *Israel's Political-Military Doctrines*, C.F.I.A., Harvard University, No 30, August 1973, and Moshe Dayan, *Diary of the Sinai Campaign*, Harper and Row, New York, 1965. For the institutionalization of the security function, see Michael Brecher, *The Foreign Policy of Israel* and Meir Pa'il, 'The Transformation of the Concept of the High Command from the Haganah to Zahal,' unpublished MA thesis, The University of Tel-Aviv, 1971. For an evaluation of Israeli military and security relations, see Amos Perlmutter, *Military and Politics in Israel 1948-1967* (Cass 1969, reissued 1977). See also Zeev Schiff, *Earthquake in October* (Hebrew), Zmora Publishers, 1974, pp. 68-72.
2. Prime Minister Yitzchak Rabin did not establish a formal NSC. The Kitchen Cabinet is no longer effective. Instead, Rabin's NSC was the full cabinet. A few individuals were more influential in security matters, e.g. Ministers Peres, Bar-Lev, Yariv, and Zadok.

3. This was written two months before Agranat's Investigation Committee's Interim Report was published on April 2, 1974; for an English summary of the Interim Report, see the *New York Times*, April 3, 1974; in Hebrew part of the Report was published in *Ma'ariv*, April 4, 1974, pp. 4-8; the full Interim Report in Hebrew was published in mimeo, *The Agranat Report*, April, 1974, Jerusalem, 33 pages.
4. Irving Janis, *Victims of Group Think*, Houghton Mifflin, Boston, 1972.
5. Erwin C. Hargrove, *The Power of the Modern Presidency*, Temple University Press, Philadelphia, 1974, p. 140.
6. Edward Jones and Harold Gerrard, *Foundations of Social Psychology*, Wiley, New York, 1967, pp. 131-132, 190-194 also 'Cognition' in J. Gould and Kalb eds., *Dictionary of the Social Sciences*, The Free Press, MacMillan, 1964, p. 99.
7. Robert Jervis, Introduction to *Perception and International Relations*, Unpublished MS, C.F.I.A., Harvard University, February 1973.
8. See Herbert Blumer, 'Science Without Concepts,' *American Journal of Sociology*: 36 (No 31) pp. 515-533.
9. Robert Jervis, 'Hypotheses on Misperceptions,' *World Politics*: 20 (No 3, April 1968) p. 455.
10. Jones and Gerrard, *Foundations*, p. 190.
11. The classic work on cognitive dissonance is Leon Festinger, *A Theory of Cognitive Dissonance*, Harper and Row, Evanston, Ill., 1957.
12. 'Perception' in J. Gould and J. Kalb, *Dictionary of the Social Sciences*, The Free Press, MacMillan, New York, 1964.
13. Lawrence Martin, *Arms and Strategy*, David McKay, New York, 1973, p. 13.
14. Ben Gurion's concept of deterrence and military balance is analyzed in David Ben Gurion's *When Israel Fights* (Hebrew), Mapai Publishing House, Tel-Aviv, 1950.
15. *Ibid.*, p. 17.
16. See Michael Handel, *Israel's Political-Military Doctrine*, pp. 21-36.
17. Moshe Dayan, 'Interview,' *Bamachane*, Israel Army Weekly, August 21, 1967, pp. 5-7.
18. A party compromise between the inner circle and their opponents adopted in August 1973 had favoured Dayan's demand for gradual and partial settlement of occupied territory in Egypt and Jordan. This document was modified in the party platform after the 1973 war.
19. Instead of transferring the war into enemy territory, the IDF 'waited' for Arab forces to take the offensive.
20. The American attitude toward Israel between 1948 and 1970 is best summarized as a moral commitment to Israel's existence and a political commitment to the 1947 partition. In the absence of a single valuable monograph on Israeli-American relations, I rely mainly on my researches for my forthcoming study, 'Israel and America, the Politics of Ambiguity'.
21. Interviews with Rabin, Peres and Dinitz confirmed this point of view, although the term 'perfect' was not used in each case. *All* gave high credence to the Nixon Doctrine ('We give the weapons and you fight').

22. Between 1967 and 1971 Israel faced a practical embargo on her supply of interceptors. During 1972 Israel received inadequate electronic and anti-missile equipment. And repeatedly, Israelis were warned by Secretary Kissinger to abandon the strategy of pre-emption now that their security could rest on detente and that, without Soviet support and resupply, the Arab aspirations for war would subside.
23. The leading Israeli expert and theoretician of Arab attitudes toward Israel is undoubtedly Professor (General) Yehoshafat Harkabi who, for over a decade, has written in both Hebrew and English the most important studies on the Arab position. I single out among his numerous essays and books, both in Hebrew and English, the following: The seminal *Arab Attitudes Toward Israel* (Vallentine, Mitchell, London, 1971); *The Israeli Position in the Arab-Israeli Conflict* (Dvir, 1967, Tel-Aviv (Hebrew)); his 'The Fog of Peace has Hidden the War,' (*Ma'ariv* (Hebrew), November 2, 1973); and his prophetic and perceptive 'Who is responsible for the persistence of the Arab-Israeli Conflict?' (*Ma'ariv*, September 26, 1973, p. 25). See also Gil Carl Alroy, 'Patterns of Hostility' in Gil Carl Alroy ed. *Attitudes Towards Jewish Statehood in the Arab World*, American Academic Assn. for Peace in the Middle East, New York, 1971, pp. 1-31.
24. See Harkabi's two essays in *Ma'ariv*, September 26, 1973 and November 2, 1973.
25. Even the Chief of Staff General Elazar complained before the Agranat Committee of inadequate Intelligence information from below.
26. Harkabi, 'The Fog of Peace has Hidden the War', *Ma'ariv*, November 2, 1973, p. 15.
27. Interviews with members of the inner circle and the 1967-1973 IDF's High Command during the summers of 1971, 1972 and 1973.
28. Private interview with Dayan, July 11, 1973.
29. See also Zeev Schiff, 'The Grand Error,' *Haaretz*, June 26, 1974, p. 2.
30. For a Zionist view on this period, see: Yehudah Bauer, *Diplomacy and Underground in Zionism op. cit*; David Ben Gurion, *Meetings with Arab Leaders* (Hebrew), Am Oved, Tel-Aviv, 1966; and Arthur Rupin, *Works*, Am Oved, Tel Aviv, Vol. III.
31. 'The Protocol of Closed Session Between Dayan and the Editors of the Israeli Press', *Ma'ariv*, November 15, 1973, pp. 22, 29.
32. *Ibid.*, p. 29.
33. The 1973 alliance has yet to prove its military strength and durability. Its military effectiveness may only have been temporary. Had it not been for the American and Soviet intervention when the Arabs sued for a ceasefire, the Egyptian armies might have been annihilated by Generals Sharon and Adan's troops.
34. *Ibid.*, 'Protocol', *Ibid.* p. 22.
35. Again, for short summary of the IDF's military-tactical doctrine, see Michael Handel, *Israel's Political-Military Doctrine*, C.F.I.A., Harvard, August 1973, pp. 51-63. See also Zeev Schiff's series of articles (six) on the failure of the Intelligence, *Haaretz*, June 22-27, 1974.
36. See Terrence Smith, 'Israeli Errors on the Eve of the War Emerging,'

New York Times, December 12, 1973. My interviews with two key members of the inner circle, several generals in the High Command as well as with retired officers on duty during the war, between October 24 and November 12, 1973, corroborated Smith's contention.

37. Matityahu Peled is at the University of Tel-Aviv as Professor of Arabic literature. He writes as well for *Ma'ariv*. Peled places the blame on the Minister of Defence, the Chief of Staff, planners within the IDF and General Chaim Bar-Lev, who had originally been recalled to serve as a special adviser to the Chief of Staff, but who took over the Southern Command when it collapsed.
38. M. Peled, 'First Lessons,' *Ma'ariv*, October 17, 1973, p. 9.
39. General Chaim Bar-Lev, 'The Lessons of War: The Tactical Doctrine Withstood the Test of War,' *Ma'ariv*, November 9, 1973, p. 18. General Ariel (Arik) Sharon, the only Israeli hero of the 1973 war, who successfully crossed the Canal on October 15, consummating the IDF offensive in Sinai, bitterly disputes Bar-Lev's contention; see Amos Perlmutter 'The Covenant of War', *Harpers*, February 1973, pp. 51-63.
40. Bar-Lev. *Ibid.* Zeev Schiff, assessing the IDF Intelligence system, argues that the major error of the latter was a distorted assessment of Arab military doctrine: (1) failure to assess the Egyptian capability for a large-scale and successful crossing of the Canal; (2) failure to assess the new technological advancement integrated into the Egyptian infantry, such as tank-seeking weapons; (3) the quantities of anti-tank weapons distributed among the Egyptian infantry and (4) no prognosis on the invulnerability of the anti-missile, anti-tank, anti-artillery Egyptian umbrella against the efficient Israeli air force. 'The Grand Error,' *Haaretz*, June 26, 1974, p. 2.
41. M. Peled, 'Confrontation between Military Defensive Strategies,' *Ma'ariv*, October 17, 1973. In an interview with editors of *Haaretz* (March 15, 1974, pp. 13, 20), General David Elazar was asked: 'Do you think that the IDF was well prepared to deal with enemy formations like those we have witnessed on the Egyptian front?' He answered: 'There is never enough [preparation]. There were several areas in which we were not sufficiently ready. There is no war that can be totally forecast. After all [in a war] two forces confront one another and sometimes there are quantities of weapons of whose existence we are aware, but whose quality we fail to evaluate correctly.'
42. M. Peled, 'Confrontation Between Military Defensive Strategies,' *Ma'ariv*, October 17, 1973.
43. *Ibid.*
44. See Amos Perlmutter 'The Israeli Army in Politics: The persistence of the Civilian over the Military,' *World Politics*, July 1968.
45. Generals Sharon, Yariv, Eytan, Adan, Handler, Zeevi and Hod. Some had retired of their own volition, seeking new careers. Others, however, as in the case of Sharon, were forced into retirement.
46. Dayan (commando) served Makleff (British Army), Laskov (British Army) served Dayan, Rabin (Palmach) served Tsur (British Army). See also Shabtai Teveth, 'Building a New Army,' *Haaretz*, February 8, 1974.

47. The Palmach really represented a caste or brotherhood, where the baton of chief of staff was passed from one Palmach officer to another: from Rabin to Bar-Lev to Elazar. In 1967, 80 per cent of the High Command were Palmach graduates. Although General Gur, the present Chief of Staff, is too young to be a Palmach veteran, he told me that in 1947 he joined the Palmach.
48. 'Hypotheses on Misperception,' *World Politics*, pp. 462-466.
49. Terrence Smith, 'Israeli Errors on the Eve of the War Emerging,' *New York Times*, December 10, 1973.
50. 'Dayan is Optimistic,' *New York Times*, December 26, 1973.

CHAPTER V

*Crisis Management: Kissinger's Middle East Negotiations (October 1973–June 1974)**

With the advent of nuclear weapons and great power competition, both the nature and structure of the international crisis have been revolutionized.[1] In the three decades since 1945, no major war among the great powers—no world war—has erupted. As Coral Bell has written, the post-war period may be characterized as 'a period of limited and peripheral wars.'[2]

The transformed nature of the nuclear international system demanded a new method for resolving international conflicts: the new structure is called 'crisis management,' and is an innovation of nuclear diplomacy.[3] Buchan sees two different types of crisis management structures: 'an allied system of crisis management and a bilateral system (US–USSR)'[4] . Bell identifies two major types of crisis management on two different levels: adversary crisis, which is conducted on the central level, and intramural crisis, conducted on the local level (e.g. Kashmir, or the Arab-Israeli conflict).[5]

The structure of crisis management has mainly developed in crises affecting the power in the central nuclear balance, as Bell has shown.[6] Crisis management between the nuclear powers is not a cordial type of exercise; it is 'a consciousness between the dominant powers, that they have solid common interests as well as sharp conflicting interests.'[7] Above all, a

*I am grateful to Professor Thomas Schelling of Harvard University for a concise definition of crisis management and for recommending that I examine the appropriate literature. I am also grateful to Robert Jervis and Murray Feld, both of Harvard, for their help.

crisis can only be managed when there is a 'preponderance of power on the side of the status quo coalition, formal or informal.'[8]

The main purpose of forming structures for crisis management is to develop rational procedures to meet unexpected contingencies and to search for options, which minimize the adversary's threats and maximize one's own self-interests, other than resorting to war. In the US a major structural reform took place during the Kennedy and Johnson administrations when the National Security Council (NSC) was re-established (it was first formed in 1947) to research, consult, plan, and take appropriate action to meet the adversary's challenge. The function of the NSC became one of crisis management, that is, the organization of decision-making on the highest national level to find means of avoiding war, short of appeasement or surrender. Decision-making techniques, troop deployment, and control over the nuclear arsenal were all to be synchronized at the highest level. Thus crisis management for the nuclear age became institutionalized.

The structure of crisis management was first operational at the time of the Cuba II missile crisis of the Kennedy administration. Gradually, however, despite much talk, research, writing, and planning, crisis management became politically routinized and bureaucratized and lost its essential purpose—to react to a major challenge both instantly and rationally. The elements of management science, such as centralized decision-making, a system of contingency planning, securing ideas, and troop deployment, failed to materialize in the case of NATO or in the conduct of the Vietnam war. Its failure to forestall the 1967 Arab-Israeli war demonstrated that institutionalized crisis management was not an effective or workable structure. As a pre-emptive political structure, crisis management failed to meet the challenges of major international crises.

When Henry Kissinger took over the NSC he substituted personal diplomatic management for institutionalized crisis management, which he saw as needlessly encumbered by its bureaucratic structure. Although the term crisis management is still used academically to refer to an institutionalized system of decision-making for contingency planning, practice has changed the structure and, therefore, the purpose, concepts and procedures of post-1962 crisis management. The term has generally come to mean the personalization of international diplomacy, a technique developed by Kissinger.

The Crisis Manager

Crisis management calls for 'crisis manager' types. According to Bell such a person must: (1) possess 'information about the other side's military capabilities and disposition,'[9] (2) exploit surveillance, and (3) the relations between antagonists based on 'adverse partnership;' (4) have access to intelligence information. Crisis managers must share a common strategic ideology 'built around the military means of the nuclear age.'[10] and be endowed, says Bell, with 'great moral and intellectual sensitivity, perception, imagination and courage.'[1] Whether Kissinger is endowed with all these qualities will be the subject of continued historical and political controversy, but whatever his own particular successes and failures, there can be no doubt that he has set the standards for the art of crisis management.

By these standards, the crisis manager, if he is to succeed, must be a super-diplomat. His method, in intra-mural disputes, is to set himself above the battle, to affect a style of innocence. The super-diplomat must appear to stand to gain nothing from the negotiations: only to ensure that the adversaries do. A super-diplomat is not necessarily a statesman. The two types have converged in only a few exceptional individuals, such as Masaryk, Bismarck, and Chaim Weizmann. The super-diplomat is a highly skilled technician; he is not necessarily endowed with the statesman's vision.

The post of super-diplomat has not been institutionalized and probably never will be. Nevertheless, men have taken the role upon themselves throughout history, and all with different styles. The purpose of this analysis is to examine how Kissinger has adapted the super-diplomat role to suit his background and personality. To this end we shall look at the first phase of negotiations in the Middle East (October

1973—June 1974) and examine the workings of Kissinger's technique of crisis management.

The Kissinger Modus Operandi

Two types of behaviour are evident in this super-diplomat: first, the understanding empathiser; and second, the mean man, the master of 'coercive diplomacy.'

The Diplomat as Empathiser

The technique is one of intimacy and empathy with the adversaries and their aspirations in the negotiations.

Networks

When he was a Professor at Harvard in the late 1950s Kissinger established a strategy-defence seminar which was designed to attract promising international politicians. In a little over a decade, Kissinger made close contacts with men who, by the late 1960s and early 1970s would become key political leaders in the Western world. In his seminar he taught such men from the Middle East as Allon, several advisers of Sadat and Faisal, and a few senior Syrian civil servants. Several senior members of the national and international media also 'served their time' in Kissinger's summer seminars and in the one-year fellow appointments at Harvard's Center for International Affairs. Kissinger remains on a first-name basis with his former students and has increased his acquaintanceship considerably since 1968, especially with the addition of Dayan and Rabin.

Understanding

The Kissinger diplomat must convince the adversary or adversaries that he 'understands' their goals and fears and is willing to modify his own goals as a result of his understanding. He also knows about their apprehensions concerning security interests and maximum and minimum national security aspirations.

Surrogate-Arbitrator

In negotiations Kissinger's ideal type of diplomat acts as a surrogate for everybody's national interests, supposedly to the exclusion of his own interests. However this understanding is conveyed to each actor only in private. He never gathers all the adversaries in one room or conference. He disdains international propaganda forums and ceremonial conferences. The approach is tête-à-tête, secretive, confidential, and intimate, in contrast to the normative conference approach of traditional diplomacy.

Insulator

The super-diplomat acts as an insulator in negotiations. He 'loves' both Chinese and Russians, Egyptians and Israelis, South and North Vietnamese. Since 'unfortunately' conflicts exist, he finds himself as the only person who can act as go-between. It is essential that he gives the impression of gaining nothing for himself, and that all the gains appear to be for the adversaries' benefit.

Confidant

Throughout the negotiations, the super-diplomat must assume the role of being the only person whom all belligerents can trust. Since he thus seems to be their trust personified, he is in a position to demand further confidence.

Kissinger as the Master of Coercive Diplomacy

The diplomat who practises the Kissinger technique learns to transfer the failure of the negotiations on to one or the other adversary, who is left to assume that he is helpless once the mediator threatens to end his services on the adversary's behalf.

Threat

An example of Kissinger's use of this technique can be seen

in his warning to Dayan in which he said, in effect, that if the Israelis did not place their trust in him, he could not promise that the US would once again airlift supplies and weapons to Israel as it did in October, 1973. Or in his advice to Sadat, that if he failed to have confidence in him as mediator, how could he prevent the Israelis from resorting to a war of pre-emption.

Having made the threat, the super-diplomat's next step is to bring forth his own solution. In Kissinger's case, such a plan was usually known as an 'American Initiative' or the 'American Proposal'. After the adversaries have confided in him, after he knows their weak points as well as those on which they would be least persistent, he 'sums up' the belligerents' demands and makes known what was really a preconceived American plan. In effect he pulls a rabbit out of a hat that has been with him since he left Washington, but acts as if it were only one hour old. By threatening them with a worse outcome, he 'convinces' the adversaries that what they have achieved as a result of his efforts is the best solution they could have reached.

Responsibility

It is important for the diplomat to make it appear that should the negotiations collapse, it is the fault of the adversaries. He must convince them that if only they could have seen the situation as he did, then the outcome of the negotiations might have been positive.

If negotiation fails, the adversary is to blame, not the insulator. The super-diplomat maintains his posture of having given all that could humanly and morally be expected of him.

The Unthinkable

Examination of the diplomat's threats to the adversaries shows that they are rarely carried out. Nevertheless, most of the time the harness of coercive diplomacy binds each adversary. The function of speed—the force of shuttle diplomacy—is designed to baffle the adversaries into believing that if the diplomat's mission fails, the unthinkable may occur. Such a blitz is the super-diplomat's most effective weapon.

Tranquillizers

Another popular super-diplomat manoeuvre could be called the use of a 'painkiller' administered to the belligerents wounded during the process of securing their agreement to the diplomat's blitz proposal. The process is furthered by a tacit message to each adversary that this may be his last operation.

Thus Israel was promised some tranquillity, as were Egypt and Syria. All three were exhausted by the shuttle blitz, confused by the promises and given the hope that their national aspirations had not been compromised. But tranquilizers are not a cure in themselves, and whether the operation was successful can only be seen when the medication wears off. Thus, while the patients are being lulled into thinking that the worst is over, the super-diplomat may be busy contemplating further surgery. Conversely, the diplomat may mistake the calm of the adversaries for lasting satisfaction only to find their disagreements and discontent as strong as ever, once his painkillers wear off.

Satellites

To institute an effective cost accounting system in the defence establishment, former Secretary of Defence Robert McNamara forced the defence industries to institute cost accounting procedures in their organizations; corporations which did not adopt the managerial technique could no longer compete effectively for department contracts.

In an analogous manner, in order to rationalize the system of crisis management, the super-diplomat has encouraged and, indeed, 'created,' crisis managers in the Middle East —notably, Sadat, Dayan, Allon, Rabin, Eban, and Fahmy. These Middle Eastern leaders have adopted the new style of diplomacy, presumably to further their own national goals. That Kissinger approves of this turn of events is seen in his praise of his 'student' crisis managers. Dayan, for example, is considered a man with 'original ideas;' Asad, although tough, is a 'tenacious man'; Rabin is a 'brilliant analyst'; Fahmy is a 'pragmatic negotiator.'

The creation of satellite crisis managers lubricates diplomatic procedures and makes all the participants feel that they are partners in a common pursuit, carefully orchestrated by their mentor.

The Dynamics and Processes of Crisis Management

The aftermath of the 1973 war in the Middle East offers a clear illustration of the dynamics of super diplomacy as refined by Kissinger. As has been mentioned, the technique itself was developed before Kissinger, during the Cuban Missile Crisis and in negotiations over arms control.[12]

The 1973 war certainly called for crisis management. At his press conference, on September 26, 1973, Kissinger emphasized that the Middle East was to get priority. Kissinger harnessed himself to crisis management on the day of attack, October 6, 1973, and a process, which began with the negotiation over Suez and the Golan Heights for the disengagement of Egyptian, Syrian, and Israeli forces, was still going on a year later. By October, 1974, it had resulted in the total withdrawal of Israel from territories occupied in 1973 and in a partial withdrawal from territories occupied in 1967.

An examination of the major American and British newspapers, and the Israeli, Egyptian, and Syrian press will supply the interested reader with the details of the day-to-day negotiations. The purpose of this analysis is to explore the conceptual, intellectual, and social-psychological framework of the Kissinger system of crisis management and its processes while drawing illustrations from the cases of the Israeli, Egyptian and Syrian troop disengagements. The analysis will demonstrate the impact of the Kissinger style on the belligerents, describe the effect of its contribution, and speculate on the possible options that may emerge from this type of diplomacy.

The newly personalized super diplomacy can be divided into the following processes, which embody the variables of the Kissinger style: (1) the conditioning of the belligerents for negotiations; (2) the promotion of their hopes; (3) the system of threat-making; and (4) the breakthrough.

The Conditioning of the Belligerents

To persuade the belligerents into accepting his services the super-diplomat must first act as their sympathizer and convince them that he 'understands' them, without having any illusions as to the difficulties that face them. Kissinger, for example, as early as September 26, 1973, told the Arab foreign ministers and ambassadors at the UN: 'There are no miracles . . . what is needed is to find ways to turn what is presently unacceptable to you into a situation with which you can live.'[13] A prolonged war in the Middle East, he said, would create a 'high possibility of great power involvement.'[14]

To woo the Israelis, Kissinger stated that 'the US will not allow the Soviets a victory in the Middle East;'[15] and to Egypt he said, 'I believe that for the first time in five years we are engaged in a real dialogue with the Arab world.'[16] The diplomacy of attrition depends upon the establishment of trust between the mediator and the belligerent party. As Kissinger said, 'I think I know the Egyptian position very well, and I have attempted to present it as fairly as I could to the Israeli side on several occasions.'[17]

In January, 1974, Terrence Smith wrote from Jerusalem on the outlook in Israel during the Egyptian disengagement negotiations: 'It is the first time that Israel has placed her faith in something other than her own strength.' Kissinger, he said, 'has managed to win the confidence and respect of the Israeli authorities. The Israelis are convinced he has played straight with them and fairly represented their views to the other side.'[18] Here Kissinger is seen as the trusted man, the confidant of both adversaries.

In Egypt Kissinger said, 'These are the roughest negotiations I have ever been involved in, the most complex, but I like the people involved. It is humanly easier than Vietnam.'[19] Arab envoys told the *New York Times*, 'Mr. Kissinger's role is a "good faith" mediator.'[20]

During the Syrian negotiations, a *Newsweek* correspondent cabled from Cairo, 'Kissinger's agony in these negotiations is that he *deeply understands* these fears. . . . More than once, he has come out of a meeting with the Israeli leadership to sympathize with the way they see their dilemma. And last week, emerging from a meeting with Syrian President Hafez Asad, he turned to aides and said, "I just wish you could sit in on this and hear for yourself the intensity of the Syrian commitment, the sense of carrying the lance of Arab nationalism, their deep commitment to Palestine." Increasingly, it has become clear that he is attempting in his mid-East travels not just to negotiate a military disengagement, but to get the Israelis and Arabs to see—as he does—*the merits of each other's arguments and understand each other's fears.*'[21]

Once the empathy/sympathy phase of the diplomatic manoeuvring is completed, the next step is to exploit the belligerents' trust and channel it into self-serving praises between the crisis manager and his satellites.

Abba Eban had this to say on the ABC TV programme 'Issues and Answers,' in March, 1974: 'Mr Kissinger's personal role refutes the view that history is the product of impersonal forces and objective conditions in which the personal human factor doesn't matter. I believe that the association of American prestige with Secretary Kissinger's skills has been crucial in creating a new climate.'[22]

When President Sadat appeared on the same programme on April 7, 1974, he was asked, 'To what extent do you think that your personal rapport with Secretary Kissinger has been a factor in the change between the US and Egypt?' Sadat replied: 'I always believe in personal contacts, and when you find a Secretary of State who knows the full details about the problem, *who is a man of trust and a man of vision*, our friendship and relations survive. I was accused by my Arab colleagues of betrayal (that is, of establishing cordial relations with the US), but it has been proved that with imagination, effort, and trust, we have reached the best conclusions (mutually). We (Kissinger and I) talk lots—lots. He is a man of strategy; myself, I am a man of strategy also; so when we sit together one cannot imagine what we discuss (that is, we discuss the range of strategic questions)—not only the area here, the Middle East, but all over the world. Dr Kissinger and I are friends. We discuss everything that friends discuss: business . . . exchange jokes, everything.'[23]

When Dayan arrived in 1974 in Washington, Kissinger characterized his proposal on the Israeli-Syrian disengagement on the Golan as 'useful', and 'very serious'. At a cocktail party given for Dayan in Ambassador Dinitz's home on March 31, Kissinger hailed Dayan as one of the original strategists in the Middle East.*

About this time, Dayan began to use the language of crisis managers: 'What we are trying to do is to negotiate with Syria. It will take a lot of work to bring the two parties together.' Taking his cue from his master, this new satellite crisis manager began to echo the language of his 'friend, Dr Henry'. Sadat too began to use such words as 'concepts', 'strategy' and 'breakthrough', all part of the crisis manager's jargon. Evidently diplomacy, disguised in the language of crisis management, has become the stock-in-trade of Eban, Sadat, Dayan, and even of the rigid Asad of Syria.

Secure in his position as headmaster of this school of diplomacy, Kissinger has rarely had his own role in negotiations challenged. On one occasion, however, the shrewd former editor-in-chief of *Al-Ahram*, Muhammad Hasanayn Haykal, challenged the 'above-the-battle' stance taken by the Secretary. Haykal described the encounter thus: 'When I met Dr Henry Kissinger at dinner on November 7, 1973, after he met Sadat, Kissinger told me quietly, "From reading several of your articles, I feel as though we have been friends for at least 20 years."'[24] But Haykal inquired, 'Who are you, Dr Kissinger? You have handled massive problems with great ability before—the Vietnam War—opening the gates of China . . . and the détente with the USSR. However, in all these problems you represented *one side of the problem* . . . in this time of crisis in the Middle East, the question "Who are you?" becomes necessary so that we may know *exactly where we stand.* Are you a party? Are you a negotiator? I don't think so. You are the first to say that Israel enjoys a will independent from the US, although you admit that you have considerable influence over it . . . this does not exactly make you a

*Private information of the author.

party . . . consequently you do not conduct negotiations . . . . Is your role one of "mediator"? . . . . but such a role calls for neutrality between the two sides.'

Kissinger admitted, 'I do not act as a mediator between the two parties in the crisis . . . . Let us say and agree that I represent America's concern over a serious crisis that is taking place in an area sensitive to us . . . an area in which we have strategic political and economic interests, as well as security interests. We want to preserve these interests.'[25]

Challenged by Haykal, Kissinger's style of 'frankness' proved effective. But Haykal, refusing to accept the satellite role assigned to him by Kissinger, was ousted from his position as editor-in-chief of *Al-Ahram*.

A senior leading member of the Israeli cabinet, and a prominent Kissinger satellite, has refuted Haykal's opinion of Kissinger. In a private conversation with the author, he said, 'After all, do you want Rusk, Ball, or Rogers as Secretary of State? They will cut off your balls. Maybe Henry is not doing all that we want, but after all, he is a member of the *family*; and if we sometimes quarrel, it is only in the family, is it not?'* By the 'family', the author at first assumed his interlocutor meant 'Jews.' Since then, it has become apparent from his actions that he meant the family of crisis managers.

The Promotion of Hopes

Acting as an above-battle arbitrator, by not taking sides, Kissinger manages to raise his adversaries' hopes.

The technique is rather simple. First, the crisis manager claims little or nothing for his personal or immediate national advantage. He told Haykal, for example, that the US had only political and strategic concerns in the Middle East. In this way, he expects to reduce the resistance of an adversary who no longer suspects him of harbouring institutional and personal aspirations. Next, he tries to engender the hope that aspirations can be fulfilled and fears alleviated.

In a press conference in Washington on November 21, 1973, Kissinger claimed 'modest' objectives for his negotiations

*Private meeting with the author in Tel-Aviv, January 13, 1974.

in the Middle East. 'Our objective was to solidify the ceasefires [referring to the Suez agreement] so that we could move forward, together with other interested parties, toward peace negotiations . . . we will make a major effort to narrow the differences between the parties, to help the parties move toward peace that all the peoples in the area need, and that the peace of the world requires. Now, this will be our policy in the Middle East.'[26]

Taken at face value, therefore, Kissinger's objectives for the Middle East have been to stabilize the ceasefire and narrow the differences of the belligerents, in co-operation with the Soviets; objectives that call for a restricted role for the Secretary—that of mediator-negotiator. But he frankly admitted to Haykal that he was more than a mediator-negotiator, that his role was one of 'concern' for American national interests in the area. Certainly these are higher aspirations than those he has claimed at his press conferences or when he meets his satellite crisis managers.

Aware of Israel's fears, mistrust, and sense of hopelessness over the Syrian attitude to conflict resolution, Kissinger made this statement on his arrival in Jerusalem on May 2, 1974: 'I come not to discuss concessions but to discuss security. The issue is not pressure, but a lasting peace.'[27] In this way, Kissinger raised Israeli hopes by substituting Israel's most cherished symbols, 'security' and 'lasting peace,' for the two symbols of fear, 'concessions' and 'pressure.' He was also protecting Dayan, who in Washington on March 30 had conceded more than the Israeli cabinet had formally authorized. Finally, by using the language of the adversary's aspirations, Kissinger offered Israeli decision-makers and his students of crisis management a demonstration of the use of language to gloss over an unhappy situation.

Using the adversary's own words and phrases that symbolize his fears and hopes has been proved an effective psychological technique in diplomatic management. For instance, in mid-May, 1974, Kissinger told journalists accompanying him[28] that 'Asad has gone a long way toward drumming up domestic support for a settlement and it could be too late for him to turn back.'[29] Thus by raising the hopes of the adversaries, he intends to lower their resistance and make his own demands (in the form of a 'solution') seem eminently reasonable.

Kissinger's next step is to portray the hope he has promoted as creating new *conditions*, previously unrealizable. Thus, in negotiating the troop disengagement he promised Israel secure borders; the Arabs were told that the pre-October 6, 1973, conditions would be tolerable and the process of an Israeli withdrawal would begin.[30] He avoids defining the secure or final borders of Israel (perhaps even to himself), nor has he told the Arabs how much territory lost in 1967 would be returned. These conditions have been left to the imagination, craftiness, and persistence of the belligerents. The secure Israeli border and the final Israeli withdrawal are not the 'American Concern'.

Incrementalist crisis management demands a minimum from the belligerents and inspires them with hope. To alleviate their frustration at not realizing their hopes—which is often the outcome—Kissinger supplies them with a version of what transpired during negotiations which is more positive. For instance, he tells the adversaries that they will *lose* still more if they refuse to negotiate or compromise. Then what they might have lost by failing to negotiate, he tells them they have gained. In effect, the adversaries are thus persuaded that each of their losses can become a gain.

On October 12, 1974, Kissinger reiterated this statement made in the midst of the October war a year earlier: 'Stalemate is the most propitious condition for a settlement.'[31] He had worked hard to achieve that type of stalemate in October 1973. The strategy was to create 'gains' out of domestic frustration within Israel and to minimize Arab 'losses' by regaining for the Arabs all the territories occupied in 1973 and some of those lost in 1967.

The System of Threat Promotion

After establishing confidence, creating conditions of credibility, and securing maximal information on the adversaries' apprehensions and fears, Kissinger will often resort to another technique, that of making a double-edged threat. On the one hand, it appears as another element of 'understanding', for a statement such as 'since I know your apprehensions, let me see what I can do for you', can be presented not as a threat but as a friendly offer. But it does, too, contain the element of a direct threat that support will be withdrawn, making the adversary believe that all will be lost. The threat, then, combines misinformation and friendly advice with a statement or an allusion concerning the withdrawal of support. Its purpose is to lead the adversary into thinking that the only possible alternative is to accept the American proposal. Finally, Kissinger uses a third type of threat, this one better known as deterrence.

A classic example of a threat which incorporated all three elements of ambiguity, withdrawal of support, and deterrence, was the American alert of October 25, 1973. According to one of Washington's national security specialists, the alert was conceived after the Soviet Union boasted that it had 'mobilized seven Russian divisions to fight for Egypt. . . .'[32] Whether this information was correct, whether it was part of a diplomatic manoeuvre by Sadat, demonstrating his fidelity to the Arabs, the fact remains that the week of October 26, 1973, was climactic in the American-Soviet struggle. After the alert Brezhnev faced a real dilemma: Was the US withdrawing from detente, or was crisis management being stretched to the limit?

The fear of a Russian withdrawal from detente must have played a key role in the American alert, which, according to the *New York Times*, was managed by Kissinger and Secretary Schlesinger alone. 'It is now certain,' wrote David Binder of the *Times* in November, 'that both the timing and exact nature of the alert were acted upon without the President's specific prior approval.'[33] Binder described all the elements of the alert, which were faithful to the style of crisis management. The actors were Kissinger, Schlesinger, Brezhnev, Gromyko, and Dobrynin (one of Kissinger's chief partners in the system of super diplomacy). 'From all this,' wrote Binder, 'it seems clear there was no *actual* crisis, but a *potential* crisis. That is why the President stayed upstairs and that is why the hot line was not used. Only after the news of the alert was broadcast, did Mr Nixon decide to *dramatize* it as a crucial, personal face-off against the Russians.'[34]

The crisis managers manipulated the alert for their own advantages, and it was carefully controlled. Secretary Kissinger said in his November 21, 1973, press conference, 'The relationship between the Soviet Union and the United States is an inherently *ambiguous* one. We have never said that detente indicated that we have parallel objectives, or that it indicates that we have compatible domestic structures.'[35] Kissinger also revealed that 'in this situation [the alert and the Soviet–American confrontation], one will always have an element, both of *confidence* and *competition*, coexisting in a somewhat ambivalent manner.'[36] The statement could well serve as a description of the inputs and orientations of the personalized crisis management system.

Kissinger went on to identify crisis management by using the term 'considerable restraints' and by pointing out that confidence exists where 'confrontation is mitigated'. The confrontation between the great powers, explained Kissinger, 'took place after the compromise of October 22, 1973 (the ceasefire had been reached, and as a result of actions which could not be fully controlled by either of the two sides [US-USSR] . . . .' But one had to consider how rapidly the confrontation had ended and how quickly the two sides had decided to move back to a policy of co-operation in settling the Middle East conflict. 'I would, therefore, say that the relationship that had developed between the two governments and between the two leaders played a role in settling the crisis, even though it had not been firm enough to prevent the crisis.'[37] Implicit in this statement was the threat that if the Soviets did not co-operate, detente would be jeopardized (as indeed it materialized in the alert of October 25).

The other side of the threat, the technique of appearing extremely understanding and sympathetic to adversaries' positions, was demonstrated when Kissinger imposed a ceasefire on the Israeli army advancing into the western territory of Egypt. Kissinger arrived in Tel-Aviv from Moscow on October 22 with a fait accompli—an American–Soviet agreement on a new Middle Eastern ceasefire, which was adopted by the Security Council as Resolution 333. Kissinger had advocated a ceasefire as early as October 6, 1973, but as this idea was not accepted by Egypt and Syria or by the USSR, he waited to see what the Arabs could and would do. According to Leslie Gelb of the *New York Times*, 'Informed American officials [in the White House and Pentagon] related that Dr Kissinger moved as soon as Moscow was prepared to support the ceasefire. These officials said he [Kissinger] was arguing that a total *Israeli victory over Egyptian forces* would make negotiations impossible.'[38] Kissinger himself claimed that he had 'requested' Israel to accept the ceasefire in view of the Soviet military threat to the advancing Israeli armies. Thus, Kissinger approached Israel in the spirit of 'understanding', warning the Israelis of the supposed Soviet threat.

Kissinger used the same technique in persuading Israel to help him negotiate a Syrian–Israeli troop disengagement. While the Israeli cabinet was discussing the Syrian proposals Kissinger had submitted, he recruited Nixon to send no less than three cables, 'asking Mrs Meir to support Dr Kissinger in his efforts, while emphasizing that he, Nixon, was monitoring his Secretary's trip with great *personal* interest.'[39]

Then Kissinger moved on to threaten the Israelis: 'If war breaks out again, many people may blame Israel for it. I doubt if it will be possible to airlift supplies to Israel as the United States did after the tenth of October. American public opinion will fail to understand Israeli stubborness [i.e. Israel's unwillingness to compromise on the Golan negotiations], and I doubt if there could be another alert such as the one issued on October 25 under the circumstances, even if the Soviets should threaten direct intervention.'[40] Support withdrawal, Kissinger's last resort, is his most effective way of reducing the adversary's highest hopes to the super-diplomat's own level. Once this has been achieved, negotiations verge on the step known as 'breakthrough.'

The Breakthrough

When the process of diplomatic attrition reaches a point at which the crisis manager believes that: (1) by threatening the adversaries' most cherished national interests, he has persuaded them of the 'advantages' of compromise; (2) they are now convinced that their interests converge with those of the super-diplomat; and (3) finds he has stretched the adversaries' nerves to the limit—he pulls out a plan which embodies *his* views of what the adversaries can and should surrender. The plan—variously labelled the 'breakthrough,' the American initiative, or the American proposal—defines the nature and structure of the compromise. The decision on the timing of the breakthrough is crucial. The adversaries are not permitted to decide at their own time and place, for the breakthrough is the super-diplomat's most guarded domain. Even his closest advisers are not aware when he will declare that the impasse has been broken.

Marilyn Berger of the *Washington Post* described the breakthrough phase in negotiations between Israel and Syria as follows: 'Kissinger's negotiating style is to wait until the last moment, so that *any American proposal* does not become a subject for negotiations.'[41] Or, as Joseph Kraft put it, 'In sum, the Secretary's essential method is to leash the dogs of war which he himself has previously unleashed. It is not nice, but it works what looks like wonders.'[42]

Past successful America proposals have been accompanied by a frantic blitz of diplomatic activity. The major ingredient is surprise. 'Diplomatic momentum produces success, success feeds success, and leads to strengthening one's position at home. Each negotiating partner is to be given the impression that everyone else is about to compromise and agree . . . the technique is to seek whatever agreement is possible.'[43] And should the technique appear to be failing, Kissinger may suddenly announce that he is desperately needed in Washington. He may thus further press the adversaries by saying that if they do not hurry up, they may find him on the way to Washington within an hour.

In the case of the Damascus–Jerusalem mediations, this technique did not produce immediate results. Though the Secretary threatened several times to return to Washington, he remained in the area for exactly three weeks after his first offensive. 'Through the negotiations he had broken "deadlines" for his departure from the Middle East; each time he thought it would be possible to reach an agreement, but each deadline spurred both sides to expedite their decisions.'[44]

The language the Secretary uses during the blitz is firm and aggressive. In the shuttle negotiations on the Egyptian–

Israeli troop separation, Kissinger told Golda Meir, 'You *must* co-operate with me on releasing the Egyptian Third Army and opening the Canal. The Russians are threatening; you'd better hurry, Mrs Meir.'* In the weeks preceding the Suez agreement of January 18, 1974, the following was the tenor of his speech and behaviour: 'Israel must adjust to the new conditions [those elaborated in the American Proposal] if it wants to secure its defence [by getting American military aid]. You must do your very best, Mrs Meir; you must not humiliate me [by failing to meet with the unconditional demand for Israeli withdrawal from the West Bank of the Canal].'[45]

As already mentioned, the American proposal is partly generated in its early stages by the adversaries, particularly through their satellite crisis managers. Dayan's visit to Washington on March 29, 1974, before the Syrian–Israeli troop withdrawal negotiations, is a case in point. Despite the fact that the Israeli cabinet had unanimously decided never to return any Syrian territory occupied during the 1967 war, Dayan proposed a withdrawal beyond the 1973-occupied territories, but said that surrendering Kuneitra would be Israel's 'last territorial compromise in this stage of the pre-negotiations with Syria'. Kissinger reminded Dayan, however, that he regarded Kuneitra as the *first* phase of the negotiations.[46] Thus after the adversary has made his first compromise, the super crisis manager pushes him a little farther, and then continues to push until the last compromise is reached. Only then does he put forth the American proposal.

The process of attrition against Israel had begun even before the Secretary left for his first shuttle. In December, 1973, he invited a group of leading Jewish intellectuals, Harvard Zionists, and pro-Israeli professors[47] to Washington and lectured them on the 'plight' of Israel. He told them that Israel had lost the war, that if it had not been for him there would have been no airlift, and that Israel was politically isolated and mortally wounded. He said that its political

*Author's private information secured from a senior Israeli negotiator, January 8, 1974, in Tel-Aviv.

leadership lacked vision, its strategists lacked ideas, the malaise in the country was serious, and the Israeli government could not carry the burden of negotiations. This method of diplomatic attrition had three purposes: (1) to convey to the Israeli leadership the need for territorial withdrawal, thus 'softening' Israeli opposition; (2) to protect Kissinger's flank from a Jewish and intellectual-liberal backlash; (3) to signal to Israel that he could be rude and ruthless. Similar ideas were related to the Executive Council of NATO late in March, 1974.*

Finally, several journalists in Kissinger's entourage played a role in the diplomacy of attrition and persuasion. Bernard Gwertzman of the *New York Times* has written: 'Because Mr Kissinger travels as a mediator on these trips, those with him also become, by extension, a sort of mediation force.'[48] Thus, even the press is harnessed to the processes of crisis management.

In the words of a key Egyptian official in Cairo on January 18, 1974, 'Kissinger produced a proposal and we accepted.'[49] What looks like an agreed compromise can, with a knowledge of the workings of crisis management, be described as a solution *imposed* on the adversaries. In the long run this type of diplomacy may prove to be little more than a whirlwind. Tactics of switching from ruthlessness to understanding, from empathy to meanness, and love to hate, make an impact, to be sure. Such emotional manipulations have produced two troop separations. But will they produce a lasting peace?

The main exercise of crisis diplomacy seems no more than a risky, short-term, collective leadership technique at the international level to *avoid* war. As Coral Bell has argued, 'if the avoidance of war is the only criterion for success in management of adversary crisis . . . this single criterion is not adequate, because it would oblige us to classify as a success, for instance, the management of the Munich crisis of 1938. War was certainly avoided on that occasion, but only to be incurred a year later, on worse terms.'[50]

The criteria for judging the success of super-diplomacy, Professor Bell cautions, should be: (1) has the probability of war increased or diminished or been mitigated? (2) what has

*Private information received by the author.

been the effect on the power position of either adversary, over the short and long terms? (3) has any contribution been made to the convention and technique of crisis management?[51]

Clearly, Kissinger's super diplomacy in the Middle East has made a considerable contribution to crisis management. But despite his brilliance, imagination, energy, and persuasiveness, the Middle East still faces the threat of war. Soviet levels of aspiration and intervention have not declined, despite the Middle East troop separation and ceasefire, nor has Soviet diplomacy and military power in the area been weakened, despite a short-term setback. In fact, since the conference in November 1974, the Soviets have re-emerged as supporters of Syrian military aspirations and as the backers of the PLO.

Detente may be operative and successful in the area of trade, arms control, and a European troop withdrawal settlement (MBFR). It may survive or even run its course in Southeast Asia. In the Middle East, however, the Soviet option of supplying the Arabs with military aid is *open*. It was never foreclosed, not even after Soviet advisers were ousted from Egypt in July, 1972. Soviet military support is the Arabs' best insurance policy against possible military debacles in the future.

The super diplomacy of Secretary Kissinger has made it more feasible for Egypt to have both a political option, i.e. that the US pressure Israel to withdraw from occupied territories, and a military option, with the Soviets to supply Egypt with the strategic weapons for the next Arab–Israeli round. Soviet military and diplomatic support of Syria throughout Kissinger's negotiations with Syria and Israel on troop separation, has only demonstrated the tenacity of Soviet military and diplomatic commitment in the Middle East and the Persian Gulf. I doubt if the USSR will be 'satisfied', to use another crisis management term, with a unilateral American proposal for the Middle East.* On the other hand, as Kissinger admitted to Haykal, the US is also 'concerned' about the area and has strategic, political and

**Pravda* gave all the credit for the successful troop withdrawal negotiations to Asad of Syria. Kissinger was not even mentioned.

economic interests there. It would be unrealistic to expect either great power to change its position vis-à-vis the Middle East in the short or the long run.

The US has improved its political options in Egypt, in the oil kingdoms and Persian gulf Sheikdoms, and among 'moderate' Arabs. But that the Egyptians have now become American 'allies', does not mean that the Sadat has lowered his level of aspirations concerning the Arab–Israeli conflict. Sadat stated emphatically in the ABC interview of April 7, 1974: 'I plan to disengage with the US, not Israel. I build no alliances, neither with the US, nor with the USSR. I only respond to friends. Egypt is neutral, and doesn't aim to play East against West. It only works to fulfil its national interests, the total withdrawal of Israeli forces from Arab lands and the economic rehabilitation of Egypt.'[52] (1974) What Kissinger has succeeded in doing has been to make the Arab–Israeli conflict more tolerable to the US. In the short run, he has certainly mitigated the great power struggle over the Middle East by deriving strength from the policy of detente elsewhere—in trade, arms control, and Europe. But he has also raised the Arab capacity to bid for more sophisticated Soviet weapons. The price the USSR must pay for Kissinger's Arab rapprochement is now higher than ever, and an influx of Soviet arms into the area can hardly be in America's interest.

As for the Arab–Israeli conflict, Kissinger has neither mitigated the aspirations of the belligerents nor reduced the probability of war. This is because Secretary of State Kissinger has chosen to abandon Professor Kissinger's wisdom that 'diplomacy, the art of restraining the exercise of power, cannot function in [a revolutionary] environment.'[53]

Professor Kissinger's most important contribution to the study of international politics is his concept of the roles of the two international order orientations—the legitimate and the revolutionary.[54] Even if Kissinger applied these concepts to international communism during the 1950s, the concepts are, nevertheless, his stock-in-trade and reflect his vision of the future of the international order.

A stable or legitimate international system utilizes international agreements, workable arrangements, and permissible aims as methods of foreign policy, and accepts the general rules of the international system: 'It implies the acceptance of the framework of international order by all major powers. . . . A legitimate order does not make conflicts impossible, but it limits their scope.'[55] Wars will be fought 'in *the name of the existing* structure and the peace which follows will be justified as a better expression of the "legitimate" general consensus.'[56] Diplomacy in the legitimate international system is 'the adjustment of differences through negotiations', something that 'is possible only in "legitimate" international orders.'[57] (Kissinger, 1957).

The revolutionary international system is dialectically opposite to the legitimate order; it does not accept the legitimacy of the structure, or its agreements and settlements. It considers the legitimate order oppressive.[58] 'The distinguishing feature of the revolutionary power is not that it feels threatened . . . but that nothing can reassure it.'[59] Diplomacy is, therefore, not the method to restrain the aspiration of actors in the revolutionary international order. '*Adjustments are possible*,' writes Kissinger of the revolutionary order, '*but they will be conceived as tactical manoeuvres to consolidate positions for the inevitable showdown, or tools to undermine the morale of the antagonist*.'[60]

There could not be found a more apt, succinct, and brilliant conceptual analysis of the Middle Eastern conflict. The tenacity of Soviet commitment to the area and its use of tactical manoeuvres to consolidate positions are matched by an even more powerful commitment on the part of the Arabs to rout Israel out of the Middle Eastern subsystem.

'The essence of a revolutionary situation is its *self consciousness*.'[61] The tenacity, dedication, and commitment of the Arabs to the elimination of Israel have not been compromised or mitigated by the crisis management of October, 1973, and June, 1974. Syrian intransigence (and Kissinger alluded to that in the *Newsweek* article quoted earlier) has demonstrated that Syrian willingness to co-operate with the super-diplomat was a tactical manoeuvre, not a general consensus, and was designed to advance Syrian military forces closer to the Israeli border and remove Damascus from Israeli artillery range. Egyptian aspirations were enunciated by former Deputy Prime Minister Abdel Kader Hatem in *Al-Ahram* in December, 1973:

> 1. The seizure of land by means of force cannot be accepted. This constitutes a blatant violation of UN principles and a direct threat to world peace; and
> 2. The Palestinian people's struggle against imperialism, Zionism and racism and for liberating their national rights is a legitimate [part] of the world liberation movement.
>
> For the sake of demonstrating these facts and gathering the support of the people and governments of the world for them, we have left no path for political action unexplored, and no legitimate means untried. We have done all of this because of our faith that the political and diplomatic battle against imperialism and Zionism is a basic part of our all-out struggle.
>
> Our work has borne fruit in numerous domains:
>
> 1. In the Arab domain, 6 October was a prominent land-mark on the road of Arab reunion which has demonstrated the ties binding the Arab nation. It also drew the Arab nation's attention to its historical responsibilities which require further efforts and sacrifices. The unanimous Arab view at Algiers was that the ceasefire is not peace and that peace requires a number of changes, foremost of which are the following two conditions:
>
> (1) Israel must withdraw from all occupied territories, especially Jerusalem.
>
> (2) The firm national rights of the Palestinian people must be restored.[62]

Egypt is using crisis diplomacy to bring Israel back to the 1967 borders. But Egypt has not given up its dedication to the Palestinian cause, which means, at the very least, the diminution of Israel. Sadat reiterated in his ABC interview that the Geneva conference would deal only with peace. When asked what he meant by peace, he answered, 'a just solution to the Palestine question',[63] which could be interpreted as a euphemism for the diminution, and with regard to the Palestinians the ultimate annihilation, of Israel. Not a single Arab aspiration—major or minor—was mitigated by Kissinger's crisis diplomacy venture involving first Egypt and Israel, and then Syria and Israel. Egypt still refuses to grant Israel a non-belligerent status.

The aspiration for Arab unity and strong military posture, the return of occupied territories without direct negotiation, the non-recognition of Israel's moral and political rights and sovereignty, and, above all, the failure to define territorial aims, the Palestinian state, or the future boundaries—all these factors strengthen the argument that the Arab manoeuvre is *strictly tactical.* Given the revolutionary orientations of the Arabs, it is difficult to see how crisis diplomacy has changed the fundamental attitude toward the State of Israel. The US and the USSR have accepted Resolution 242, but the Arab dictum of Khartoum still prevails, however 'modified' or disguised, and it does not accept the political sovereignty of Israel.

Not only did Kissinger fail to root out the sources of the conflict, he also planted hopes in Egypt, and certainly in Syria, that what is lost by war and violence can be restored by super diplomacy. What is thus gained by such diplomacy the Arabs view as the next step toward the final and victorious military solution of the Palestinian problem.

Thus, war has not been permanently avoided. 'The whole domain of crisis management,' concludes Bell, 'is a sort of no man's land, sour with uncharted minefields of such problems. And it must be repeated that even a high rate of success in the management of crisis does not necessarily end the underlying conflicts.'[64]

In the case of the Middle Eastern conflict, the exercise of super diplomacy had been admirable for its courage, style, technique and performance. But it has ended where it began. The brutal Arab-Israeli conflict, the political instability of the area, and regime insecurity make the Middle East the most revolutionary international subsystem of the 1970s. In the words of Kissinger in a different era, 'The revolutionary system pushes and erodes the legitimate political order.'[65] No super diplomat could possibly drain off the motivations of the revolutionary order. 'And because in revolutionary situations the contending systems are less concerned with the ties, diplomacy is replaced either by war or by an armaments race.'[66] So wrote Professor Kissinger in 1957.

NOTES

1. Coral Bell, *The Conventions of Crisis: A Study in Diplomatic Management* (London, Oxford Paperbacks, 1971), p. 49.
2. *Ibid.*, p. 49.
3. Alastair Buchan, *Crisis Management: The New Diplomacy* (Paris: The Atlantic Institute, 1966), p. 20.
4. *Ibid.*, p. 18.
5. Bell, *Conventions of Crisis*, p. 8.
6. *Ibid.*, p. 7.
7. *Ibid.*, p. 50.
8. *Ibid.*, p. 69.
9. *Ibid.*, p. 39.
10. *Ibid.*, p. 61.
11. *Ibid.*, p. 84.
12. See John Newhouse, *Cold Dawn: The Story of SALT* (New York: Reinholt Holt, 1973).
13. *Washington Post*, September 26, 1973, p. 1.
14. *Ibid.*, October 13, 1973.
15. *New York Times*, December 4, 1973, p. 1.
16. *Ibid.*, November 7, 1973, p. 1.
17. *Ibid.*, January 6, 1974, p. 1.
18. *Ibid.*, January 18, 1974, p. 1.
19. *Washington Post*, January 15, 1974, p. 5.
20. *New York Times*, February 21, 1974, p. 7.
21. *Newsweek*, May 20, 1974, p. 13. (Emphasis added.)
22. Quoted in *New York Times*, March 17, 1974, p. 15.
23. Interview: Anwar el-Sadat, *ABC*, April 7, 1974. Taped by author (Emphasis added.)
24. Muhammed Hasanayn Haykal, *Al-Anwar*, November 16, 1973, p. 1.
25. *Ibid.*
26. 'Press conference by the Honorable Henry A. Kissinger, Secretary of State, November 21, 1973,' Department of State, No. 423, p. 5.
27. *Washington Post*, May 3, 1974, p. 1.
28. Roger Morris, 'Henry Kissinger and the Media: Separate Peace,' *Columbia Journalism Review* (May/June, 1974).
29. *Washington Post*, May 14, 1974, p. 4.
30. 'Press Conference by the Honorable Henry A. Kissinger, Secretary of State, December 27, 1973,' Department of State, No 435, p. 6.
31. *Washington Post*, October 13, 1974, p. 5.

32. Murray Marder, *Washington Post*, May 1, 1974, p. 1.
33. 'The October 25, 1974 Alert,' Review of the Week, *New York Times*, November 25, 1973, p. 3.
34. *Ibid.* (Emphasis added).
35. Department of State, November 21, 1973, p. 19.
36. *Ibid.*, p. 20. (Emphasis added.)
37. *Ibid.*
38. *New York Times*, April 21, 1974, p. 4. (Emphasis added.)
39. Yoseph Harif, 'The Three Nixon Cables,' *Ma'ariv*, May 10, 1974, p. 19. Nixon had also cabled Mrs Meir between October 19 and 22, 1973.
40. See *Ibid.*
41. Marilyn Berger, *Washington Post*, May 24, 1974. (Emphasis added.)
42. Joseph Kraft, 'The Kissinger Technique,' *Washington Post*, May 5, 1974.
43. Leslie Gelb, *New York Times*, March 22, 1974, p. 3.
44. *Washington Post*, May 24, 1974, p. 1.
45. Yoseph Harif, 'The Draft for the Peace Treaty with Egypt is Ready,' *Ma'ariv*, December 7, 1973, p. 15.
46. Yoseph Harif, 'The Separation of Forces,' *Ma'ariv*, March 22, 1974; also author's private information.
47. 'Kissinger's Document–Jewish Meeting,' *Haaretz*, January 4, 1974, p. 5.
48. Bernard Gwertzman, *New York Times*, May 23, 1974. (Emphasis added.)
49. *Washington Post*, January 19, 1974.
50. *Conventions of Crisis*, p. 11.
51. *Ibid.*, p. 12.
52. Paraphrased by author from taped interview.
53. Henry Kissinger, *A World Restored* (Boston: Houghton Mifflin, 1957), p. 2.
54. *Ibid.*, pp. 1-6.
55. *Ibid.*, p. 1.
56. *Ibid.*, p. 2.
57. *Ibid.*, p. 2.
58. *Ibid.*
59. *Ibid.*
60. *Ibid.* (Emphasis added.)
61. *Ibid.*, p. 3. (Emphasis added.)
62. Abdel Kader Hatem, *Al-Ahram*, December 10, 1973, pp. 3-4.
63. Paraphrased by author from taped interview.
64. *Conventions of Crisis*, p. 124.
65. *A World Restored*, p. 3.
66. *Ibid.*

CHAPTER VI

Kissinger and Middle East Negotiations–Phase Two

By the end of 1974 Henry Kissinger had succeeded in achieving a separation-of-forces agreement and a temporary ceasefire among Israel, Egypt, and Syria. Such an act had been unnecessary in 1967. At that time Israel had won a clear and decisive military victory. The Arab armies had been defeated and Israel's borders extended to their geographically logical limits—the Suez Canal in the south, the Jordan River in the east and the Golan Heights to the north. The 1967 ceasefire agreement was not guaranteed by the Americans, who had evidently learned from the difficulties they had experienced in keeping their promise to guarantee the 1957 withdrawal agreement.

Due partly to American obstruction neither the Syrian nor Egyptian armies were so decisively defeated in 1973 as they had been in 1967. On the day when the US and the USSR imposed a ceasefire, October 22, 1973, the Israelis were in the middle of the third phase of the war. During the first, defensive phase, they were threatened on two fronts by the massive and highly mobilized armies of Egypt and Syria. Though the Israelis faced an uphill fight, by the third day they had halted the advancing Arab armies. Gathering momentum in the second, counter-offensive phase, the Israelis pushed the Syrian army toward Damascus. Meanwhile, by October 15, 1973, General Ariel (Arik) Sharon had achieved the remarkable military feat of establishing an Israeli enclave on the western side of the Suez Canal and encircling the Egyptian Third Army. The Egyptian Second Army on the east bank, holding what had been Israeli-occupied territory in Sinai, was also in danger of being encircled. Suddenly, Israel seemed on the threshold of military victory. The road to Cairo was wide open to an IDF offensive that could have annihilated the Third Egyptian Army and halted the Second Army. It was in this third phase of the fighting that the Israeli advance was halted by the superpowers.

The Israeli people were eventually made aware of the reason for their failure to make further advances. In December 1974, Dayan admitted that 'the Americans did not want the Egyptians to surrender. They issued an ultimatum that if Israel did not permit the cut-off force of 80,000 men (Third Army) to get supplies from their main forces, they, the Americans, would do it themselves with helicopters . . . the Americans wanted to show the Arabs how effectively the United States could help them.'[1] Sadat was quick to claim a military and political victory, in that his army had crossed the 'Canal of Shame.' The Syrian army, although defeated, was not routed and retreated in relatively orderly fashion toward Damascus.

The ceasefire left the Arabs with an option they had not enjoyed since 1967, that of taking military action against Israel. However, Sadat's alleged victory was won by a crossing of the Canal with Soviet military aid, and then ensured by American diplomatic pressure on Israel. Sadat had accepted the mediation of the two superpowers; Israel accepted only Kissinger's mediation. Israel hoped that the price Kissinger had already exacted (the unfinished offensive against the Arab armies) would give Israel leverage both in bargaining with the US and in subsequent negotiations with the Arabs. Sadat hoped that the US in 1973, as it had done in 1956, would pressure Israel into withdrawing from all Arab occupied territory. The Israelis hoped that Kissinger's mediation would give teeth to any agreement it reached with the Arabs.

The aspirations of the belligerents, both immediate and long-range, were utterly asymmetrical. Egypt hoped to exploit the American desire to play a key role in the Middle Eastern negotiations and at the same time to keep a Soviet military option open. Israel hoped for a step-by-step peace arrangement with the Arabs via Kissinger. Meanwhile Kissinger, who had halted a final IDF offensive, hoped to secure a role for America in the affairs of Egypt, which, as the most important Arab country, would secure American influence in the rest of the Arab world.

The Diplomacy of Mediation Phase Two
June 1974—March 1975

Despite the single-minded tenacity shown throughout the Mideast negotiations the people represented by the negotiators were never of a single mind. There are among both Arabs and Israelis optimists and pessimists, hawks and doves, militants and moderates. It is least possible to speak of the Israelis as a united, ideologically and politically consolidated, cohesive bloc when it comes to their attitudes toward a settlement with the Arabs. After Kissinger's Phase One negotiations, new leaders and forces emerged in Israel with new orientations toward settlement.[2] A government was established by Yitzchak Rabin[3] and the cabinet of 1967-1973 was replaced. Rabin's government opted for what was apparently a new stance: that it would no longer tolerate a return to the 1967-1973 status quo policy. Further, this new government orientation was clearly moderate and it seemed inclined to keep up the momentum of negotiations begun by the Meir-Dayan government after the October war.[4]

The Arab world, after the troop separation agreement, seemed as though it was again dividing into two camps, the moderates and the militants.[5] Sadat and Egypt demonstrated throughout Phase One that not only was Egypt politically the senior Arab State, but that among all the Arab leaders, Sadat seemed the most reasonable and moderate especially in his attitude toward the US. Jordan supported Egypt; King Faisal, however reluctantly, also supported Sadat's rapprochement with the United States.[6] On the other hand, the most militant and non-accommodating Arab leader (apart from Libya's Colonel Ghadafi) was Syria's Asad. The Syrians were reluctant to join Phase One even if they were rewarded with the return of all the territory they had lost in 1973 plus Kuneitra, the capital of the Golan Heights.[7] The PLO did not change its orientation concerning both accommodation with, and recognition of, Israel. In fact the PLO after 1973 became more militant and firmly backed its plan for an authoritarian Palestinian state—or, as they euphemistically called it, a democratic, Christian-Muslim-Jewish Palestine.

During the Rabat Arab summit conference of October-November 1974, the extremists were expected to collaborate with the moderates, who wished to accept Kissinger's mediation. Nobody expected to modify the PLO stance but it was hoped that the Arabs would agree to Sadat's collaboration with Kissinger. Instead Syria, supported by the USSR and Algeria, turned the summit into a virtual PLO conference. Sadat betrayed Jordan, by establishing in September 1974 a joint front with Asad to recognize the PLO as the single Palestinian representative. Neither Faisal nor Boumedienne ever tried to swing the conference. In fact with Faisal's betrayal, Jordan remained isolated. Rabat was a clear victory for the Syrian-PLO camp.[8] Hussein apparently had little choice other than to reluctantly accept the dictum of Rabat. Thus despite Sadat's support for the Kissinger mediation, he curtailed his chances for negotiation with Israel by supporting the PLO. These actions seemed to cast a deep shadow over Kissinger's high hopes for a negotiations momentum. It seemed that the USSR had gained the upper hand, that its political and military support of Syria had paid off, and that it had helped to legitimize the PLO.[9] To revive the spirit of negotiations in the Kissinger style, there was only one actor remaining—Egypt. Sadat, aware of the crucial importance of Rabat, was not however ready to abandon his 'American connection.' By acting in good faith vis-à-vis the Arab militants in Rabat, he hoped to rebuke the Soviets for their negative attitude toward the further rearmament of Egypt, now militarily inferior to Israel. Sadat also conveniently accepted Kissinger's continued negotiating efforts, after having covered the moves of his radical Arab flanks. Despite the Rabat setback, Syrian and PLO intransigence, and Soviet pressure to resume the erstwhile Geneva Conference, the Egyptian and Israeli aspirations to continue the negotiations under the aegis of Secretary Kissinger made the latter begin his preparations, explorations and search for a consensus. Looking for the right formula to successfully complete Phase Two, Kissinger was back in business late in 1974.

The processes of Phase Two can best be analyzed by

considering them as follows: (a) the conceptual framework of Phase Two, (b) its expected results, (c) the Egyptian and Israeli positioning for the negotiating processes, (d) the Geneva and rejection fronts, (e) The American diplomacy and (f) the reasons for Phase Two's failure.

A. *The Conceptual Framework for Kissinger's Diplomacy Phase Two*

The apparent success of Phase One, plus the expectations of the behaviour that the belligerents would display under particular conditions, convinced Kissinger that only a step-by-step, gradual and evolutionary process stood a reasonable chance of success in the Middle East. Kissinger became convinced that an all-inclusive Geneva conference, sponsored by the superpowers and dominated by a collectivity of Arab states, would leave the US with restricted diplomatic leverage, and Israel in an increasingly isolated state. Another Geneva conference, Kissinger perceived, would produce mountains of propaganda, rhetoric and, much worse, consolidate the militant Arab States at the expense of the moderates. The result could lead to Israel returning to its pre-1973, non-compromising, posture. Geneva as constituted at the end of October 1973 would not only have failed to bring about the desired orientation toward the resolution of conflict, but might inflame the mood and raise the expectations of the belligerents. It could also strengthen the Soviet hand, and give political leverage to the militants in Israel and the Arab world. And if the conference were then to fail, Kissinger reasoned, without recourse to another diplomatic structure, the parties might again turn to their traditional military stance, possibly leading to another and this time more brutal Arab-Israeli war and, above all, ruining Kissinger's record of diplomatic success. So Kissinger categorically insisted that the negotiations proceed on a step-by-step evolutionary basis and on a country-by-country approach. The process of negotiations would essentially be bilateral i.e. between Israel and one Arab State. Several such bilateral negotiations could be conducted simultaneously i.e. Israel-Egypt, Israel-Jordan, Israel-Syria and possibly Israel-the PLO.[10] The link which would bind each set of negotiations would be the mediator,

Kissinger himself, the representative of the only superpower accepted by all the parties involved including the militant Arab states and the PLO. The major purpose of the simultaneous negotiations was to promote a gradual Israeli withdrawal from most if not all of the pre-1967 occupied territories. The question of political recognition of Israel was left for Israel to ponder. The matter was not part of the Secretary's duty, even if Israel hoped that he might persuade Egypt to come forward with some political formula. Kissinger planned to channel the new momentum for a settlement through Phase Two negotiations. A break-through could mean the end of belligerence and the beginning of some type of co-existence, at least between one or two of the Arab confrontation states and Israel, to be guaranteed by increased American support both to Israel and to the Arab states, and this would help to change the mood from war to co-existence. Thus a minimum consensus between Israel and the confrontation states was to be sought as a basis for the step-by-step, bilateral negotiations—a plan conceived, prepared, and executed by Kissinger. Kissinger's purpose in Phase Two was to achieve for Sadat an Israeli withdrawal. He did *not* commit himself to fulfilling Israel's goal of securing an Egyptian commitment to non-belligerence.

B. *The Expected Results of the Negotiations for the United States*

The decline of American global influence also changed the nature of the rivalry with the USSR. The two powers were no longer competing for global hegemony but confined their competition to men, resources and regional influence. National defence no longer depended on the superpowers' unrestricted strategic nuclear arms race—the reign of terror had passed. Still, this change did not entail curtailing capacity for retaliation, at least in the early 1970s, nor did it signify reluctance to take vigilante action at the regional level.

The SALT I and SALT II talks were events that enhanced orientations toward detente. As the US withdrew from South East Asia, the Middle East became a focus for superpower rivalry. Since the October 1973 war, the Arab–Israeli conflict and the political future of the Persian Gulf have brought the US back into the area with full vigour. The American intervention involved multi-faceted diplomatic action, arms supply and a concerted effort to stabilize the area and aid moderate regimes. Chief American interests in the area were now linked: search for stable, moderate, and if possible American-inclined, governments and support for client regimes. To achieve stability and moderation and to guard the economic prosperity of the US (and Western Europe) the Nixenger Team concentrated on refusing regional conflicts as a means of countering the favourite Soviet tactic—manipulating local, ethnic and regional conflicts. Therefore, the de-Sovietization of the Mid-East regimes was a concomitant factor in the efforts to restore stability and establish American hegemony in the region. And if an aspiration for hegemony appears an unlikely goal, an alternative contention would be that the US seeks influence in the area, and that American interest in this case was to frustrate Soviet aspirations in the area. There is little doubt that Soviet-American competition in the area is in the armaments field: the arsenal now found between the Persian Gulf and the Nile River could easily match that of World War II, and the superpowers have found no convention upon which to establish a system of limiting the arms race in the area.

To supplement American influence in the area, in the era of diffusion of power, American policy was partly directed at strengthening the political regime and military arsenal of the regional powers of Iran, Israel, and Saudi Arabia. In view of Egypt's Soviet option and the Arab-Israeli conflict, Egypt was not considered an American-oriented regional power, but no longer was it considered Soviet-oriented either, and it appears that the Nixenger gamble was to try to tilt Egypt in America's direction. The payment to Egypt was to be made in Israeli coins, i.e. an Israeli withdrawal under American pressure which would promise the de-Sovietization (in the military sense) of Egypt.

To guarantee a successful Israeli withdrawal and an American role in Egypt, the following actions were to be taken:

(a) Preparation of a minimum consensus agenda between the antagonists.

(b) Aggrandizement of the American mediator role in a

series of step-by-step bilateral negotiations under the aegis of Secretary Kissinger.

(c) Neutralization of obstructionist-interventionist actors.

(d) Actors were to be persuaded that the mediator was their trustee.

(e) 'Reasonable' and carefully studied objectives for the bilateral mediation process, within the range of 'acceptability' to the belligerents, were to be proposed.

(f) The actors were to be reassured that the dynamics of Phase Two would lead toward peace and enhance further negotations.

To achieve the above objectives the Secretary laboured for over sixteen months (October 1973—February 1975). The process was complex, speedy and determined, in terms of what the Secretary prefers to call 'sustaining momentum': in other words 'no let up.' His methods have become predictable. The essentials of Kissinger's *modus operandi* were clearly manifested in the stretch of time between Phase One and Phase Two of his Middle Eastern super diplomacy.

C. *The Israeli and Egyptian Positioning for Phase Two*[11]

(a) Israel:

Frustrated, shocked and bewildered, robbed of its military victory, Israel went through Phase One like a sleepwalker. The post-Agranat[12] new regime began the uphill climb toward the political, military, economic and psychological recovery of Israel. Unquestionably the disengagement agreements were in the circumstances a psychological necessity. The new government of Prime Minister Rabin, although politically insecure and seemingly an interim regime, was set not to repeat, if possible, the errors of its predecessor. Like the Secretary, Rabin and his cabinet advocated the need for 'momentum' in negotiations and in breaking out of the previous impasse. No longer could or would Israel opt for the status quo. Phase One had to continue (as in fact it did in the last months of the Meir-Dayan regime responsible for the disengagement of Israel in Phase One). Once the troops were separated and the IDF was slowly recovering, together with the rest of the country, helped by massive American aid,

Israel was searching for a partner and a mediator. It became obvious that the Israeli aspirations for *direct* negotiations with the Arabs were not yet to be fulfilled. Phase Two was to be negotiated via a mediator. Continuing the essential policy of the Meir-Dayan regime, the Rabin-Allon-Peres team found a partner in Egypt and a mediator in Kissinger. The Israel positioning however was not a simple process. Through the exposure of ideas in Israel's open marketplace, the 1967-1973 consensus was torn asunder. The Rabin government's decision-making processes were widened and were seemingly more democratic than those of its predecessor, and an inner circle was no longer in existence—yet it failed to derive an equal and acceptable legitimation to that granted to the Meir-Dayan regime. Not only that, the 1967-1973 'hawk-dove' dichotomy was reversed and the nation reluctantly accepted Rabin's government. But the cabinet was clearly divided among the new 'doves', Rabin and Allon, and the old hawks, Peres and Yaacobi. If the 1967-1973 trio exclusively dominated the highest levels of national security decision-making in the government, the Rabin cabinet heterogeneously possessed greater autonomy. Additionally, in view of the fact that the new labour ministers were elected by the party's Central Committee, the powers of the cabinet became evenly divided—something unthinkable in the Meir-Dayan regime. The power of the Labour-Alignment coalition and its partners was also augmented. In sum, during Phase Two's preparations, no national consensus existed in Israel. An obstructionist opposition (led by Begin, Sharon and the *Likud* bloc) and a cabinet, composed of several relatively autonomous ministers, made Rabin's a vulnerable regime with obviously restricted powers.[13] The authority of Rabin was dependent to a large extent on what kind of legitimation it could establish. The only way it could restore national consensus and national unity was to establish its legitimacy in *successful negotiations.* Thus Phase Two became the political crucible for the Rabin regime but especially for the Rabin-Allon pair.

This situation obviously restricted Rabin's 'momentum'. Yet later both he and Secretary Kissinger ignored the risks of his own political vulnerability which promised dire consequences for Phase Two. How did Rabin position himself for Phase Two? In an interview with the Israeli daily, *Ha'aretz*, Rabin argued that to traverse the 'seven lean years' (i.e. the constellation of Arab oil, money and weapons) 'Israel's chief goal must be to buy *time*.' Time was to be purchased to restore Israel economically, psychologically and militarily. The major aims of Phase Two for Israel were (1) to disengage the USSR's interests from those of Egypt, and (2) to separate Egypt from Syria. 'Our immediate and practical interest should be to prevent Egypt from returning to the Soviet orbit', Rabin said, and to achieve this, Israel was prepared for an additional partial agreement. But, he predicted uncannily, 'in this type of arrangement [Phase Two] Israel might risk straining its relations with the United States.' Nevertheless Rabin concluded that even if non-belligerency, i.e. the political orientation of Egypt toward peace, were not to be realized, 'I would not insist that *I am not ready to go along with military arrangements*'. (italics mine).[15]

As Yoel Marcus wrote following the interview, 'my impressions are that the government would not, ab initio, reject an Egyptian demand that the next phase be negotiated on the military plane, as long as its practical implication would be political.'[16] Thus in December 1973, Rabin was ready to relinquish his well-proclaimed demand that the next phase with Egypt would unequivocally be directed toward the political fulfilment of an Egyptian commitment to non-belligerency. In fact, said Marcus, Rabin would accept a second phase withdrawal as long as (1) Egypt would not move into evacuated Israeli territory, (2) that the Sinai passes remain in Israeli hands[!] (3) that under no condition could Phase Two begin before the UN mandate was renewed and that the UN mandate would no longer be restricted to short-term periodic renewals.[17]

The Israeli-American interim bargaining was based on certain Rabin-Allon assumptions that were disputed by Secretary Kissinger. While they spoke of the principle of non-belligerency of some type, of 'political commitment on a bilateral basis,'[18] Sadat flatly rejected non-belligerency,[19] and Secretary Kissinger was hoping that Rabin would follow his own advice to move into Phase Two 'as long as the practical implication [of a military arrangement] be political.' This issue remained vague. In an interview with the *Washington Post* just before Kissinger departed for his last mission hopefully to conclude Phase Two, Rabin said that in 'the context of an interim agreement it [sic] should include at least three elements: first, a political commitment [sic] on a bilateral basis . . . second, it has to include certain physical security arrangements on grounds that assure that certain territories we have evacuated would not be used against us. Third the [political] commitment—should be translated into a change of behaviour on the part of Egypt or the part [sic] of Israel in a way that it will not just be a paper statement.'[20]

Thus from an emphatic non-belligerency stance Rabin moved to the political implication of military arrangements and back to a political commitment on the part of Egypt to change its behaviour. If non-belligerence is a vague non-legal, non-political concept, a political commitment to alter the behaviour of the adversaries sounds an even more ambitious goal. It seemed that Kissinger and possibly Rabin at the time assumed that the latter would settle for the political, practical implications which would flow from additional military arrangements.

When the Israeli cabinet was set for its final positioning and appointed the team of Rabin-Peres-Allon to represent it in the negotiations, it reiterated its commitment to non-belligerency. Thus, to separate military from political commitments, the Israeli cabinet proceeded with two separate procedures for Phase Two. One was a military withdrawal known as the mini-plan. Should Egypt refuse to accept the principle of non-belligerency or to offer Israel even a vague political commitment Israel would then return 30 miles of desert east of Suez, but keep the Sinai straits and oil fields under its jurisdiction.[21] If, however, Egypt were politically accommodating i.e. accepted some type of political commitment, then Israel would relinquish the Sinai passes and the Egyptian Sinai oil fields on the conditions of demilitarization, a more stable UN mandate system, and Israeli purchase of oil from Egypt. This was the maxi-plan.[22]

Thus the Israeli positioning for Phase Two was complex. And Kissinger, who was informed by the Israelis in his last exploratory trip (March 10—March 15) of Israel's two proposals, nevertheless must have assumed that Israel would opt for the 'political, practical implications' i.e. for the maxi-plan, while Egypt, he well knew, was not prepared to change its posture. So he went on his mission aware of the Israeli determination to get an Egyptian political commitment.

(b) The Egyptian positioning:

Contrary to the relative political weaknesses of the new Israeli regime, Sadat's strength had only grown. A relatively unknown Nasser lieutenant, who had never committed himself frontally to oppose Nasser's policies, even if he apparently must have abhorred much of them, Sadat emerged after the October 1973 war as an Egyptian and Arab national hero. In the words of Hasanyan Haykal, 'Sadat and Egypt crossed the Canal of Shame.' Sadat did not begin his career after Nasser's death by immediately assuming the upper hand. In fact, Egyptian and foreign observers misjudged Sadat, as a lesser Nasser crony, and as an interim ruler. These judgments were based on substantial data. The personalities, issues and circumstances that faced Sadat were monumental: the death of the charismatic Nasser in a praetorian society[23] and the powerful opposition to Sadat by ambitious heirs, Ali Sabri, Sharawi Gouma'sh and Sami Sharaf. Coupled with these challenges were the post-1967 political and military frustrations of Egyptian society, and the apparent Israeli superiority and lack of compromise. Furthermore the US failed to take decisive action to support the Egyptian claims, and this led to the relative isolation of Egypt, not only from America but also from Syria and Saudi Arabia. Egypt's total dependence on the USSR, in addition to all these other factors, legitimately raised the experts' doubts that a lesser Nasser lieutenant would be able to withstand such insurmountable events. Gradually, with patience, cunning and political intuition and intrigue, Sadat succeeded in foiling a highly organized coup, which was supported by such institutional forces as the ASU, Intelligence, the army and the Presidential Office, led by Sabri, Gouma'sh, Sharaf, and the Minister of War, General Fawzi—the most powerful political personalities in Egypt. Sadat suspected that the USSR supported, if not engineered, the plot. He was ready to take action against the USSR, which he did in July 1972 by ousting 20,000 Soviet advisers from Egypt.[24]

These actions were misinterpreted by the US and Israel as acts of weakness;[25] that Sadat was exhausted; that the 1971 coup had undermined his position among the armed forces; that the Soviet ouster was a serious setback to the Egyptian armed forces. Sadat's proclamations, year in and year out between 1971 and 1973, that this was the 'year of decision' made him the laughing stock of Egypt, Israel and elsewhere, and only confirmed the Tel-Aviv—Washington misperceptions. Such was the pronounced judgment of experts at home and abroad. Nevertheless, the master counter-coup-maker and coup-unmaker, has since silently and successfully become the dominant politician in Egypt. After the 1971 coup he purged, arrested and discredited his rivals. He brutally crushed student demonstrations. He appointed his own men to run the army, now led by loyalists, professional and non-political officers, Marshals Sadiq and Ismail Ali and Generals Sa'ad Shazli and Abd al Ghani al-Gamasi. He re-established praetorian rule and dominion over the armed forces and the intelligence services; he drained the ASU of its content, purging leading ASU opponents and replaced them with his own men led now by Said Marai, thus making the ASU an all-but defunct state organ. But above all, Sadat forged a new military alliance with Syria, and a political axis with Nasser's arch rival, the late, powerful fundamentalist, oil-rich Arabian desert potentate, King Faisal, as well as with the new potentates in Gulf Sheikhdoms. The years 1972-1973 were active and busy years for Sadat. He abolished Nasser's oppressive decrees at home, introduced a greater freedom of the press, abolished abortive 'Arab Socialist' experiments, cultivated the new urban intelligentsia, recruited its sons into the army and above all broke out of Nasser's international isolation and total dependency on the Soviets. His new axis with Asad and Faisal and his concerted efforts to court the US and become autonomous of the USSR were political actions designed to break through the 1967-1973 Israeli-American imposed status quo. He was not going to be 'forgotten and forlorn' (to reiterate Haykal). Thus Sadat shrewdly calculated and courageously risked a military initiative. In alliance with Syria and assured of Soviet military support, he attacked Israel on two fronts. Despite the heavy price in men and material that both he and Asad paid and the chance of losing his entire armed forces, caught between the Israeli pincers, Sadat came out of the war with the upper hand, having demonstrated Egyptian military capability and determination, and having successfully persuaded his new allies, Faisal and the Arab Gulf Sheikhs, to exercise the oil weapon. Sadat also exploited Soviet military aid despite his strained relations with the USSR, demonstrating that he has the leverage over the Soviets and not vice versa. Above all, Sadat exploited Kissinger's desire to re-establish the America influence in the area and he used Kissinger to save the Egyptian Third Army from capitulation.[26] Sadat further took advantage of Kissinger's ambitions for close relations with Egypt to bring about an Israeli withdrawal from Western Egypt which gave him control over the Canal to the point where Egyptian troops again are stationed on its east bank.

Unquestionably at the end of Phase One, Sadat emerged as the dominant figure in Egypt and the Arab World. After all, Nasser's policies had left Egypt defeated and isolated. The only option which had been left to Sadat was to call the world's attention to Egypt's cause by resorting to violence however risky that might be. After the war, Sadat clearly was master of Egypt although, as is the case with all praetorian regimes his major source of support remains the armed forces whose prestige he helped restore after the October war of 1973, and whom he must continue to cultivate. Sadat was positioning for Phase Two essentially on the basis of Kissinger's concept of 'momentum'. As the manager of the Arabs, after the successful crossing of the Canal (notwithstanding the near collapse of his armed forces) and having successfully concluded Phase One, Sadat's position at home, in the Arab world, and internationally was much strengthened. Substituting the role of the 'manager of Arabs' for Nasser's pan-Arab leadership, Sadat was more flexible than Nasser in championing an Egyptian 'go it alone' policy, despite being handicapped by the dicta of Rabat, Syrian opposition, and PLO intransigence. Nevertheless, as manager of the Arabs and chief organizer of the 1973 alliance, Sadat opted for bilateral mediation-negotiations with Israel over the future of Sinai. The Syrian and PLO opposition was manifest, so was that of the USSR which advocated the resumption of the Geneva Conference. But with the support of Faisal, the tacit consent of Boumedienne, and the armed forces behind him, Sadat ventured into Phase Two without fearing a Syrian-PLO-Soviet retaliation.

In fact, despite the Soviet demand that he end the Kissinger process, the USSR has continued, however grudgingly, to slowly replenish Egypt's 1973 losses.[27] How did Sadat—now confident, possessing American political, and Soviet military, options—perceive his role in Phase Two? Sadat's major aims were (1) to regain all of Sinai via Kissinger and (2) to disengage the US from Israel, thus, in effect, rejecting a direct political commitment to non-belligerence on the part of Egypt. Sadat made it clear to Kissinger that he would pledge non-belligerency only as part of an overall settlement. His advisers, nevertheless, hinted that assurances might be given to the US, not to Israel, 'that Egypt will not go to war while there is reasonable progress toward peace'.[28]

Sadat's goal in participating in Phase Two was to disengage the United States from its heavy commitment to Israel and tilt, if possible, the balance towards Egypt. A clear reference to this point was made in an ABC television interview (March 1973), when Sadat said that his major aim was to 'disengage the United States'—i.e. from Israel. He sought to defuse the situation before going to Geneva, and saw Phase Two as a single step before a total Israeli withdrawal. Sadat made clear that Phase Two entailed a military disengagement only, and that he adhered to the Egyptian interpretation of Resolution 242 that there would be no political commitment to Israel unless it totally withdrew from *all* the 1967-occupied territories. 'I am imagining the whole (the step-by-step process) like this: the Israeli pullback is a gesture of peace and at the same time, according to Resolution No. 242 of the Security Council, they must withdraw from our land. So they must make this gesture and then after that we shall be going to discuss the whole problem in Geneva.'[29] Thus his proposition was made clear to Kissinger, who was to fulfil what Jarring had failed to do, i.e. achieve the military withdrawal of Israel; 'discussions' in Geneva would then follow. However, he strictly adhered to his opening position on Resolution 338, which introduced the concept of negotiations and of buffer zones between the belligerents. But when he spoke of negotiations, he meant mediation, and he interpreted 'buffer zones' as the pre-1967 border: an Egyptian buffer zone east of the Nile River and an Israeli demilitarized zone west of the Negev. However, he clearly stated to Geyelin, '*I am not ready to make a settlement agreement with Israel.* I am ready to argue for a *gesture* of peace from the side of Israel to pull back so that we can create a new atmosphere toward permanent peace'.[30] (italics mine).

Sadat's position in the context of Phase Two was a strictly military arrangement for an Israeli troop withdrawal, and a rejection of any political commitment. 'We concluded the disengagement agreement before last year. In the same *context*, we can work.'[31] (italics mine). Any non-belligerency proclamation was to be postponed for Geneva. In response to Geyelin's query for 'a removal of any further challenge to the territorial integrity and sovereignty and the right of Israel to exist,' Sadat equivocally answered that it was for all the Arabs to acknowledge this. More significantly, Sadat had this to say on a long-term political settlement: 'The coming generation will decide what happens here and in Israel.'[32] Sadat's generation's job was just 'to end this state of belligerency. Time is on our side. I am sure of it.'[33] Haykal, the discredited former chief editor of *Al-Ahram* and Nasser's *porte parole* and confidant, although seemingly more hawkish than Sadat, clearly spelt out Sadat's perception of time and the Egyptian strategy. In an interview with *Newsweek*, he was asked what he felt was the minimum Egypt could accept in the next stage. 'Nobody,' answered Haykal, 'could refuse the Sinai passes and the oil. That also means the entire Gulf [of Suez] Coasts of Sinai—otherwise, the oil could not be defended, nor could we ensure the safety of traffic to the Suez Canal. *But* if we take this and wait several years for the next stage, as the Israelis demand, we will destroy what's left of our military option by widening the demilitarized disengagement zone.'[34]

Sadat's Phase Two exercise was well summarized in his own statement to Geyelin: 'We require an agreement in principle from Israel that the rest of the territories be yielded.'[35]

It could hardly be argued that the Israeli and Egyptian opening positions were symmetrical. The positions of the USSR, Syria and PLO were not so far from the Egyptian position, even if they aimed to neutralize Kissinger's efforts and prevent him from bridging the gap between Israel and Egypt before he could enter his final mediation-negotiation stage.

D. *The positioning of the Geneva 'Rejection Block' USSR-Syria-The PLO*

Three actors were adamantly opposed to the Kissinger-Sadat-Rabin negotiations: the USSR, Syria and the PLO.

The USSR

As analyzed elsewhere,[36] the evolution of Egyptian-Soviet relations since 1953 was not necessarily set in an evolutionary spiral but in a protracted, permanently suspicious, relationship. Brezhnev in contradistinction to the volatile Khruschev has proven more cautious and less impetuous.[37] This, however, did not change the basic asymmetry of Soviet-Egyptian relations: Egypt wishing to restrict the USSR to the role of an arms supplier, while the USSR demanded a greater involvement, going beyond the field of arms. Since the October war, the USSR as co-chairman of the Geneva Conference has insisted on active participation in all the phases and processes of negotiation. Yet, despite its heavy investment in Egypt and Syria, the Soviet interventionist role was curtailed in the summer of 1972. After October 1973 Sadat further severed his political option with the USSR, in conformity with his policy in 1972 of ousting the Soviet advisers. The initiative for dominating the negotiators over troop separation and the preparation for Phase Two were clearly Kissinger's. The USSR was being isolated from Egypt and had severed its relations with Israel, leaving the arena open for Kissinger diplomacy. The Soviet Union was also politically frustrated.

For a while Egypt, Israel and the US seemed satisfied, each for different reasons, with the negotiations that had achieved the separation of forces on the Canal and in the Golan Heights. As for the USSR, however, when the Golan agreement was signed in May 1974, it seemed to have been pushed out of Egypt and excluded from the negotiations. Kissinger, in fact, became the messenger between the confrontation states and the USSR. Nixon's triumphant trip to Egypt in May 1974 appeared to establish a pax Americana in the area. All this was intolerable for the Soviets. After more than twenty years of Russian military and political support to Egypt, Syria and the other radical Arab states, the Soviets could not allow themselves to be deprived of a role to play.

On October 19, 1973, both superpowers had signed Resolution 338, whereby it was agreed that they would supervise the ceasefire and play an *equal* role in a forthcoming Arab-Israeli peace conference to be held in Geneva. Kissinger pre-empted Geneva, and during a year-long, whirlwind negotiation solo, aided by the Arab-Israeli separation agreements, he worked to re-establish American influence in the area. Kissinger's super-diplomat achievement was, however, a Pyrrhic victory.[38] When Nixon left Egypt after his colossal, Caesar-like tour, the Soviets perceived that if they did not manage to play a role equal to Kissinger's, they might as well foreclose their Middle Eastern interests and investments. The result was their decision to support Syria and the PLO. As in 1973, when the Soviets did not need to push the Arabs into war, so in 1974 they did not have to activate Syrian or PLO belligerence.

Syria, although beaten by the IDF in 1973, had not changed its basic position on the Arab Israeli conflict. Although in 1973-1974 the Egyptians spoke of some kind of Israeli-Egyptian military arrangement, the Syrian attitude toward the conflict was based solely on a military option. The separation agreements raised serious doubts in the minds of the Syrians as to whether they could continue to pursue a military option in the conflict in order to reconquer the Golan. Syria suspected Egypt's unique role in the negotiations and feared that Syrian interests would be compromised; that a pro-American Egyptian policy would advance Egyptian interests only; and that in view of the geographical-topographical nature of the Golan, little could be secured from Israel. Syria thus opted for a tough line. What helped Syria to sustain its militant stance was precisely the American-Egyptian, and the Israeli-Egyptian, diplomatic progress. As a result of Syrian militancy, Asad succeeded in persuading Sadat that if he neglected Syria's territorial interests in favour of his own, he would forfeit his role as manager of the Arabs.[39]

To challenge the unity of action forged between Syria and Egypt prior to 1973, a challenge Sadat could not tolerate, Syria found a natural ally—the PLO. Syria engineered the task of rescuing the PLO from its political mothballs, and, with the aid of Boumedienne-Faisal, who torpedoed Sadat, turned the Rabat Summit Conference (September 1974) into a PLO conference. In this way Syria imposed a commitment on Egypt, while the PLO, which had feared that its political interests might blow away in the Kissinger whirlwind, became a factor in Arab and international politics. In an interview with Philip Geyelin of the *Washington Post*, Asad made his points clear. (1) The construction of peace 'can only be realized through a collective Arab movement (i.e. Geneva). Separate moves (step-by-step) which American diplomacy is trying to achieve are leading in the opposite direction.' (2) Asad proposed an international conference 'combining the Palestinian, Syrian and Egyptian fronts.' Contradicting Sadat, Asad said that 'We are talking with the United States' i.e. that while Sadat wished to disengage the Americans, Asad did not believe it was possible through incremental diplomacy since only Israel stood to gain. According to Asad, the United States was Israel's patron and would support Israeli interests. Asad also considered step-by-step diplomacy an American-Israeli effort to separate Egypt from Syria. Concerning Phase Two negotiations, Asad clearly stated that we do not expect them to succeed.' Diplomatic 'manoeuvres' i.e. Phase Two 'may succeed in blocking the road toward peace'. Prophetically Asad declared, 'I rule out the suggestion that President Sadat is in sympathy with *separate moves.* I believe that President Sadat is desirous of a common Arab move.' Asad added: President Sadat *gives the impression* of sympathy with separate moves in the light of the narrow choices put before him by American diplomacy.'[40] The Soviets, meanwhile, found the Syrian–PLO alliance ripe for harvest. By exploiting the Rabat Conference as its vehicle for re-entry into the Middle East, the USSR managed to circumvent the American–Egyptian and American–Israeli step-by-step negotiations.

The short era of pax Americana disappeared in Kissinger's jet stream. As Tad Szulc wrote in October 1974:

> Secretary of State Kissinger has dangerously misjudged Soviet intentions in the Mideast, despite secret personal warnings to him by Chairman Leonid Brezhnev last March in Moscow that there would be no peace in the Mideast if the United States persisted in 'going it alone' diplomatically with the Arabs and Israelis. At that time, Brezhnev accused Kissinger of 'ruses' and 'trickery'.
>
> The cumulative result of Kissingerian miscalculations —some diplomats call it Kissinger's 'greed' in freezing out the Russians—is the latest crisis raising the threat of a new Arab–Israeli war.
>
> Kissinger, in effect, helped to create a situation in which the Arabs, frustrated by the lack of diplomatic 'movement' with Israel which he had promised them after the 1973 war, have turned again toward Moscow for political and military help. For similar reasons, a new sense of unity against Israel emerged from the recent Rabat summit with the all-out support of the financially powerful oil-producing states.
>
> The Soviets, feeling vindicated, are obviously delighted to oblige. They have been heavily rearming the Syrians for some time. And all indications are that Soviet military supplies will start flowing anew to Egypt even before Brezhnev visits Cairo in January.[41]

If in June 1974 the feelings of the Arab world were tilted toward the US, after Rabat there was some swing back towards the USSR. The Soviets used their only leverage in the Middle East—military rearmament of the Arabs—to good advantage. They ingratiated themselves with the Arab radicals by completely re-supplying Syria with arms, and by politically legitimizing the PLO.

The next Soviet step was to come to terms with Sadat. Deprived of military equipment and modern weapons, the Egyptian generals put pressure on Sadat to invite Chairman Brezhnev to Egypt on January 15, 1975. Brezhnev did not commit himself to re-supplying Egypt's arsenal to the same level as Syria's. But the USSR nevertheless armed Egypt. The price he demanded and received was an Egyptian acceptance of a return to the Geneva conference. Sadat, however, kept the American political option open. The Soviets thus failed to achieve equality with the US and the initiative remained with Kissinger. But by exploiting radical Arab aspirations, as they have always done, they did advance their potential role at a new Geneva conference. At best, Kissinger had only one more chance to pursue his incremental step-by-step diplomacy.

The Soviet rearmament of Syria was challenged by an Israeli mini-crisis in the Golan Heights on November 16, 1974. Israel called for partial mobilization of the IDF and Defence Minister Shimon Peres said 'that Israel has taken countermeasures against Syrian military movements'—an indication that Israel would not tolerate Syrian military aspirations. Israel also flatly refused to negotiate with the PLO as representative of the Palestinians. The Israeli alert signaled that the radicalization of the conflict by the re-entry of the USSR would lead to another Arab-Israeli war. Israel was also telling Kissinger that he should make detente *operational* in the Middle East. By the end of January 1975 Kissinger's diplomacy seemed to be over a barrel. At the summit conference of December 2, 1974, held at Vladivostok, the futility of unilateral super-diplomacy was apparent. The USSR was no longer willing to play a role subordinate to Kissinger's, and the US might be forced to accept, in good faith, the principles set forth in Resolution 338 of October 1973: Soviet-American co-operation in the Middle Eastern negotiations, that is, the reconvening of the Geneva conference.

America still has several diplomatic options open to it, but the options are running out. As Joseph Kraft wrote, 'far from exulting about breakthroughs, American officials ought now to be especially wary. The Russians are on the move, and this is just the wrong time to let down the guard.'[42]

E. *The American Diplomacy in Phase Two*

For eight out of seventeen months (November 1973–March 1975) and in exploratory contacts elsewhere, Kissinger was engrossed in diplomatic discussions that included no fewer than six trips to the Middle Eastern capitals. These culminated in the March 12–23 shuttle that ended in failure. The Secretary had been both confident and hopeful. 'Mr Kissinger's Middle East diplomacy [Phase one] was successful because *he encouraged the Arabs to think that he would regain for them their lost lands while he kept Israel satisfied* that her security was not being endangered . . . Mr Kissinger created the belief in the Arab world that Mr Nixon and Mr Kissinger, known as "the magician" in the Arab press, *will bring about a complete pullback*'[43] (italics mine). The attempt was to consolidate the 'moderate' trend in the Arab world, and to improve Arab–American relations at the expense of Israeli territorial concessions.

Phase Two was to begin with simultaneous Egyptian–Israeli and Jordanian–Israeli negotiations. However as a consequence of the Rabat conference, the Jordanian option was removed from the Secretary's agenda. Now Kissinger concentrated on an Egyptian–Israeli disengagement. Among other reasons, he undertook the November 1974 trip to salvage his diplomacy from the Rabat ruins,[44] and he did establish that there was still a role for Egypt to play in revitalizing the incremental diplomacy. Thus, he concluded on November 7, 1974 'that possibilities do exist for further American-sponsored diplomatic progress in the Middle East despite hard-line decisions of last week's Rabat Summit

Conference of Arab states', and that 'everyone agrees the United States' effort should continue.'[45]

In between trips, Kissinger consulted with key decision-makers of the Arab countries and Israel. He conducted lengthy 'exploratory' talks with Rabin, Allon, Dinitz and Peres of Israel. His discussions with Sadat, Fahmi and Faisal convinced Kissinger that both Israel and Egypt were interested in another accord. To cover his flanks, Kissinger met American Jewish leaders in Washington, and also received the blessings of Faisal, the oil-rich king of Saudi Arabia. Thus from February 9-14, 1975, Kissinger undertook final exploratory trips in order to conclude Phase Two before the reconvening of the Geneva conference. The accord was intended to achieve some Egyptian political commitment for Israel (although the Secretary abstained from concurring with the Israeli demand for non-belligerency), and an Israeli withdrawal from the strategic passes and the Egyptian oil fields. Though the Egyptians expected an Israeli withdrawal, Sadat 'has so far not indicated publicly *what, if anything, he would give in return.*'[46] Kissinger nevertheless claimed that discussions with Sadat 'yield progress' and that 'Sadat was satisfied'.[47] While the Israelis made it clear that in return for tangible territorial concessions they demanded political non-belligerency, Sadat openly rejected their demand.[48]

Thus the last exploratory tour ended with Kissinger proclaiming that he was 'prudently optimistic.' Hopeful, heartened, prudent—all these adverbs certainly indicate high expectations. Kissinger obviously confided in no one what made him prudently optimistic, in view of the fact that Sadat flatly rejected political concessions.[49]

The final shuttle began on March 5, 1975 and ended in failure on March 23, 1975. The reasons for the failure will be discussed in the next section. First, however, some observations can be made on what did happen during this shuttle: (1) Kissinger spoke of Phase Two as if it would be a peace negotiation while it was no more than a second phase troop withdrawal, to be engineered before the Geneva conference supposedly reconvened. (2) As always, Kissinger made open and closed deals which, in the end, were clear only to him—Sadat was to make pledges to Kissinger rather than to

Israel while the Israelis suggested to Kissinger that Egypt renounced war.[50] Most of the negotiations were kept secret and journalists reported only on 'moods.' Despite Kissinger's hope that Israel would accept intangible pledges for a tangible withdrawal, Rabin made it clear to Kissinger on March 13, before he left for Aswan, that an Egyptian move unaccompanied by a political commitment would not be accepted by the Israeli cabinet.[51] On March 15 the Israelis seemed apprehensive of the Egyptian ideas which apparently failed to yield a political commitment.[52] By March 18 renunciation of war was the crux of the Israeli argument. The Israelis offered 'an end to acts of belligerence' to be linked to a demilitarization, a larger role for UNEF, and, hopefully, an end to the Arab diplomatic and economic boycott of Israel.[53]

According to a *New York Times* article on March 21 newsmen were told of the following developments in negotiations:

> Both sides agree that any mutual declaration on renouncing use of force would be made public.
>
> Egypt has agreed that most of the territory that Israel would give up would be demilitarized and manned by United Nations forces.
>
> The United Nations force would have a life span longer than the current six-month renewable periods, but Egypt rejects an indefinite life for it.
>
> The accord would be carried out in phases lasting several months, the exact time to be worked out after a basic agreement is reached.
>
> The agreement would stand on its own and not be conditional on any other steps such as a reconvening of the Geneva peace conference.
>
> The two sides have also begun discussing with Mr Kissinger the exact placement of the disengagement lines, with maps being consulted.[54]

On March 23 Kissinger dropped the Sinai accord bid, after having reached a deadlock between Egypt and Israel. He announced this failure to reach an agreement on withdrawal in Sinai, suspended his peace mediation, and returned to

Washington.[55] How significant that Kissinger defined Phase Two as an 'agreement on an Egyptian political commitment', that he had suspended 'peace talks' when in fact he had suspended a Phase Two troop separation in Sinai. Thus the Americans bemoaned the 'failure of peace' and looked for someone to blame—not Kissinger of course who had created and nurtured Phase Two. Officially, the blame was laid 'neither on Israel nor on Egypt' while privately Kissinger laid[56] the burden of failure on Israel's doorstep. George Will, *Washington Post* columnist, has this to say on the mission's failure: Kissinger, wrote Will, was not after peace but merely an adjustment in the Sinai armistice agreement, a piece of paper which would symbolize a personal victory in the 'de-institutionalized, personalized spectacle' of shuttle diplomacy. Israel, he continued, was ready to take military risks to get an Egyptian political gesture, principally an Egyptian declaration of non-belligerence. When Egypt refused to consider such a declaration seriously, 'Israel made an extraordinary offer . . . [to] return the Abu Rodeis oil fields and [to] agree to Egyptian forces moving forward to occupy the current UN buffer zone [and to] withdraw its forces half-way through the (Sinai) passes.'

Egypt would not agree. Believing ' . . . that the United States is desperate for a Mideast agreement—almost any agreement', Egypt saw that 'it could win a political victory in Washington' if instead it took the action of ' . . . turning the negotiations into a charade.' The Egyptians gambled, says Will, that the US would blame Israel for any breakdown in negotiation. Will concludes:

> The fact that Washington is debating whether Israel's intransigence foiled Kissinger's mission indicates that Egypt won its gamble. Egypt made Israel a frivolous offer that Israel had to refuse, and this refusal triggered a preposterous debate in the capital of Israel's bewildered ally.[57]

F. Why Did Phase Two End in Failure?

Those who would trace the roots of the failure of Phase

Two's negotiations could easily find themselves going in several different directions. The blame is shared by all parties, in particular by the extremist rejection fronts.

However, the fundamental error was made by Kissinger himself, a compilation of misconceptions resulting in misguided diplomatic tactics.

(1) Belief in his personal diplomatic prowess.

(2) His misperception of the Egyptian and Israeli abilities and/or willingness to deliver under the pressure of the American 'momentum.'

(3) Refusal to recognize the internal constraints imposed upon the Israeli and Egyptian regimes.

(4) His previous success with personalized, and highly centralistic regimes, and his failure to perceive the different nature of the Rabin from the Meir-Dayan cabinet.

(5) His failure to perceive Israeli doubts on American guarantees which some writers assumed would replace Israeli concessions for withdrawing its forces from strategic positions, in the absence of a binding Egyptian political commitment.[58]

(6) His misperception of the strength of Arab political options resulting from a built-in Soviet 'insurance' policy to supply Egypt and Syria with superior strategic weapons, coupled with a misjudgment of the strength of Arab expectations of Soviet intervention in a crunch as was the case in the 1956, 1967 and 1973 wars.

Before analyzing the above factors, it is necessary to make a fundamental critique of the Kissingerian step-by-step concept of incremental diplomacy, and his conceptual allies, which include the government of Israel. Kissinger, and to a certain extent, the Rabin-Allon pair made the following errors in analyzing the fundamental sources of political instability and of the roots of the Arab–Israeli conflict: (a) undervaluing the longevity, tenacity, and brutality of the Arab–Israeli conflict, the commitment of the belligerents (even if not with the same vehemence) to basic—if not atavistic—integral nationalist stances; and (b) undervaluing the extraordinary role played by the superpower rivalries and the ability of the USSR, as well as Syria and the PLO, to torpedo Kissinger's diplomatic concept, process and output.

Incremental diplomacy was initiated in an endeavour to overcome the above two basic impasses. The failure of Phase Two demonstrates its futility. The history of diplomacy, however replete with incrementalism, does not necessarily demonstrate that processes of diplomacy *ipso facto* evolve into reasonable and incremental processes of progressive concession by belligerents. There is no evidence as yet that incremental diplomacy, harnessed to the step-by-step momentum, guarantees better results than an all-inclusive collective security conference (comprising the superpowers, Arab states, the PLO and Israel.) If incremental diplomacy was designed to avoid an impasse, limit the options for conflict resolution, lower the levels of aspiration and expectation of the belligerents and lead to some type of political settlement, the technique fell far short of its goals. In fact, it may be cautiously argued that the failure of Phase Two will have resulted in a hardening of everybody's position if and when the Geneva conference reconvenes. The argument in support of Kissinger's incrementalism, i.e. that, in the absence of a *real* diplomatic structure for conflict resolution, the step-by-step structure could serve as a buffer against old aspirations and practices—should also be doubted. After all, is it not equally reasonable to assume that the collapse of a collective conference would produce the same result as the collapse of Phase Two and that there is no evidence that the parties would resort to war as Kissinger anticipated?

To say that the Secretary made a conceptual error is a serious challenge to his *Weltanschauung*. Nevertheless, the charge is justified; the source of error *is* conceptual. The Kissingerian framework was built, in my view, on a series of misperceptions. A surge of self-confidence in his diplomatic prowess carried him along through successful negotiations in the Far and Middle East. Vanity, mass adulation, media manipulation, the clandestine Nixon years and, above all, his style were all factors contributing to his errors of judgment. His *modus operandi*—the muting of opposition within the NSC, the elimination of options and closure on feedback from other men and agencies, compounded by the de-institutionalized Department of State—greatly contributed to his conceptual errors and magnified his misperceptions. Having got the Soviets off his back, at least for the duration of the second phase, with the Syrians and the PLO if not isolated, partially paralyzed (by indirect tacit Soviet consent for this one last incremental solo), and with support from Faisal, Kissinger felt that all that remained was for him to persuade Egypt, desirous of its territories, and Israel, over which he wielded considerable leverage. Having temporarily removed the rejection fronts, he misjudged the difficulties and may have been misled by both Egypt and Israel. To begin with, he gave the two regimes greater credit for the *capability* or willingness to deliver even the minimal concessions for a successful conclusion of Phase Two. Kissinger certainly misjudged Egypt's willingness to make concessions as agonizing as those he expected from Israel, or Rabin's ability to produce an agreement without any reasonable Egyptian concessions. It is clear from the processes and actions between the end of Phase One and the end of Phase Two that Kissinger treated Israel in a coercive way, while restricting his role to that of a mediator with regard to Egypt. This difference in attitudes was not because Kissinger is malicious or ill-intentioned toward Israel. On the contrary, Kissinger essentially acted in good faith in order to help Israel. But obviously he had *more* leverage on Israel and little or none on Egypt, now that he was no longer in a position to save its Third Army. In fact, as Henry Tanner, the Washington correspondent of the *New York Times* in Cairo wrote, Egypt was ready to deliver only 'minimal concessions'. An outline of what these concessions were had been known to Kissinger since the fall of 1974, according to Egyptian officials. They added that he did not question these limits, and that he 'expected to find an agreement within that perimeter.'[59] Thus it seems that Egypt, not incorrectly, having perceived Kissinger's leverage on Israel, envisaged the 'momentum' as tantamount to American pressure for a unilateral Israeli withdrawal, and therefore was prepared to offer very little in return. (The Egyptian offer to refrain from war was the only 'political' concession made in the negotiations.)

In the meantime the Israelis saw American influence crumble like the proverbial dominoes in Portugal and South East Asia. Simultaneously, Israel also witnessed the reemergence of the Arab Eastern front (Syria-the PLO-Iraq), the collapse of Kurdistan, and the antagonism between the President and Congress especially in the area of foreign aid. Little wonder they were unreceptive to an offer of possible American guarantees in the absence of any significant Egyptian concession. The Egyptians, although supporting Phase Two, clearly left wide open the option to return to Geneva. In fact, Sadat clearly told Geyelin that with regard to long-term security: 'You must keep this for Geneva: for the whole solution (sic).' Thus Sadat clearly envisaged that non-belligerency would be dealt with at Geneva, and a political settlement would be postponed until the next generation.[60]

Another serious misjudgment was Kissinger's overconfidence in the authority of the Rabin-Allon team. Although he became an expert in the internal politics of the Israeli cabinet, passed judgment on its personalities, and was aware of Rabin's vulnerability, he failed to perceive the change of mood and public opinion in Israel. To begin with, Rabin's popularity was low. Kissinger knew that. Yet his own popularity in Israel dropped considerably toward the end of Phase Two.[61] The impact of Cambodia, Vietnam, Portugal and the fall of Kurdistan only increased Israel's apprehensions and mistrust of American guarantees. Thus the internal constraints on the cabinet were considerable. Rabin's lack of authority over the cabinet and the Labour Party, and the fierce Likud opposition were well known to Kissinger. Despite protest to the contrary, the impact of domestic factors on Israeli foreign policy were not carefully studied.[62] Kissinger failed to consider the impact of the Israeli *vox populi* on the calculus for Phase Two.

The Secretary was aware of Rabin's abandonment of the demand for non-belligerency in December, 1974, and its modification in a less ambitious formula. Nevertheless, during his exploratory tour (March 10-15, 1975), he ignored the factors that made the Rabin government finally insist on changed tactics and positioning for the negotiations. Unexpectedly the Rabin cabinet (though this may have been debated between Kissinger and Allon during the exploratory period) suggested a two-tier negotiations proposal (a mini-withdrawal of 30 miles proposal, and a maxi-withdrawal including the straits and the oil fields). These new proposals stemmed from the hardening of public opinion, and its impact on the cabinet. Kissinger expected a Meir–Dayan inner-circle duumvirate system and style of deliverance; instead, rather late, he found that the broadening of decision-making in Israel and the democratization of the cabinet produced an unexpected obstacle. Kissinger's superdiplomacy and crisis management in the past depended on—and thus produced results only with—authoritarian or semi-authoritarian regimes and decision-making styles. He could 'finish' business with Chou en-Lai, Le doc-Tho, Brezhnev, Faisal, Sadat, and the Greek junta—but in a non-personalized, non-authoritarian, managerial and democratic type of regime, Kissinger's superdiplomacy proved a failure. This was not just a case of misjudgment. It was a case of misperception—that the seemingly doveish, accommodating, vulnerable Rabin cabinet would produce the necessary concessions for a successful conclusion of Phase Two. The nature of the regime did not lend itself to authoritarian superdiplomacy. In the case of Sadat, Kissinger knew that he had little leverage but did not realize just how *meagre* the Egyptian commitment to Kissingerian diplomacy was. As Mr Tanner reported of Sadat: 'He came at his suggestion, not ours.'[63] Sadat clearly sought Kissinger's mediation to protect his American option. Nevertheless, the American political option was not a sufficient inducement for Sadat to offer, at this stage of the diplomatic process, the minimum concessions required.[64] Hoping to exercise his leverage over the Israelis, Kissinger found to his dismay that this cabinet, however divided, was nevertheless representative of a public opinion which was suspicious of Kissinger and doubted Egypt's intentions.

Next, Kissinger failed to cancel the Egyptian and Soviet military option. Kissinger moved into the final stages of the negotiations despite the flow of Soviet arms to Egypt which was resumed early in February, 1975.[65] In the absence of any press reports to the contrary, it appears that neither in Vladivostok in December, 1974, nor thereafter, did Kissinger succeed in persuading the Soviets to agree to an arms control in the Middle East. Why did he expect, once the USSR stood behind Syria and the PLO and was sending arms to Egypt, that Egypt would abandon its Soviet option by substituting step-by-step negotiations for the Soviet-coveted Geneva conference? Why should Sadat abandon his open options with the superpowers, who in 1956, 1967, and 1973 stopped Israel short of the total destruction of Arab forces and their political humiliation? Sadat remembered well that the US forced an Israeli withdrawal from Sinai in 1956. In 1973, the USSR not only supplied and constantly airlifted weapons to Syria and Egypt, but induced the US to impose a cease-fire on Israel, and even threatened military intervention to save the collapsing Egyptian armed forces. Why should Sadat have been accommodating while the Soviets supported the Arabs? Sadat's insurance policy was that in the event that he resorted to war and lost, the USSR would bail him out politically and militarily. The case of Syria is similar. At no time did Kissinger make a real effort to cancel this insurance policy, so that he could have greater leverage which would enable him to lower the level of Arab military aspirations. Faithful to his policy of detente, Kissinger made no effort to remove the Soviet military option in the area. The USSR remained free to supply the Arabs with a modern arsenal, and indirectly participate in Arab–Israeli wars through monumental airlifts. What leverage did Kissinger have over Sadat at the very time he was to conclude the diplomatic process of Phase Two?

The onus of responsibility for the failure of Phase Two must be laid on the shoulders of Secretary Kissinger whose incremental diplomacy reached a *cul-de-sac* and whose perceptions proved to be wrong. Nevertheless, both Egypt and Israel share with Kissinger a considerable part of the burden of the failure. Rabin-Allon's policy was not only convergent with Kissinger's, but evolved as both men sought and cultivated the Secretary, his concept and his style. Both invested an overabundance of hope in his superdiplomatic skills and as late as his last exploratory trip (March 10-15), neither Rabin nor Allon had frankly admitted this fact to Kissinger. Nor did the Israeli ambassador, Simcha Dinitz, appraise Kissinger correctly, take note of the mounting public criticism of his style, or the Israeli suspicions of American security guarantees. No attempt was made to dissuade Kissinger from

pursuing Phase Two, not because Rabin and Allon were insincere (they were most sincere) but because they did not foresee the problem of delivering to the cabinet the frivolous type of concessions Egypt offered. For two weeks at least Kissinger *knew* that Egypt was making 'intangible' concessions, but he hoped either to twist Rabin's arm (which he could not do in view of the tenuousness of his position), or that his advice would be accepted despite the mounting difficulties. Rabin, Allon, and the cabinet had informed the Secretary of the difficulties involved in persuading their people, but Kissinger's drive for 'momentum' gave them little time to go to the country to persuade the nation that the benefits would outweigh the losses incurred in a second phase dis-engagement. The cabinet adamantly demanded that Sadat produce something tangible—not mere words and intangible concessions. Kissinger was known to have said to the Israelis that 'in the negotiations, the problem for Israel would be to "relate the tangibles of territory to the intangibles of recognition and expression of a desire for peace".'[66]
The Egyptian offer did not persuade the Israelis to accept Kissinger's hopeful advice. In fact as Terrence Smith reported: 'It was an offer Yitzchak Rabin had to refuse—assuming, that is, he wanted to avoid the collapse of his coalition government, a revolt within his own party, and an abrupt end to his career as premier. Granting at least that degree of self-interest, Mr Rabin had no choice but to reject the deal that was being offered at the end of Secretary of State Kissinger's two weeks of shuttle diplomacy in search for a new Sinai accord with Egypt.'[67] Rabin-Allon may have misjudged their ability to deliver considerable concessions for so little in return—against popular opposition. 'This time Israel resisted. Mr Rabin said "No", despite his firm belief that close co-operation with the United States is the cornerstone of Israeli foreign policy.'[68]

In the case of Egypt, Kissinger was working to neutralize Syrian and PLO pressure on the Egyptian president; by temporarily disengaging the USSR, Kissinger hoped, furthermore, that he could induce Sadat to become more co-operative. Kissinger's serious error was that this time he had no Egyptian Third Army as hostage. This time the Egyptian army, recovered and rearmed, did not impose on Sadat the necessity to hurry. As Sadat related to Geyelin, 'I am a patient man.'[69] Sadat's position as manager of the Arabs, although apparently unchallenged, was not completely autonomous. 'It would almost certainly be false to say that it was pressure from other governments that kept President Anwer el-Sadat from making a non-belligerency pledge in exchange for a partial Israeli withdrawal, no matter how extensive. The Egyptian president is a nationalist, and his intimates say that he meant every word he said, that he would not abandon the right to go to war as long as a part of his national territory remains under Israeli occupation.'[70]

Sadat's hands were not as tied as some journalists and American political visitors made them out to be. (In fact, it was Asad who was relatively isolated.[71]) The PLO presented no serious threat with which to pressure Egypt; and the Soviets continued to deliver strategic weapons to the Egyptian army. What Kissinger misjudged was:

(a) That Sadat was not desperate as he had been on October 25, 1973.
(b) That Sadat would not relinquish his Soviet military option.
(c) That Sadat was not as committed to Phase Two and the Kissingerian step-by-step approach as the Israelis were.
(d) That Sadat possibly saw a chance to achieve at a Geneva conference what he was unable to in Phase Two.
(e) (This is only a reasonable conjecture) that if Phase Two collapsed, the chances were that Israel and not Egypt would be blamed.

It was not that Sadat deceived Kissinger and lured him into a trap that could only produce friction between Israel and the US. Rather Sadat's policy was to isolate the US from Israel. That this was his intention has been reiterated on numerous occasions by Arab leaders to their American interlocutors; still it is probable that Sadat hoped to achieve a military disengagement with as little concession as possible during Phase Two. Kissinger's grand error was in failing to be persuaded by what he knew—that Sadat had his option open in Geneva. Why should Sadat have exerted himself in Phase Two, which Rabin said was, from an Israeli point of view, designed to isolate Egypt from Syria, since Israel had no intention of returning to the pre-1967 borders?[72]

The failure lies in the concept of incrementalism. The agenda for a Middle Eastern political settlement must be all-inclusive—not incremental. The concept of a Geneva conference (but not as the Soviets or the PLO perceive it) is more promising, where the major items on the agenda would be the issues which underlie the fundamentals of the Arab–Israeli asymmetries and conflict. A political settlement would mean the political recognition of Israel in exchange for all the 1967-occupied territories; in effect, peace for territories. All outstanding issues should be open and negotiable: the settlement of boundaries, the Palestinian question, the political recognition of Israel; cultural and human exchange and transfer; arms limitations, and reasonable co-existence. If such a conference were to be dominated by the USSR, as the advocate for the Arabs, thus torpedoing all possible arrangements, it certainly would justify Kissinger's fears. But I doubt it. The USSR highly values its role as co-chairman and would not forfeit such a chance; it is committed to the conference's success and not to its failure. In truth the only mediator both the Arabs and the Israelis accept is the US, but the USSR could not be excluded from a final settlement. There will be no settlement if the USSR were to be in the chair at Geneva —neither, it seems, would there be a settlement unilaterally chaired by the United States. The concept of a Geneva conference must be divided into two tiers, or two structures, for peace: first, an American–Soviet understanding, the agenda of which should include among other objectives a limitation on the arms race and whose function would be to guarantee the second tier. What would be achieved in the second tier is a directly negotiated Arab–Israeli peace conference, whose chances would be better than the bleak view expressed by Secretary Kissinger once the belligerents were aware of the United States–USSR compromise. The chairmen would be the two superpowers who would not exploit their position to threaten one party or to act as the other party's solicitor. Such a conference would be dependent on a superpower imprimatur for what the second tier had agreed upon. The political concept and framework for a settlement must be just the opposite of Kissinger's incrementalism. It should be a maximalist conference endowed with an over-ambitious agenda to settle the major and most stubborn issues first. The Arab–Israeli conflict is cumulative, brutal, and integral. Trying to dismantle it layer by layer is to needlessly handle political dynamite. Years of belligerency, non-recognition, and mortal combat cannot be disentangled incrementally. There is no way but the hard way to peace: to deal with all the major and outstanding issues, the generalities—however vague—and to end the process with practical, step-by-step, political and military withdrawals and disengagements, as outlined and agreed upon by principles around which a Geneva agenda must revolve if it is to succeed: peace for territories; political recognition for military withdrawal; and cultural and social exchange to replace garrisoned borders. If between 1967–1973 this was not possible in view of the Khartoum *diktat*, the Israeli adherence to the *status quo*, and the lack of great power political momentum, the post-1973 conditions may have made the opportunity more propitious.

Incrementalism as a concept has utterly failed. The misperceptions of Kissinger must *not* be repeated. The only incentive to conflict resolution in the end is not what Arabs and Israelis do or say, but what the superpowers are willing to sacrifice. The chances for an all-embracing conference, in view of the contemporary realities of international politics, are still not promising. But the concept is. Step-by-step diplomacy has proved bankrupt. To try to redeem it is tantamount to stalemate. One concept has led to paralysis, the other one could not be any worse, and can, at least, offer a small hope of success.

NOTES

1. 'Dayan says US Blocked Victory', *The New York Times* (December 19, 1974), p. 6. See also 'The Speech that was not Delivered,' *Ma'ariv* December 27, 1974, pp. 21-22.
2. On Israeli attitudes towards foreign policy, see Michael Brecher, *The Foreign Policy of Israel*, Yale University Press, Vol 1 (1971) and Vol. 2

(1975). For the different view of Israelis, one should consult the Israeli press. See especially *Ma'ariv, Haaretz* and *Yediot Aharonot* and the periodical polls taken by *DAHAF*, Public Opinion Survey Corporation, and the Guttman Institute in Jerusalem. On the Israeli political system see Moshe Lissak, *Social Structure in Israel*, Israel Universities Presses, Tel-Aviv (1970).

3. Following the Interim Agranat Report on April 1974, Mrs Meir resigned and along with her, Dayan, Eban and Sapir, the key members of the cabinet. Only Galili, the last member of the former inner-circle, remained. To some extent Allon is a representative of the former regime. Rabin, elected by the Labour Party Central Committee, received only 45 per cent of the vote. Peres, a representative of the smaller faction, Rafi (8 per cent of Labour) received over 40 per cent of the vote.
4. In fact, Dayan is responsible for the Kissinger initiative. It was Dayan who suggested several ideas that were later adopted by Kissinger. Troop separation and its conclusion reflects Dayan's 1971 plan. Dayan, defying a cabinet decision, suggested returning Kuneitra to the Syrians. Dayan fully supported Kissinger and the Meir-Dayan team was dedicated to the step-by-step approach.
5. The moderates are now led by Egypt, Jordan and Saudi Arabia. The militants are led by Libya, Algeria, Syria, Iraq and the PLO. The former accepted incremental diplomacy; the latter advocated the immediate reconvening of a full scale Geneva Conference.
6. Bernard Gwertzman, 'Sadat and Faisal support Kissinger's Mideast Aims,' *The New York Times* November 7, 1974, pp. 1, 7. See also James Reston, *The New York Times*, April 28, 1974, p. 21.
7. On the Syrian attitude toward Phase One, see Philip Geyelin, excerpts of interview with President Asad, *The Washington Post*, March 5, 1975, p. 10. Sadat 'Interview,' *Le Monde*, January 22, 1975.
8. Shimon Shamir, 'The Spirit of Ramadan,' *Ma'ariv*, March 20, 1975, p. 20. See also footnote 9.
9. For American recognition of the PLO, see 'Arabs Draft Palestine Resolution,' *The Washington Post*, November 18, 1974, p. 1: *The New York Times*, November 12, 1974, p. 1: 'Arafat offers Olive Branch, Gun at UN.' *The Washington Post*, November 13, 1974, p. 1: Terrence Smith, 'Hussein' and 'Arafat,' Week in Review, *The New York Times*, November 10, 1974, p. 4: Jim Hoagland, 'Arafat Chooses Life with Israel,' Outlook, *The Washington Post*, November 10, 1974, p. 1: George Will, 'Knowing One When You See One,' *The Washington Post*, November 14, 1974, p. 17: 'Statement of American Delegate in General Assembly Debate on Palestine Question,' *The New York Times*, November 22, 1974, p. 15: for the Rabat Conference see, Henry Tanner. 'Arab Issue Calls for a Palestinian State,' *The New York Times*, October 29, 1974, p. 6: Yoseph Harif, 'Kissinger Wants to Mediate Between Hussein and Arafat.' *Ma'ariv*, October 25, 1974 p. 15: Henry Tanner, 'Palestinian Chief Meets with Arab Leaders,' *The New York Times*, October 31, 1974, p. 4: 'Arabs Hail Leaders on Declaration of

a Palestinian State', *The New York Times*, October 30, 1974, p. 18; Terrence Smith, 'A Reporter's Note Book: Rabat Summit Conference', *The New York Times*, November 4, 1974, p. 12; 'Mr Kissinger Faces a New Middle East', Week in Review, *The New York Times*, November 3, 1974, p. 4; 'Guns and Olive Branches', *Time Magazine*, November 25, 1974, pp. 43-46. There were no minutes in Arabic published at the Rabat Conference.

10. Yoseph Harif, 'The Americans Search for a Palestinian Formula in Geneva', *Ma'ariv*, July 5, 1974, p. 17; Yoseph Harif, 'Washington Inquiries of Israel: Ideas for Negotiations with Jordan', *Ma'ariv*, June 28, 1974, p. 19; Henry Tanner, 'Geneva Role Set for Palestinians', *The New York Times*, June 9, 1974, p. 1.

11. On the Egyptian positioning for Phase Two, see Arnaud de Brochgrave interview with Haykal, *Newsweek*, January 27, 1974, p. 41; Muhammed H. Haykal, 'Pulling Back from the Mideast Regime', *The New York Times*, January 16, 1975, p. 41; Henry Tanner, 'Kissinger Flies to Cairo to Assess Talk Outlook', *The New York Times*, November 5, 1974, p. 4; B. Gwertzman, 'Kissinger Hopeful of Sinai Formula', *The New York Times*, January 28, 1975, p. 3; H. Tanner, 'Sadat Still Pins Hope on Kissinger', *The New York Times*, December 18, 1974, p. 14; B. Gwertzman, 'Kissinger Says Talk with Sadat Yields Progress', *The New York Times*, February 13, 1975, p. 1; 'The Step-by-Step is Still in Business', *Time Magazine*, February 24, 1975, pp. 28-30; Henry Tanner, 'If Sadat Does Give in, He May Do So Privately', Week in Review, *The New York Times*, February 16, 1975, p. 3; Philip Geyelin, 'Sadat Stresses Flexibility on Territories', *The Washington Post*, February 17, 1975, pp. 13, 1, 10; 'Egypt Studies Peace Pledge', *The Washington Post*, February 13, 1975, pp. 1, 14; Anwar el Sadat, 'Interview' *Le Monde*, January 22, 1975, p. 1; On the Israeli positioning see Yoseph Harif 'Allon to Washington', *Ma'ariv*, December 13, 1974, p. 15; Yoseph Harif, 'Ford-Allon Meeting', *Ma'ariv*, December 20, 1974, p. 15; Yuval Elizur, 'New Sinai Pullback Favoured', *Washington Post*, December 26, 1974, p. 13; T. Smith, 'Israel Rejects a Pact Deadline', *The New York Times*, January 23, 1975, p. 6; B. Gwertzman, 'Allon and Kissinger to Confer on Mideast Outlook', *New York Times*, November 27, 1974, p. 10; T. Smith, 'Dayan Doubts that a New War is Imminent', *The New York Times*, January 21, 1975, pp. 1, 24; Yoel Marcus, 'How to Cross in Peace: The Seven Lean Years', *Haaretz*, December 3, 1974, p. 9; Editors, 'Interview with Prime Minister Rabin', *Ma'ariv*, September 25, 1974, pp. 13-14; R. Bashan, 'Interview with Prime Minister Rabin', *Yediot Aharonot*, July 26, 1974, pp. 1-3, 18; T. Smith, 'Israeli "Hawk" Scorns Kissinger's Plan', *The New York Times*, February 6, 1975, pp. 1, 4; Philip Geyelin, 'Rabin Outlines Israeli Plans for Settlement', *The Washington Post*, March 1, 1975, pp. 1, 12; P. Geyelin, 'A Conversation with Shimon Peres', *The Washington Post*, March 12, 1975, p. 17; T. Smith, 'Kissinger Hears Israelis on Sinai', *The New York Times*, February 11, 1975, pp. 1, 4; B. Gwertzman, 'Israelis Believe Sadat is Now Set for Sinai Talks', *The New York Times*, January 18,

1975, pp. 1, 4; Y. Harif, 'Rabin Requests Freedom of Action from the Cabinet', *Ma'ariv*, February, 28, 1975, p. 15.

12. On the Agranat Committee, see Amos Perlmutter, 'Political Misperceptions and Military Errors: The Israeli Lessons' (of 1973). Unpub. MS Washington, January, 1975.
13. For the first time in the political history of Israel the Prime Minister was neither the head of the party, nor in direct control of the defence ministry, not a legitimate member of pioneer Zionism, nor a member of the inner circle of Histadrut, the Labour Party or the Kibbutz and Agricultural movements, which comprise the major political and economic institutions of the State. Rabin's influence within the party was meagre, and he wielded little influence over the party secretariat. In fact, Peres, a representative of 8 per cent of the Labour electorate, won over 40 per cent of the party's central committee vote in his race for the premiership.
14. Yoel Marcus, 'Interview with the Prime Minister', *Haaretz*, December 3, 1974, p. 2.
15. *Ibid.*
16. *Ibid.*
17. *Ibid.*
18. *Ibid.*
19. Philip Geyelin's Interview with Prime Minister Rabin (Excerpts from Text) *The Washington Post*, March 1, 1975, p. 12.
20. *Ibid.*
21. For the debates within the Israeli cabinet on the issues of non-belligerency, American-proposed military arrangements, and Israel's two-tier (minimum and maximum) plans, I have relied on personal interviews with the chief of the Israeli negotiating team, the Chief of Staff, several cabinet members, former and present senior political advisers in the defence ministry, Israeli journalists specializing in national security affairs and colleagues at the universities of Jerusalem, Tel-Aviv and Haifa.
22. See 'Egypt-Israel Gap Still Big After Kissinger's Probing': *The New York Times*, March 15, 1974, pp. 1-9.
23. For a detailed analysis of Nasser's Egypt and the rise of Sadat, see Amos Perlmutter, *Egypt, the Praetorian State*, Transactions Books, New Brunswick, 1974.
24. On the 1971 Coup, see *Ibid.*
25. Check with the Israeli press (*Haaretz*, *Ma'ariv* for the months July-August 1972).
26. See Moshe Dayan, 'The Lecture That Was Not Delivered', *Ma'ariv*, December 27, 1974, pp. 21-22; 'We and the Soviets', *Ma'ariv*, January 3, 1975, p. 15.
27. 'Egypt Said to Get Soviet Arms Again Despite Sadat's Denials', *The Washington Post*, February 29, 1975, p. 25; Jim Hoagland, 'Soviet Arms Said to Flow Again to Cairo', *The Washington Post*, February 8, 1975, p. 1; Drew Middleton, 'Soviet MIG 23 Shipment to Egyptians', *The New York Times*, February 10, 1975, p. 1.

28. Henry Tanner, 'If Sadat Does Give in He May Do So Privately', *The New York Times*, February 16, 1975, p. 3.
29. See excerpts of interviews with Sadat, Philip Geyelin, *The Washington Post*, February 17, 1975, p. 10.
30. *Ibid.*
31. *Ibid.*
32. *Ibid.*
33. *Ibid.*
34. Arnaud de Borchgrav, 'Interview with Haykal', *Newsweek*, January 27, 1975, p. 41. It is interesting that Haykal's view converges with that of Dayan. In an interview with *Ma'ariv* Dayan has this to say on the Israeli disengagement with Egypt: 'The Israeli Government is mistaken: We should have conducted a simultaneous interim settlement with both Egypt and Syria. There is a logic in the Egyptian argument that they cannot open the Canal and rehabilitate its cities as long as they are within range of Israeli artillery.' *Ma'ariv*, March 21, 1975, pp. 22, 24.
35. *Op. cit.*, p. 10. *The USSR and the Yom Kippur War*, CUP, 1977.
36. On Soviet-Egyptian relations, see Galia Golan; Paula Stern, 'Egypt and Soviet Policy', *The Washington Post*, March 3, 1975, p. 17; Victor Zorza, 'Bickering Between Moscow and Cairo', *The Washington Post*, February 13, 1975, p. 19; 'Moscow-Cairo split Considered Serious', *The Washington Post*, December 30, 1974, p. 6; Christopher Wren, 'Soviet-Egyptian Tension Seen by Moscow Diplomats', *The New York Times*, January 2, 1975, p. 1; 'Gromyko in Cairo, Hints Views Differ', *The New York Times*, February 4, 1975, p. 2; Drew Middleton, 'Moscow Said to Link Arms Aid for Egypt', *The New York Times*, February 8, 1975, p. 2.
37. Paula Stern, 'Egypt', *The Washington Post*, *Ibid*, p. 17.
38. 'Dayan Says US Blocked Victory', *New York Times*, December 19, 1974, p. 6. See also 'The Speech That Was Not Delivered', *Ma'ariv*, December 27, 1974, pp. 21-22.
39. Itamar Rabinowitch, 'What Makes Asad Run', *Ma'ariv*, November 29, 1974, p. 18.
40. Excerpts from the text of an interview with President Asad, *The Washington Post*, February 5, 1975, p. 10.
41. Tad Szulc, 'Kissinger's Miscalculations', *The Washington Post*, October 8, 1974, p. 17.
42. Joseph Kraft, 'The High Price of Detente', *The Washington Post*, February 12, 1974, p. 17.
43. Bernard Gwertzman, 'The President's Mideast Gamble', *The New York Times*, June 10, 1974, p. 3.
44. Bernard Gwertzman, 'Kissinger Plans to "Salvage" Visit to Middle East', *The New York Times*, November 1, 1974, pp. 1, 6.
45. Bernard Gwertzman, 'Kissinger Tells of Mideast Possibilities', *The New York Times*, November 9, 1974, p. 4.
46. Bernard Gwertzman, 'Some Questions and Answers on Kissinger's Trip to Mideast', *The New York Times*, February 9, 1975, p. 20.

47. Bernard Gwertzman, 'Kissinger Says Talk with Sadat Yields Progress', *The New York Times*, February 13, 1975, p. 1.
48. On Israeli position, see Geyelin's 'Interview with Rabin' *op.cit.*
49. Gwertzman, 'Some Questions', *The New York Times*, February 9, 1975, p. 20.
50. Bernard Gwertzman, 'Kissinger Hopeful on the Eve of New Trip to the Middle East', *The New York Times*, March 5, 1975, p. 5.
51. Yoseph Harif, 'Face to Face: Kissinger and Rabin', *Ma'ariv*, March 14, 1975, p. 4.
52. B. Gwertzman, 'Israelis Indicate a Cool Reaction to Egypt's Ideas', *The New York Times*, March 15, 1975, pp. 1, 6.
53. B. Gwertzman, 'Israel and Egypt are Now at the Hard-Bargaining Stage', *The New York Times*, March 19, 1975, p. 4.
54. B. Gwertzman, 'Kissinger Efforts Focus on a Territorial Issue', *The New York Times*, March 23, 1975, pp. 1, 9.
56. Bernard Gwertzman, 'Kissinger Home, Sees No Renewal of Mideast Role', *The New York Times*, March 23, 1975, p. 1.
57. George Will, '"Instransigence" and Peace', *The Washington Post*, March 29, 1975, p. 15.
58. Amos Perlmutter, 'The Illusions of American Guarantees to Israel,' *Ma'ariv*, February 7, 1975: and Geyelin, 'Rabin Interview,' *op. cit.*.
59. Henry Tanner, 'Mr Sadat, Nationalist and Wants All Sinai Back,' in 'The Week in Review,' *The New York Times*, March 10, 1975, p. 4.
60. *Op. cit.*, p. 10.
61. See John Goshko, 'Israelis Grow Suspicious of Kissinger,' *The Washington Post*, March 13, 1975, p. 32. According to *Haaretz*'s Poll, 33.8 per cent were 'clearly dissatisfied' with Kissinger's approach to the Middle East; 24.4 per cent were partially dissatisfied. (In June, 1974, his popularity was as high as 63.8 per cent.)
62. For over three months (January–March, 1975), the major Israeli papers, *Haaretz* and *Ma'ariv*, were vehemently opposed to Kissinger's policies.
63. Henry Tanner, *op. cit.*
64. From the information available on the negotiations, it is abundantly clear that Sadat was not going to make even 'practical political' concessions which would flow from the expected, and offered, Israeli military concessions at this stage. See Henry Tanner, 'Cairo Sees No Gain by Kissinger', *The New York Times*, November 9, 1974: and Henry Tanner, *op. cit.*
65. Jim Hoagland, 'Egypt Said to Get Soviet Arms Again Despite Sadat's Denials', *The Washington Post*, February 9, 1975, pp. 1, 25.
66. Bernard Gwertzman, 'Kissinger Hears Israeli View on Sinai Accord with Egypt', *The New York Times*, February 12, 1975, p. 7.
67. Terrence Smith, '"Yes" Would Make Rabin Ex-Premier', *The New York Times*, 'The Week in Review', March 30, 1975, p. 4.
68. *Ibid.*
69. Philip Geyelin, 'Interview with Sadat', *Washington Post*, February 7, 1975, p. 9.

70. Henry Tanner, *op. cit.*
71. Ihsan Hijazi, 'This Time, Syria is Standing All Alone', *The New York Times*, 'The Week in Review', March 9, 1975, p. 5.
72. See Geyelin's interview, *op. cit.*, p. 10. 'I said, even in a context of a peace treaty with Syria, I don't see Israel going down from the Golan Heights.' See also Dov Goldstein, 'Interview with Prime Minister Rabin', *Ma'ariv*, September 25, 1974, pp. 13-14.

CHAPTER VII

Phase II of Shuttle II

Henry Kissinger is not a man to accept defeat. Magnanimity is not one of his personal or diplomatic characteristics. Although there was a 'Gentleman's Agreement' between Kissinger and Rabin that the former would not blame either side (Egypt and/or Israel) for the March failure, as soon as he arrived in Washington Kissinger did not keep his word.[1] Not only was the President misinformed about Israel's responsibility for the failure of phase one of Shuttle Two negotiations, but Kissinger began an open campaign against the Israeli negotiating team by putting all the onus of blame upon them. The major weapon of the administration was the so-called policy of 'reassessment', which did not mean actually reassessing American military aid to Israel (although the administration went through the motions of reassessment[2]) but was rather intended as a clear threat: the US would contain (with an option of imposing an embargo on) the sale of strategic weapons to Israel, especially sophisticated electronic equipment and the like.[3]

The second weapon employed against Israel was an intensification of the relationship with Egypt. Kissinger arranged for a special summit between Presidents Ford and Sadat in Salzburg with the purpose of persuading the latter to move further toward the American orbit. Sadat was under heavy political pressure from his army, having failed to convince the Soviets of the need to re-equip his armed forces, depleted after the 1973[4] losses, and in view of Egypt's economic plight, found an excellent political outlet in the Kissinger summit with Ford.[5]

The Salzburg summit, in my view, turned out to be more than a desperate trip for Sadat, or a public opinion stunt for President Ford (as suggested by some journalists) intended to create an image of a President in charge of foreign policy;

the Salzburg principles, indeed, became the foundation stone for a new Egyptian–American alliance. If the Nixon Trip to Egypt symbolized the Egyptian–American rapprochement, the Salzburg summit established a new political alliance between Egypt and the US, even if it was not so designated.

Egypt conceded its political one-sidedness in global politics. The strained political relations with the USSR, accelerated by mutual suspicions, since the Soviet effort to topple Sadat in 1971,[6] was now matched by the USSR's denial of strategic arms to Egypt. In exchanging Egypt's political options Sadat still left open a military option with the USSR (however unsatisfactory it might have seemed to the Egyptian military establishment). In return for siding with the US in the US–USSR rivalry in the area the US *guaranteed* to Egypt the acceleration of an Israeli withdrawal from occupied Egyptian territories. In other words the price the US was to pay Egypt for its 'political revolution' was in Israeli coin. Thus the road for an American hegemony was paved, as it seemed to the Kissinger–Ford Team. Prime Minister Rabin was 'invited' to the US in the middle of June to be informed of the Salzburg Egyptian–American understanding, to be 'told' personally by President Ford that Israel had to continue the momentum of retreat and actually abandon the strategic passes of the Mitla and Jidi in Sinai. The pressure on Rabin was monumental.[7] Rabin returned to Israel and before a closed session of the Labour Alignment declared, 'our choices are either an uncomfortable agreement [Phase II], or a damaging general agreement (Geneva), the latter being accompanied by a serious American threat to restrict Israeli military and economic aid'.[8] Rabin insisted that the step-by-step 'strategy' was the correct policy and that the Israeli negotiating team, as well as the government, had to choose between several unattractive options. It gradually became obvious to members of the team and several Cabinet Ministers that Rabin and Peres opted (Allon openly stated his position) to surrender the Sinai passes lest the American 'reassessment' became a permanent policy of the US.[9] Yet Rabin was not in a position to dictate his preferred options to the team, the government, or the people, for reasons I have elaborated earlier. What seemed clear was that the Israeli refusal in March, if revised, would not carry the political leverage it possessed earlier. In other words, negotiations for Israel this time would take place under the shadow of Salzburg, and an American reassessment policy. The negotiations for Israel therefore did not start with the pre-March position but with the latest Israeli concession in March.

By 22 March 1975, the last day of the abortive Phase I Shuttle II, Israel abandoned the following political principles: one, there was no more talk of demanding an open declaration of nonbelligerency from Sadat. Two, it became clear that it was not Israel negotiating with Egypt, but the US, on behalf of Egypt, negotiating the surrender of the Sinai passes from Israel. Three, the unequal relationship also demonstrated the new American–Egyptian entente and the eroding of the 'special' American–Israeli relations which were the foundation for the first interim agreement. Israel was to give territory of considerable strategic and economic value for an Egyptian agreement to have Kissinger mediate and for the possible estrangement of Egypt and Syria,—a Rabin–Kissinger political goal. Rabin summed up the condition under which Israel was to negotiate: 'Israel's main problem is to *understand* American *needs* in the Middle East, not to oppose them but to make sure that politically nothing will be done at the expense of Israel'[10] (emphasis mine).

There was little doubt where Rabin and Allon (who favoured signing the agreement in March and vigorously defended it now) were leading. Peres now seemed the only stumbling block.

The Israeli position for negotiating Phase II of Shuttle II

The Negotiating Team (Rabin, Peres, Allon) were cognizant (a) of the Salzburg arrangement and of the fact that the US would not tolerate freezing the negotiating 'momentum' (to reiterate a much-used Kissinger term), (b) that concessions would be *made to the US* not to Egypt, (c) that an interim agreement could hopefully result in some kind of 'loss of contact', if not nonbelligerency, with the Arab world's major power—Egypt, (d) to buy time in hopes of a change in the American elections of 1976, in OPEC's power and attrition, and in the uneasy but existing Arab political and military alliance.

Thus Rabin, when asked what change he found in the Arab position since March, summarized the following points (which became the negotiating terms when Kissinger arrived in August to help sign the interim agreement).

1. The time framework of the agreement. For how long would the interim agreement be intact (until replaced by another)? Israel was hoping for a three years' renewal of the UN Mandate. 'We have discovered that the presence of the UN gives a sense of reality (*mamashut*) to the tenure of the agreement.'[11]
2. The military positioning of the Israeli and Egyptian forces once Israel retreated from the passes.
3. The symbolic increments of the agreement i.e. symbolic gestures on the part of Egypt to reduce the mood and level of its belligerency.

The negotiating team planned that the interim agreement would guarantee:

1. That the two sides (Israel and Egypt) declare that they envision the interim agreement as only the first phase in a process that would lead towards permanent settlement: withdrawal, signed peace treaties, demilitarized zones and international guarantees.
2. The components of demilitarization and an Israeli presence in the demilitarized zones, i.e. command over reconnaissance sites.[12]

What were the military considerations of the Israelis?

1. What would be the implications of the strategic loss of the passes?
2. What would constitute the enemy's capability to pre-empt, given the new line?
3. How defensible (economically, militarily and politically) would the new line be?
4. Would the new line constitute an Egyptian advantage in case of a strategic surprise decision? The Suez line was already in the hands of the Egyptians. What, in Israeli eyes, would it be necessary for Egypt to do in order to widen

Egyptian defensive capabilities over the Suez line?

Concerning oil, although it was not a military consideration, nevertheless it would play a role in the sense that Israel would lose its supply, which was of more significance than what Egypt would gain. The last Egyptian strategic objective would be the Gulf of Suez. Here Israel aspired to keep dominance, at least as viewed by Zahal's High Command. While the Egyptian considerations were frankly military, the Israeli military considerations were linked to the political posture of Israel in the post interim-agreement era. Thus the Israeli military considerations were dictated by political determinants. Nonetheless, Israel was opting for a wider neutral zone, i.e. to widen the scope of demilitarization,[13] and to remain dominant in the reconnaissance system in Sinai, i.e. command over the strategy of pre-emption and over the first move in a possible military campaign.

The strategy of the IDF was clear: to *widen* and *deepen* the military contact with Egypt.[14]

An American Trojan Horse?

The thunderbolt that ignited the forces for and against the agreement was not so much the unfulfilled Egyptian demands; paradoxically, it was a proposed American military guarantee. For some time, the State Department, the NSC and several analysts in foreign affairs journals, (*Foreign Affairs* and *Foreign Policy*,) were debating the possibilities of an American guarantee to Israel as a substitute for territorial security for Israel.[15] Historically the Israeli position concerning American intervention was clear. In the words of Moshe Dayan on June 2, 1967, 'We do not ask for American soldiers to fight for us. Give us the weapons, we will do the job.' Ever since the early days of the Haganah, the issue of the autonomy of the Jewish community in Palestine over the instruments of defence was fiercely fought.[16] By 1941 it was resolved, with the formation of the Palmach, that the military instrument must be clearly controlled by the Jewish authorities, the Jewish Agency for Palestine. The formation of the IDF in March 1949 was clearly the first act of Jewish independence after the declaration of the State in May 1948. Between 1951-1954 Ben

Gurion did occasionally entertain the idea of an Israeli participation in NATO. With regard to the IDF, however, there was no question that it was composed, organized, controlled and dominated exclusively by the Israeli government. Intervention in the IDF's doctrines, training, programme and plans by foreign elements was totally excluded. The IDF grew into the single and most autonomous bureaucratic instrument of the newly-established state. Zahal is jealous and proud of its traditions, successes and reputation and tolerates no intervention in its organizational autonomy from internal and especially external sources.

Nevertheless since 1973, the dependence for the first time on considerable American military supply, in view of the length and intensity of the war, as well as continuous Soviet replenishment of the Syrian forces, made the issue of American military aid crucial. The nature of warfare and weaponry changed with the Soviet involvement and supply of the Arab military establishments. The policy of reassessment—the policy of pressure on Israel—was precisely directed towards the curtailment of military aid. The American political pressure concentrated on its real leverage—military and economic aid to Israel. In view of the fact that it was clearly perceived by the negotiating team that Israel must relinquish the Sinai passes as a gesture to the US, some members of the cabinet, but especially the Minister of Defence, Shimon Peres, proposed a way to relieve the political pressure, possibly resolve the military-economic aid issue to Israel's satisfaction, and hopefully to attach political strings to the US in the absence of an Egyptian political concession. Peres proposed to the negotiating team the idea of *involving* the US politically and militarily in the interim agreement. His idea was that the US, the only party credible to the two belligerents, *participate* in the peace-keeping once the interim agreement was concluded. Peres adopted an idea Sadat proposed in January 1975 for American supervision over the reconnaisance systems in the Sinai. The idea was that, in addition to the independent Egyptian and Israeli reconnaissance stations on either sides of the Mitla and Jidi passes, a sizeable group of American 'technicians' police the newly established demilitarized zones.

Rabin was reluctant to accept the idea, as were some

military leaders. Nevertheless when Peres on behalf of the team proposed the idea to Kissinger in one of his short trips to the area,[17] the latter seemed to be receptive. Why Kissinger seemed agreeable is left open only for speculation in view of the fact that little is known about how Kissinger himself became convinced of the desirability of an American peace-keeping mission in the Sinai, and persuaded the President to accept the idea. I offer a desperate effort by Ford–Kissinger to achieve an agreement as the most plausible interpretation of Kissinger's motivation in advancing the Peres idea which Sadat had originated. Peres, at a secret meeting with the Rafi faction of the Labour Party, convinced the latter:

(1) that the American technicians would be no substitute for an IDF reconnaissance control over the passes;
(2) that this would *not* entail any or partial American intervention in the IDF's structure and function;
(3) that in this way Israel would turn the tables on Kissinger, for instead of Israel being politically pressured, the burden would fall on Kissinger to convince the President, the Congress and American public opinion of the political legitimacy of an American 'intervention' in a post-Vietnam era;
(4) that it was Ben Gurion who for years sought an American *political* guarantee for Israel, and that the 'American technicians' could be the first step in an American policy that thus far had refused to commit itself *politically* to Israel;
(5) that the American technicians symbolized the American commitment to Israel and would therefore reduce the level of Arab aggressive aspirations—although it was not exactly a wedge it would essentially serve Israeli political interests;
(6) that this type of American involvement was not a Vietnam-like, under-the-table commitment; a public commitment of an American President, confirmed by Congress, would constitute a serious and credible American political commitment. Thus the interim agreement would be provided with 'American teeth';
(7) the political commitment in Sinai was to be coupled with a steady and stable American military supply to Israel, no longer subject to periodic reassessments.

The negotiating team and the Cabinet went along with the Peres idea and this led the more militant wing of the Labour Party into committing itself to the Rabin–Kissinger step-by-step diplomacy. Peres argued before the closed Rafi session that Israel could not rely on the caprices and moods of the UN, and that it would certainly 'be safer to trust the US with the responsibility for guarding the passes. After all, four American civilians are equal to a thousand UN soldiers.'[18]

The International Scene and the Interim Agreement

The Israeli 'American technicians' idea was not really the outcome of the above rational thesis. It was as much an effort on the part of Peres and Rabin to exploit Sadat's idea in order to maintain the integrity of the Rabin government as the result of conclusions drawn from the validity of their arguments. The government and the Rabin leadership desperately sought legitimacy. It was governing the country in the absence of the former 'giants' of Labour, and never before had an internal political struggle and positioning influenced so considerably national security policy.[19] The policy differences between Rabin, Peres and Allon were less significant than their political ambitions and future. Thus, the domestic sources of foreign policy since 1973 have become a critical variable in explaining Israeli national security policy. Personalities, not ideologies or controversial security positions, divided the negotiating team. In fact, as one important Cabinet member clearly said, 'Whatever Rabin decides—the cabinet will approve. The cabinet is divided evenly. So if he decides to reject the American proposal the cabinet will go along with him. He also has all the necessary votes to dictate the opposite course. This is not a cabinet [in the old Mapai sense], it is a board of directors!'[20] The even division in the cabinet was reflected in public opinion. A poll of 1,192 representing a sample of the population above 18 years of age conducted at the end of July 1975 revealed the following close division: when asked

(a) whether opinion was in favour of or against the interim agreement for a period of years viz. giving up the Western part of the passes but with continued American aid, 45.8 per cent voted in favour, 39.5 per cent voted against; when asked (b) on the American presence in the passes, 44.5 per cent voted against, 39.1 per cent were in favour.[21]

Beginning with Kissinger's arrival in Israel in the middle of August, and culminating on Friday-Saturday, September 1 and 2, violent anti-Kissinger and anti-American demonstrations took place, particularly in Jerusalem and Tel-Aviv. The opposition to the treaty was represented by a coalition of hawks and centrists, NRP-Likud-Rafi, but soon to be led by dedicated nationalists and idealists, the youth movement of the NRP and its settlement leadership *Gush Emunim* (the Bloc of the Faithful/Faithful of the Land of Israel). Never was the nation more angry, confused and wounded. To the demonstrators and their supporters the interim agreement represented a grim picture indeed. Israel was negotiating not directly with Egypt, not even for symbolic non-belligerency, certainly not for peace, but with the US. The negotiation was taking place with a giant upon whose political goodwill Israel was now becoming dependent for both weapons and economic aid. Unquestionably it was the Ford–Kissinger administration that forced Israel to return the Sinai passes in 1975 for no political return from Egypt.[22]

The Egyptian Position

The American pressure was clearly on Israel and not upon Egypt. In comparison with Israel, Sadat stood to gain whatever he wished from the process of Kissingerian 'momentum'. Sadat's options were already clarified during the March shuttle: rapprochement with the US, and an Israeli troop withdrawal.

1. The rapprochement with the US would yield the following:
   (a) Autonomy from political dependency on the USSR.
   (b) Good prospects for American economic and possibly even military support.
   (c) Greater political manoeuvrability at home, among the other Arab states, and with the superpowers.
   (d) Stabilization of Sadat's regime.
   (e) A new economic renaissance for Egypt.

(f) The goodwill of Western public opinion and the media for playing the game and giving the image of the moderate.

2. Concessions from Israel would yield:
   (a) That no *political* commitment on the part of Sadat supposedly be made until Israel completely fulfilled the Egyptian interpretation of UN Resolution 242 (i.e. a total Israeli withdrawal to the June 5 1967 borders).
   (b) That the agreement was to be a *purely* military arrangement like the first interim agreement.
   (c) That he would remain an Arab leader and would receive back territory even if no other confrontation state (Syria, Jordan, or the PLO) concomitantly benefited from the interim agreement.
   (d) That Egypt would receive valuable strategic areas and, above all, refuse the Israeli demand for a demilitarization of the evacuated zones.
   (e) That he would receive increased support from his own military establishment.
   (f) That Egypt would stand to gain military advantages from its new policy with the US.

In Salzburg, Sadat enhanced his new foreign policy that had begun when Kissinger released the Third Army captured in November 1973.

Sadat's policy, as I have indicated in earlier chapters, was clearly to widen all options including *political and military* support from the super powers. Closer relations with the US enabled Egypt to exercise greater pressure for economic and political support from the oil-rich, conservative, Arab states, which were America's loyal allies (Saudi Arabia in particular). Egypt's relations with Iran improved. A new Cairo–Riad–Tehran axis was forged under the aegis of the American–Egyptian rapprochement. Sadat and Kissinger had helped create a new balance of power in the Middle East, in the Arab world and possibly in the Arab–Israeli conflict (although, in my view, the latter may prove transient). The policy of using the US as a lever over Israel, of clearly abstaining from coming in contact with 'cancerous' Israel and above all creating a wedge between Israel and the US and

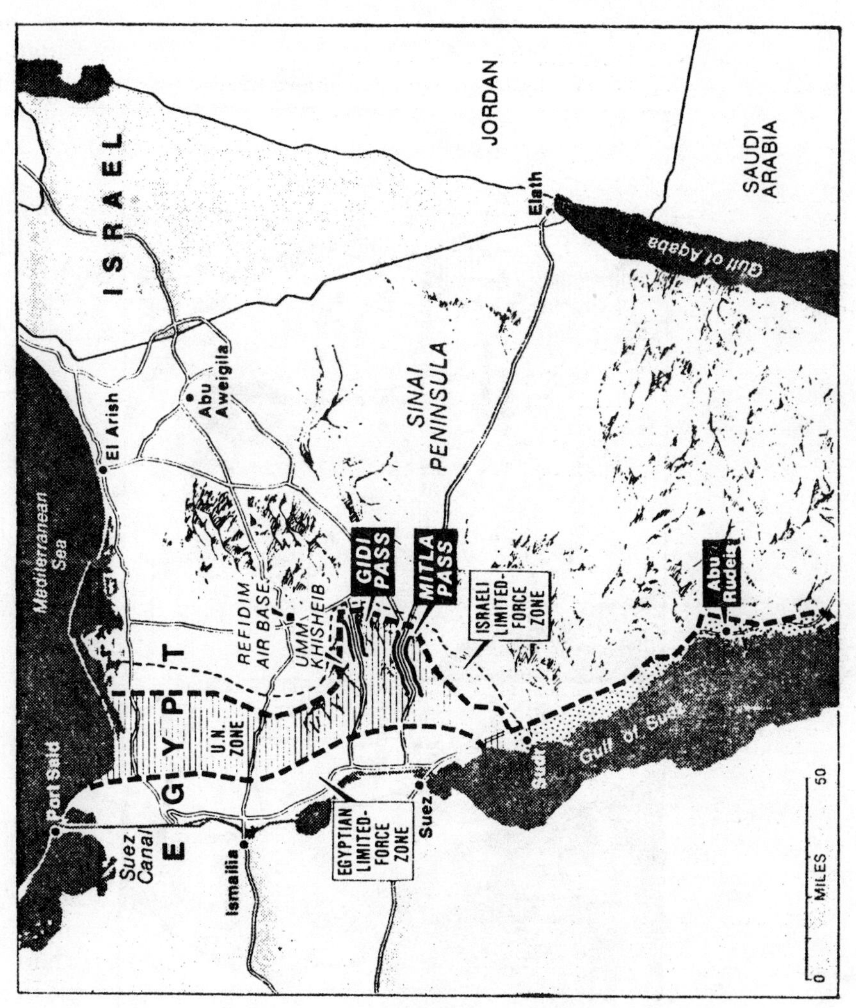

From the New York Times

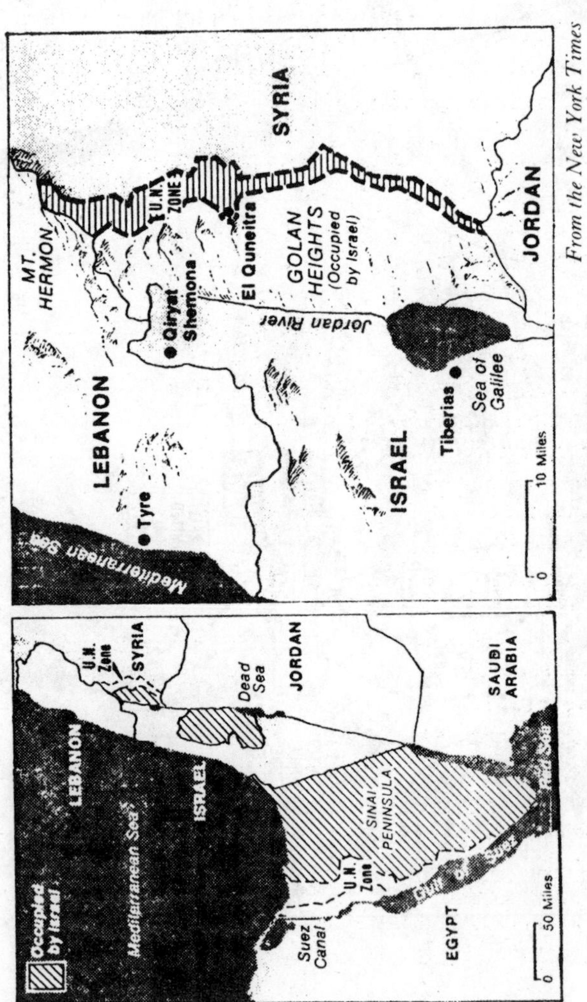

From the New York Times

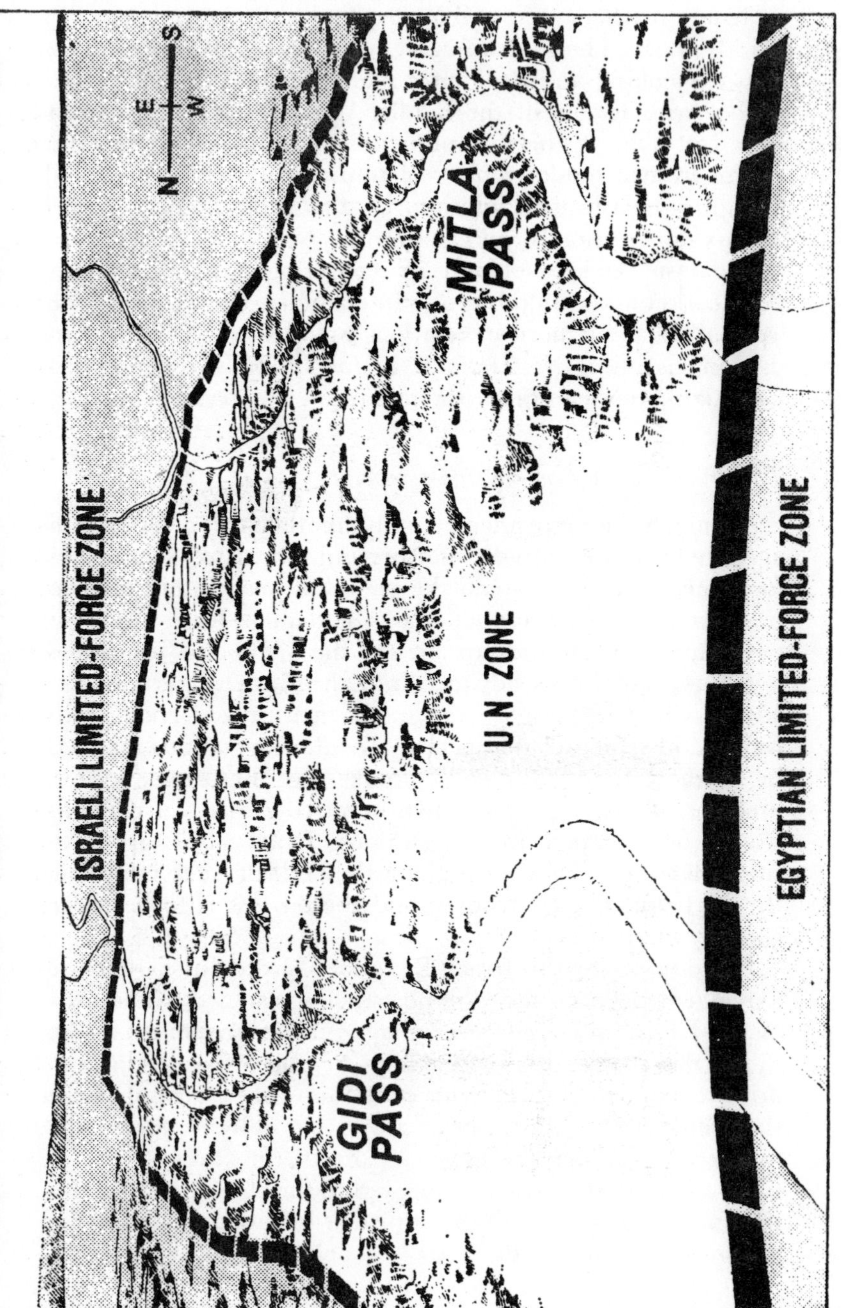

Schmatic drawing by Martim Avillez

widening it whenever possible gave Sadat the initiative in the Middle East. The interim agreement for Egypt represents a forward-looking and brilliant diplomatic coup for Sadat. He is the Arab leader in the saddle. Without Egypt, no Arab state can achieve their unfulfilled aspirations which run the gamut from a modest policy of return of the 1967 occupied territories to a radical solution, i.e. the annihilation of Israel and its substitution by a PLO state.

Sadat succeeded not only in recovering territory without political remuneration but also in changing the nature of the 'special' Israeli-American relations established after the Jordanian civil war (1971-1972) in favour of an open-ended Egyptian-American rapprochement.

The structure of the Sinai interim agreement

Although the agreement is only another troop separation agreement and essentially another military truce, it provides for a mechanism to extend the period of peace and build up trust between the combatants. The Israeli forces were to withdraw from the Eastern parts of the Mitla and Jidi passes and Egyptian forces advance into the Eastern parts of the passes, while UN forces stay in the neutralized zone. Both Egypt and Israel would operate surveillance stations manned by no more than 250 men. To make sure the posts were not used for offensive purposes two hundred American civilians would be assigned to the stations. Israel also agreed to surrender the narrow strip along the Gulf of Suez including the oil fields of Abu Rudeis, and the oil loss is to be made good by the US.

In addition to the Israeli-Egyptian agreement a separate agreement between the US and Israel was signed.[23] The texts of the Egyptian-Israeli agreements on disengagement in the Sinai desert appear more than a truce separation and armistice document: its terms contain a 'peace' arrangement, the 'conflict ... not to be resolved by military force', the 'parties ... undertake not to resort to the threat a use of force'. Nevertheless when compared to the 1949 armistice this document pales. The 1949 Armistice included the *concept of non-belligerency* and of the need to conclude peace agreements.

In the present agreement the gain is clearly an Egyptian and American one and Israel has to take a chance for future peace. Its gain is in the realm of expectation. Yet the agreement exhausted some of the goodwill between Israel and the US in view of the pressure exerted upon Israel.

To pressure Israel further would only damage chances for continuing the processes of negotiation.

Since the agreement, the US is no longer in control of the arms race in the area, nor can it dictate when the belligerents may begin a new arms build-up. It certainly has no control or leverage over whether the Arabs will start a new war, and none on Arab aspirations, strategy and tactics. A military guarantee, in fact, would give America better control over Israeli policy than over that of the Arabs.[24]

The American Involvement and Its Consequences for Middle Eastern Peace

The Administration's struggle over the ratification of the Sinai Interim Agreement II and over the 'American technicians' in Congress clearly demonstrates the revolutionary nature of this new American commitment in the Middle East. A peace mission, directed by a superpower, is not equivalent to a Swedish or even a UN mission. This is no meagre American involvement but an American intervention between Egypt and Israel. The civilian technicians are Americans who could resort to the use of force to protect their mission. And, if they do not intend to fulfil their mission of separating the forces, and acting as a warning system for both Israel and Egypt, then the commitment to Israel is of no value, and could exacerbate not only Israeli–American relations but the conflict as well. The Interim Agreement and the so-called 'American guarantees' were more than mere expediency on the part of the Kissinger–Ford team. The agreement, notwithstanding escape clauses and congressional opposition, certainly enhanced the American interest in Egypt and among the moderate Arab states, as well as the reputations of Secretary Kissinger and President Ford—no mean achievement. Yet if it works, it precludes several options that were previously open before it was initialled by Israel and Egypt:

a. The American involvement releases Egypt from making serious political concessions in the future to Israel. The Egyptians will expect the 'American guarantee' to act as a substitute for their own concessions.
b. It alienated the radical Arab countries and enhanced the political position of the Soviets in Syria, and precipitated the PLO, Radicals and Syria into the Lebanese civil war.
c. The agreement consolidated the rejection front and turned Jordan toward the radical Syrian-PLO coalition.
d. It made the US more vulnerable to blackmail by an oil embargo.
e. No longer can the US buy Arab-occupied land from Israel for a higher price.

If the American guarantees to Israel are *fulfilled* it secures Israeli military and economic needs for three—five years. And if they are not going to be fulfilled, the US will not only lose its credibility with Israel, but be unable to use the diplomatic style the Arabs prefer—successful pressure over Israel. In fact, the US has lost its leverage over Israel if it fulfils the promised guarantees, for Israel's military and economic satisfaction will reduce its dependency on the US. The US has already lost its leverage over the Syrians who refused to see President Ford, aware that the US was not able to buy the Golan Heights from Israel as it did the Sinai passes, and if American leverage over Israel (the *essence* of the Kissingerian policy) declines then what good can the US do for Egypt? The American involvement on the one hand has given Kissinger's hegemonial aspirations in the area considerable hope i.e. that as long as he acted as an arbitrator, he dominated the belligerents' aspirations and actions, and thus, Middle Eastern politics. On the other hand in the absence of leverage (none over the Arabs, and now less over Israel) he could not move the belligerents into a meaningful next phase (i.e. withdrawal from Golan and the future of the Palestinians). At best he could achieve insignificant further Israeli withdrawals in Sinai. He has not changed the revolutionary nature of the area. Arab aspirations are higher and not lower since September, 1975. The 'moderate', conservative Arab states have American political and military options (Egypt, Saudi Arabia, the Gulf Emirates) and the radical states and groups have Soviet political and military options (Syria, the PLO, Iraq and Libya) and all these *without surrendering significant political concessions to Israel.* How long did Secretary Kissinger believe that he could deceive the Israelis by buying Arab land for American support if that support no longer becomes necessary? Depriving the USSR of Egypt has not made the Soviets withdraw. In fact since the signing of the agreement the Soviets are well entrenched in Syria. Just after the signing of the agreement Syria launched a PLO campaign in the UN with the active and open support of the USSR. The USSR stood behind the new system—Jordan, the PLO and the Eastern Front—and was tacitly involved in the Lebanese civil war. The emergence of an Eastern Front, blessed by the USSR, was created to challenge Kissinger's Sinai Agreement. The solution of the Palestinian state, the real Middle Eastern powder keg, has been further removed after the interim agreement. This is particularly true in view of the collapse of historical Lebanon. If the US makes a commitment to the PLO, it has destroyed the secret understanding with the Israelis upon which the agreement rests. It cannot make the PLO recognize Israel or modify its stance, since the Israelis are the real losers of the agreement, which pushed Jordan toward Syria. Israel is now facing a serious Syrian-Soviet military alliance. If a war begins in the north, once the north is not being pacified as Egypt was, then the chances for US-USSR confrontation are greater now than they were in October, 1973. The Soviet commitment to Syria goes deep, more so after the end of the Lebanese civil war. They will not abandon Syria in case of war, for that would mean their final expulsion from the Middle East. Excluding the Soviets from the interim agreement was performed in a perfect conspiracy of silence on the part of the American Administration and the American media. Thus, since 1973, revolutionary and unstable international conditions have been enhanced while stability has actually decreased, despite the facade of peace-mongering by Sadat and his Saudi allies, because:

1. Arab aspirations are higher;
2. Arab political and military options have improved;

3. the threat to Israel is growing greater on the northern front;
4. the American involvement suggests higher risks for Soviet–American confrontations than previously; and
5. the Palestinian problem is no less volatile now, as dissatisfaction of the PLO may radicalize, not modify, temporary Middle Eastern balance achieved in September, 1975.

The American involvement could lead to a modification or an acceleration of the conflict. I see no signs of modification of the revolutionary conditions. Lip-service is being paid by the radical Arabs to a Geneva conference. An American involvement—Kissinger style—may achieve contrary results; instead of pacifying the area, it may unwittingly help to ignite the next Arab–Israeli war. The road charted by Kissinger, the step-by-step approach, has reached its end. The hope is that the next Administration will learn the lesson that a rapid 'momentum' in the Middle East is counterproductive. The Arab–Israeli conflict must be resolved piecemeal, through gradual stages, and not by fiat of temporary peace declarations that issue from moderate Arab capitals. The process of negotiation is long and protracted, with no end, as yet, in sight.

NOTES

1. *Haaretz*, August 15, 1975, 'On the Threshold of the Agreement', p. 10, Mati Golan.
   Haaretz, July 4, 1975, 'A Balance of Leaks', p. 14, Zeev Schiff.
2. *Ma'ariv*, June 20, 1975, 'Interview with Rabin', p. 13, Dov Goldstein.
3. *Haaretz*, July 11, 1975, 'The Price for Going Down the Tree', p. 13, Yoel Marcus.
4. *SRI*, Draft Background paper, Arlington, Virginia, August, 1974, 'Arab Israeli Conflict and the Military Balance', 31 pp.
   Haaretz, July 31, 1975, 'Egypt still wants an Agreement', p. 9, Oded Zarai.
   Galia Golan, *The Soviet Union and Egyptian Syrian Preparation 1973*, 1974 SRI, Washington unpublished manuscript, 100 pp.
5. *Haaretz*, June 20, 1975, 'Salzburg', p. 14, Mati Golan
   Haaretz, June 25, 1975, 'The Bargaining in Sinai', p. 13, Zeev Schiff.
6. Amos Perlmutter, *Egypt: The Praetorian State*, New Brunswick, Transactions, 1974, pp. 188-199
7. Private information obtained from Rabin's team at Blair House, June 10-15, 1975.

8. *Haaretz*, July 2, 1975, p. 2, *Yediot Aharonot*, June 2, 1975, p. 3.
9. The following information rests on a three month research field trip in Israel, June, July, August and early September 1975 where I had the chance to interview Ministers Rabin, Peres, Yaacobi, Zadok, and Generals Gur, Tamir, Sharon, Tolkowski and Tal and the chief advisers of the PM and the Defence Ministers. I also took an indirect role in the Kissinger negotiation of August-September that brought to a conclusion Phase II of Shuttle II and the Egyptian-Israeli interim agreement of September 10, 1975. During my stay I extensively interviewed leading journalists. Marcus, Golan, Dan, Zack, Avnery and received support from the media, especially the staff of *Ma'ariv*. I also spent considerable time with opposition leaders such as Begin, Hammer, Ben Meir, Sharon and leaders of *Likud*, *Rafi*; national religious parties and leaders of *Gush Emunim*, the militant anti-Kissinger political force in Israel.
10. Dov Goldstein, 'Interview with Prime Minister Rabin,' *Ma'ariv*, June 20, 1975, p. 13.
11. *Ibid.*
12. Mati Golan, 'The Interim Agreement,' *Haaretz*, July 4, 1975, p. 14.
13. Zeev Schiff, 'Bargaining in Sinai,' *Haaretz*, June 25, 1975, p. 13.
14. Mati Golan, 'The Depth of the Compromise,' *Haaretz*, June 19, 1975, p. 11.
15. Brezhinski, Ullman, Avineri and Perlmutter, 'An Exchange,' *Foreign Policy*, 21
16. On the role of the independence of Haganah and Zahal see Amos Perlmutter, *Military and Politics in Israel 1948-67*, 1969; 2nd ed. Frank Cass 1977.
17. On July 27, 1975, private information by author. See also Peres interview on Israeli TV, August, 1975.
18. Yoel Marcus, 'Interview with Shimon Peres' *Haaretz*, July 28, 1975, p. 2.
19. Ron Kislev, 'Rabin's Entrenchment in Power', *Haaretz*, August 13, 1975, p. 9.
20. Private interview, Tel-Aviv, July 1975.
21. 'Yediot Aharonot Poll', *Yediot Aharonot*, August 1, 1975, p. 3.
22. Avraham Schweizer, 'Back to Dulles', *Haaretz*, June 27, 1975, p. 9.
23. 'Mr Kissinger's Handiwork', *The New York Times*, 'Review of the Week', September 7, 1975, p. 3.
24. Amos Perlmutter, 'An Exchange Over Foreign Policy,' *Foreign Policy*, No. 21.

CHAPTER VIII

Civil-Military Relations in Israel: 1973-77

1. *Political Parties, Voters and The Election Year of 1973*

In the 1973 election year Israel inevitably elevated private and mute concerns into the public realm. Unfortunately, the public political debate was futile, given the unique combination in Israel of a highly institutionalized-centralized political structure, nepotistic parties, and the indifference of the Israeli voter.

A basically articulate and concerned public was gasping for fresh air in this politically polluted atmosphere where everything has been politicized—sports, soccer, universities, businesses, banks, unions, religious authorities and institutions. Most modern functional elites were politically silent and outside the political system. A closely inter-locked system between party and state meant that the *Parteistaat* was in command. The *Knesset* (parliament) became a tool of the parties, and a lackey of the three political blocs of Israel (the *Ma'arach* Labour, the *Gahal* Liberal-right, and Hazit Ha-Datit i.e. the religious parties' bloc), and lost its political significance. The internal party blocs were replete with functionaries and apparatchiks whose world vision ceased in the 1930s. To them ideology either belonged to the forlorn past or became a facade that enhanced the party politicians' tenure and longevity in office.

The political system of Israel is neither rational, progressive nor dynamic. Structures of authority have been highly institutionalized, integrated and centralized. Complemented by a semi-Leninist *Parteistaat* system and buttressed by a tame, conformist electorate, a mockery has been made of the concept of real and functional representation. Parties, being etatist in scope, particularly the Socialist-Zionist parties, do not exercise their true political function as broker between the electorate and its representatives. This internal party oligarchy combined with voter apathy and the absence on his part of civic virtues has produced a system of rulers.

Political behaviour in Israel in 1973 was characterized by a highly conservative electorate. Newly built incentives were needed to change this pattern—incentives that would mobilize the thousands who were dissatisfied with the internal political status quo. The Israeli voter was still pre-occupied with the great issues of defence and foreign policy, which are the domain of the few, even in the most representative democracies. The need in 1973 was for this nation of patriots to be re-educated in order to become a nation of citizens. Political democracy could no longer be restricted to futile, often irrelevant, debates in the *Knesset*, or to ceremonial party conventions. Political democracy should also mean alternative options for representation, which, to be effective, must be accompanied by the integration of the public interest with civic consciousness. This did not seem forthcoming in the Israeli elections scheduled for 1973.

It was a decisive year in Israeli politics. For the first time in the political history of the state, the ruling Labour party was seriously challenged by a new coalition formed into the *Likud* bloc, which gained momentum early in July when General Ariel Sharon unwillingly resigned his post as Commander of Israel's most sensitive southern (Egyptian) front to become the *Likud*'s lynchpin. But most significantly, for the first time in Israeli Socialist politics a splinter of Labour, the State Party (*Mifleget Ha'Am*, formerly Ben Gurion's faction), joined *Likud*). The *Likud* challenge was certainly formidable. The conservative Israeli voter had for some time been in search of an alternative to the centralistic and monopolistic Histadrut-Labour domination. *Likud*, although essentially the old *Gahal* Bloc (*Herut* and General Zionists), nevertheless seemed a reasonable alternative to the septuagenarian and exclusionary Labour power elite. *Likud*, which offered more style than substance, more glitter than deeds, nevertheless succeeded in creating an image of a renovated coalition, a meagre option, perhaps, but nonetheless an outlet for the independents, previously without real electoral power. While the

Labour party was totally dominated by the Sapir *apparat*, the *Likud* party offered a fresh choice, an open coalition.

The elections of 1973 proceeded in two phases: the pre-October war and the post-war electoral campaigns. The emergence of *Likud* before the October war was, in my view, the catalyst that brought about the decline of the Socialist, Labour domination.

2. *Officers and Politics: 1973*

While there is military praetorianism in the Middle East, Bonapartism in Latin America, and the growth of militarism among the superpowers, to argue that the military is the most effective instrument of political reform is antiquarian, apologist and inaccurate. Between 1950-1973 military 'Progressives' in the Middle East and Latin America have not only failed to solve the socio-economic problems of their societies, but have contributed to the political instability of already precarious states.

Yet a progressive and civilian-oriented military can and does play a reformist role in stable progressive political systems where military intervention can easily be crushed by popular government support. In Israel retired military men who entered politics had succeeded in capturing the enthusiasm of the electorate. All these aspirations have now gone underground again. The 1973 war changed the nature of the 1973 elections for it clearly demonstrated to the Israelis that their lease on the good life had fewer years to run. The seven prosperous and confident years were over. The war changed everything and reminded the Israelis once again of their insecurity.

The single elite of merit mobilized into the *Parteistaat* system were a small group of 1967 veteran generals, the senior retired officers who had established their reputation in the military field as well as outside it. Here we must however distinguish two generations of Israeli officers in politics. The first group of officer-politicians belonged to the pre-state generation, when the military was still an instrument of the *Yishuv* political system (persons like Dayan, Allon, Galili and Carmel, who established their reputations in both the underground military force and in Labour Socialist politics). In the pre-state *Yishuv*, it should be remembered, civil and military functions, as in other revolutionary nationalist liberation movements, were blurred and interlocked. Since 1948 they have been functionally and organizationally separated. Depoliticization and nationalization of the IDF created a new group of officers and a new type of professional, civic-oriented officer, who was not involved in party politics before 1948. Rabin, Bar-Lev, Yariv, Lahat, Sharon, Pa'il and Geva are all products of the post-1948 officers generation, without experience in pre-state party politics. Their crucial role in Israeli politics and survival was unsurpassed in two areas: the formulation and implementation of national strategy and security and in leading a peoples' reserve army successfully in two wars, (1956 and 1967). The 1973 war further elevated the political assets of the military. This war, however, unlike those that preceded it, restored forgotten officers. The reputation of General Ariel (Arik) Sharon, the conqueror of the Egyptian west bank of the Canal, has grown proportionately to his stunning military success. While Sharon enhanced his reputation immensely, the reputation of Dayan suffered considerably in view of the fact that, as Defence Minister, he failed to alert the IDF and so prepare the military for the initiative, and above all, that he failed to prevent the all-but-catastrophic conduct of the first days of the war. The reputation of Bar-Lev was enhanced by his resumption of military duty during the Syrian-Egyptian surprise attack. General Yariv, as an adviser to the Chief of Staff and the Prime Minister, and his role as negotiator with the Egyptian Third Army also scored, while the reputations of Generals Rabin and Weizmann were neither diminished nor enhanced by the war. The events immediately after the October war, the political and military fiasco that preceded it, and the future of Arab-Israeli relations were to become the chief campaign issues. Since the elections were conducted at a time when most Israelis were in uniform, the Labour coalition was in real danger. The outstanding fact of the post-war period was that the Six Day War generals loomed large in politics, both the successful and unsuccessful. The former division into doves and hawks no longer held good as both were found to have been wrong. The doves had hoped to modify Arab behaviour by a moderate, non-annexationist policy and thus make negotiations attractive. The hawks pursued a policy of frustrating the Arabs through an annexationist policy, hoping that because of the political and diplomatic stalemate, the Arabs would opt for an Israeli solution — an unequal treaty. Both misperceived the Arabs. This was clearly reflected in the different orientations and styles of the 1967 war heroes.

The post-state generation generals were the authors of Israel's military and geo-political strategy. From 1947 to 1963 military strategy was shared between the High Command and the Defence and Prime Minister, David Ben Gurion (with the exception of the two years between 1953-1955, when Lavon took over the Defence Ministry from the Prime Minister). Between 1963 and 1967, however, Arab intransigence, the escalation of the Arab–Israeli conflict into a total warfare, the growth of military technology and dependence on military experts, and the military inexperience of Israel's cabinet, gradually turned the authorship of military strategy and its political consequences into the hands of the High Command.

During the War of Attrition (1969-1970), the cabinet became even more dependent on the advice of the High Command. General Dayan, the Defence Minister, and former Chief of Staff, like Ben Gurion, relegated military strategy to the generals.

Thus, since 1967, the Six Day War generals gained considerable influence in security policy-making and implementation. In the social-ethnic field, as well as in dealing with problems of health and welfare, the officers have gained considerable experience through their daily contact with recruits, and this experience enabled them to make a claim for political office. Israeli officers are trained not only as technologists of warfare, but also as human leaders; as junior officer they are in charge of recruits who represent the citizenry of Israel, where conscription is universal between the ages of 18–21, for both men and women, and where the reserve army of some 400,000 meets the small (40,000) professional officer core. Reserve duty comprises between 30 and 90 days a year. Officers thus become experts in personal therapy and social welfare, and are trained to pay particular attention to conscripts coming from deprived Afro-Asian Jewish backgrounds, who constitute a sizeable number of the recruit intake. As an example of this high value orientation of Israeli military professionals, General Yariv told me that when he served as Commander of the Golani division, Israel's crack unit, he made a point of visiting the families and homes of the recruits and urged his junior officers to give particular attention to the problems of the deprived.

Thus, the young (40-45), retired military technocratic-professional elite, well-versed in questions of strategy-security, but also in human relations and resources, were regarded as capable of carrying out political tasks and also as catalysts to challenge party nepotism. The senior Israeli officer is a unique breed in that, among the public and intellectual elites, he is the one who has so far demonstrated the greatest dedication to the public interest, as well as remarkable personal integrity, courage, and political consciousness. A garrison state must produce thinking officers if it is to survive. These officers are graduates of Israel's most distinguished technocracy and comprise the few harbingers of merit (except for members of the kibbutzim) who exhibit dedication to the public interest and civic virtue. The challenge of the officers was taken seriously by the electorate, which hoped that the retired officers would considerably contribute to reforming, rejuvenating, and invigorating Israel's petrified institutionalised political parties. For the Israelis this was the promise to be kept by the war heroes.

The Egyptian-Syrian attack not only pre-empted the army but created a new type of electoral contest, previously scheduled for November. The debacle of the first two days accelerated the War of the Generals, especially the rivalry between Bar-Lev and Sharon over the Bar-Lev line strategy and the Canal crossing in 1973, opposed by Bar-Lev, and finally approved by Dayan. The crossing of the Canal symbolised to Israelis more than a military victory for their war hero Arik Sharon: it was a crossing of the political Rubicon for the conservative and inactive Israeli voter-citizen. Labour, fearful of finally losing its half century hegemony, became desperate. After all it was the Golda-Dayan inner circle that was responsible for the initial conduct of the war, and for giving up the encircled Egyptian Third Army after monumental American pressure. However Sapir and company in the apparat did not lose their nerve. They called for postponement of the elections until December. Israeli troops for the first time in their history remained as occupying forces in an enclave west of Suez and deep in Syria, toward the gates of Damascus. The nation was anxious to have the boys back home. The loss of close to 4,000 dead and some 6,000 wounded left the nation confused, bitter, and frustrated. Demonstrations were launched against the Golda-Dayan-Sapir party and government. To out-manoeuvre the nation, the Labour apparat promised that a peace conference would take place shortly in Geneva which would finally bring about direct negotiations with Arabs and a 'real' peace. Manipulating an exhausted nation's anxieties, woes and fears, the Labour oligarchy outmanoeuvred the *Likud* by purporting to be the party of peace and security. The fatal error of *Likud's* 'one and only' leader, Menachem Begin, was that his platform refused to surrender 'one inch' of territory, i.e. he advocated a return to the 1967-1973 status quo. The nation, however, furious with the Labour government's *Mehdal* (as its failure to anticipate the war came to be called) refused to return to a non-negotiation stance which was clearly implied by Begin's electoral strategy. *Likud's* insistance on territory was defeated by the Labour strategy of the 'Geneva spirit'. Thus an historical opportunity for a political realignment in Israel was lost. Labour won the elections even though it was badly damaged and lost five mandates, as well as its reputation for integrity. The Labour Party ruled with a majority of one. *Likud* came back reinforced with thirty-eight members to the *Knesset*. Labour was now facing the largest and most formidable opposition to Socialist-Zionism since 1920.

3. *The Decline of Authority*

The *Mehdal* was followed by several crises: the freeing of the Third Egyptian Army under American pressure; the harried and confused Egyptian–Israeli disarmament talks at Kilometer 101 in Egypt; and, above all, the pressures of the Kissingerian step-by-step troop separation avalanche. With the publication of the Agranat Report in May 1974 public opinion was unleashed against the Meir-Dayan government, which was finally forced to resign because of severe national pressure and the dissension within the cabinet between the two small factions of Labour: United Labour and Rafi. Into the political vacuum, two individuals, Yitzchak Rabin and Shimon Peres entered, both running for the premiership. Not since the establishment of Histadrut and the historic United Labour Party in 1920 have the Socialist–Zionist parties elected their leader at a party conference; previously he was elected by a small inner circle of senior party notables. This time Rabin and Peres needed the consent of 1,000 party delegates to the conference. This so-called democratic procedure was the first crack in the monopolistic Labour Party. Despite the dismay of its chief apparatchik, Pinhas Sapir, Peres became the leading candidate. Fearing a take-over by the small, hawkish, Rafi Party, Sapir mobilized the apparat to vote for Rabin. Thus to his own surprise, not enthusiastically supported by his party, Rabin became Prime Minister and official head of a Party to which he was a stranger and junior member. To pacify the other militant United Labour faction, the leadership was forced to offer Yigal Allon a senior cabinet position as Foreign Minister, and Shimon Peres of Rafi took over the next senior position in the cabinet as Defence Minister. For the first time in the history of Socialist–Zionism, the Party became headless. The cabinet was led by a member whose roots in the Party were not deep and the key ministries were dominated by non-Mapai officers. Again as in Lavon's time, the defence portfolio was split from the Prime Minister's. The erosion of authority, the national malaise that followed in the wake of the 1973 earthquake produced a disunited cabinet which had to contend with Kissinger's step-by-step diplomacy. The Israeli team, composed of Rabin, Peres and Allon, was a terribly uncomfortable group. Rabin's former chief in the Palmach, Allon, did not accept Rabin's seniority, which has created considerable friction between the two. Peres and Rabin continued their rivalry, the former being reluctant to accept the latter's authority. Shimon Peres, although a former deputy Defence Minister, a Ben Gurion protégé and for years the Ministry's Director-General, has not succeeded in dominating the powerful IDF. Having little or no military experience, Peres was slightly regarded by senior IDF Commanders and by Rabin, himself a former Chief of Staff. Peres opted for a tacit alliance with Chief of Staff, General Mordechai Gur. The struggle for power between the three, Rabin, Peres and Allon, has led to a cabinet paralysis since its inception in the middle of 1974, and thus it will probably remain until the elections scheduled for early 1977. The death of Sapir in 1975 was another blow for the dwindling apparat, the last of its kind in Israeli politics.

The Prime Minister barely holds his own among his party colleagues and at best acts as a chairman of the board at cabinet meetings. Rabin, obsessed with his American expertise, played the role of Foreign Minister and Ambassador to the US as well as Israel's chief negotiator in the Kissingerian diplomatic shuttle system. General Gur has become, in the absence of Peres's military authority, a powerful interventionist Chief of Staff, and is the first to participate personally in Kissinger's mediations, having become an *ex officio* member of the government negotiating team (Rabin, Peres, and Allon). His adamant refusal to appoint General Sharon, the hero of the Canal crossing and his former chief, to a senior military position demonstrated his ability to overcome the Prime Minister's objections who wanted Sharon to re-enter the IDF. Through the tacit alliance Gur has established with Peres, he successfully prevented Sharon from returning to active duty. Rabin has ignored the recommendations of the Agranat Committee to establish a National Security Council while in office. Thus the absence of clear, defined relationships between the Prime Minister, the Defence Minister and the Chief of Staff (although the Law of the High Command was passed in 1975 formally delineating the lines of authority between the Chief of Staff and his responsibilities to the Prime Minister, Defence Minister and the Cabinet members) has strengthened Gur's political influence. The Chief of Staff has assumed political responsibilities and has made a contribution to national security policies only rivalled by that of General Moshe Dayan between 1954 and 1957.

4. *Civil-Military Relations in Israel: An Overview*

Three decades of military and politics in Israel has demonstrated that the lines of demarcation between civilian and military functions are integral and fusionist. An analysis of this relationship must cover three areas of interaction between civilian and military authorities in Israel: one, the political-psychological; two, the institutional-structural; and, three, the personal interaction and perception of the elites governing civil and military structures.

The political-psychological, i.e. the political and perceptual relationships between the two most authoritative heads of the two systems, the Minister of Defence and the Chief of Staff, on the whole were convergent. No Minister of Defence since David Ben Gurion has selected a Chief of Staff whose political ideology and security perceptions radically diverged from his own. Clearly, it was the Defence Minister and his style to which the Chief of Staff would have to adjust. Those who did not resigned, as in the cases of Generals Yadin, Makleff and Laskov under Defence Minister David Ben Gurion who imposed his style on the IDF, via his Chief of Staff and the High Command. Ben Gurion's political philosophy and his concept of the subordinate role of the military was clear, and he did not tolerate deviation from his norms, even if they were never formalized. Next, the IDF *ipso facto* removed the Minister from direct personal intervention in the High Command, even if Ben Gurion, for instance, was a notorious interventionist and would demand from Dayan, on occasion, detailed information on minor military operations. On the whole Dayan succeeded where Yadin and Makleff failed, to reorientate Ben Gurion's policies, not necessarily in conformity with the latter's political perception. Nevertheless, the symbiotic (although clearly unequal) relationship between Ben Gurion and Dayan created one of the most harmonious periods in the IDF–Defence Ministry relationships.

Structurally, the critical relationship between the two was on the personal level, and much of civil–military relations in Israel were dictated by the following: 1) the degree of accessibility of the Chief of Staff to the Defence Minister and, inversely; 2) the scope and degree of the Minister's intervention in the structural and institutional practices of the IDF, but especially of the High Command; and 3) the respect that the Defence Minister held for the professionalism of the Chief of Staff.

Each Defence Minister attempted to define, informally of course, the role of the Chief of Staff. Ben Gurion never allowed him to become his main military adviser, and his Chiefs of Staff hardly participated in cabinet meetings or testified before the *Knesset*'s foreign affairs and security committees, or, for that matter, before the Mapai (now defunct) military affairs *ad hoc* committee. Ben Gurion was clearly a commander in chief and acted without much regard for the political views of his chiefs. Lavon, although ignorant of national security matters, tried in vain to undermine Dayan's military authority. His debacle and expulsion stemmed precisely from his unsuccessful effort to dethrone the Chief of Staff and do what Ben Gurion never tried to do—to intervene in the Chief's realm, viz. the internal conduct of the High Command, and his authority over senior subordinate officers. While Ben Gurion dominated military strategy, Lavon's inability to do the same made some analysts in Israel at the time confuse the issue and view it as a political stunt engineered by Dayan to oust Lavon. Eshkol, however, clearly perceived Rabin's role as his chief military advisor and it was in this capacity that Rabin served during the critical days of May-June, 1967. Dayan, in his capacity as Defence Minister dominated military policy, but did his utmost not to intervene in military operations recommended by the High Command led by Bar-Lev and Elazar. General Gur, however, whose military professionalism supersedes that of Minister Peres, is acting as his chief military adviser, not unlike Rabin under Eshkol.

Clearly, the relationships depend on the personalities of the Prime Minister, the Defence Minister, and the Chief of Staff. This was demonstrated in the Ben Gurion era, and especially during the short and unhappy Lavon tenure. As an assertive Defence Minister, Lavon clashed with an ambitious and controversial Chief of Staff, Moshe Dayan, whereas the cases of Yadin's and Laskov's short tenure demonstrate Ben Gurion's undisputed personal authority. Eshkol, a less assertive and domineering person, had a splendid relationship with Rabin, a highly professional and successful staff officer who, with the consent of Eshkol, built the IDF's first professional and modern army machine that was instrumental in the 1967 victory. General Elazar was not Dayan's choice. Nevertheless, the relationship between the two was correct. Dayan's concept of administration was to maximize the delegation of authority to his subordinates and minimize his personal intervention, leaving the IDF to its professionals. This was one of the reasons among others, why the Agranat Commission did not find Dayan responsible for the 1973 *Mehdal*, and placed the total responsibility for it on the Chief of Staff and his Intelligence officers. General Gur's cordial relationship with Peres and the latter's respect for the Chief of Staff again leaves the IDF senior command professionally autonomous from the Minister's domination.

The evolution of the structural relationship between the Prime Minister, Minister of Defence, and the Chief of Staff, was cyclical. Under Ben Gurion authority flowed from his undisputed personal leadership and charisma rather than from his combined function as both Prime Minister and Defence Minister. This was no longer possible with Ben Gurion's successors, Lavon, Eshkol, Dayan and Peres. Lavon, the first Defence Minister after Ben Gurion, failed not for lack of institutional authority, i.e. the separation of the portfolio of defence minister from the prime ministership, but from his personal inability to impose the necessary authority over a recalcitrant Chief of Staff and a contemptuous High Command. Thus it was not the separation of portfolios or an absence of a legal-formal authority residing in the defence office that disadvantaged Lavon, but rather his formal inability to establish his authority in an already autonomous and institutionalized High Command and IDF system. The history of the Hagannah's and the IDF's High Command is a history of three decades of institutionalization. By 1954, when

Lavon thought he could assert command over the IDF as he had over the Histadrut, the IDF was well institutionalized and successfully rebuffed the Defence Minister.

Prime Minister Eshkol who also served as Defence Minister illustrates the point made above: Eshkol assumed Ben Gurion's joint formal authority, Prime Minister–Defence Minister, but, nevertheless, lacked his personal authority. His influence over the IDF was nowhere near Ben Gurion's and he left Chief of Staff Rabin and the High Command on their own. However, despite the growing power of the IDF and its rapid institutionalization between 1963 and 1967 (Eshkol's tenure as Defence Minister), in the crucial days between May 15 and June 5, 1967, the Prime Minister *succeeded* in rebutting recommendations for an immediate resort to the use of force. The latter, convinced of Israel's decisive victory, was pushing for an early pre-emptive attack on the Arab states but the IDF did not persuade Eshkol until early in June when his cabinet was ready to pre-empt. Thus the decision to go to war rested with Eshkol, even if the three senior officers lobbied for earlier pre-emption. Dayan, who served as Defence Minister in 1973, and whose influence on Golda Meir was considerable, overruled Chief of Staff Elazar's call for the mobilizing of a great part of the IDF a few days before the Egyptian-Syrian forces were ready for the surprise attack of October 6, 1973. The IDF was thus dominated by Dayan, even if he left the latter considerable leverage and autonomy.

Chief of Staff Gur, as mentioned earlier, commands the largest Israeli army in its history. Now double its 1973 size, the most professional and best equipped army in the Middle East, it is, nevertheless, responsible to the Defence Minister and the cabinet. In case of a crisis, Gur carries considerable weight in cabinet decisions. But he can be overruled, as he has already been on several crucial military–political decisions since 1974. Thus Gur is no more powerful than key cabinet officers, but more powerful than former Chiefs of Staff in the area of national security policy.

Thus, in a state under garrison conditions, with the largest military machine it has ever had, and faced constantly with critical decisions on national security policy, it is not possible to establish simple formalistic lines of demarcation between the different functions of national security, its different structures, and, above all, of the type of personality–authority relationships that develop. The above combinations are not simply superordination–subordination relationships. Personal, institutional and structural–bureaucratic relationships dictate civil–military relations as they do in other democratic systems, especially the US—the political and military power of the western world. Modern civil–military relations in highly developed countries (this includes the USSR) are fusionist.

5. *The military organization is motivated to play a key role, if not to supersede other groups in the making of national security policy*

The concept that military professionalism removes the military from politics is derived, among others, from the classical tradition of administrative theory and American public administration which was built on the premise that politics is separated from administration, i.e. that policy-making (the responsibility of elected officials) is separate from policy implementation (the responsibility of appointed officials). This conceptual distinction was advanced to explain the separation of experts from politics. It no longer holds good. The new administrative theory is fusionist i.e. the recognition that bureaucracy and politics, government and administration experts, and politicians are all symbiotically connected. Inherently this is a pluralistic concept that power in a society is diffuse and that advanced societies are characterized by highly complex and highly differentiated organizations that hypenate experts and non-experts, policy makers and policy implementers.[1]

Richard Betts advances an interesting division between theory whose priority is efficiency, its process, command obedience, and its political behaviour neutral; the other, the priority of the revisionist is political control, its administrative process is negotiations, and it is highly involved in politics. Betts accordingly divides the policy makers into three types: (1) the professional politicos, the sub-cabinet political appointees with bureaucratic experience, (2) the politicized professionals—again, members of the joint chiefs, generals, and civilian bureau chiefs—and (3) the pure professionals—military officers and civil servants.[2]

The authorities of the modern industrial state have imbued the professional military organization in recent times with a sense of belonging. The military professional in a state that possesses a nuclear arsenal is highly skilled in the sciences of management and nuclear strategy. He understands that he *shares* with the authorities not only the conception of strategy and the maintenance of the bureaucratic hierarchical orientation, but a participation in the making of national security policy. Thus, antagonism between the professionals and the bureaucrats is mitigated. The nineteenth-century discrepancy between being a professional and a bureaucrat has almost disappeared and the two are becoming fused. Concomitantly, the virtues of bravery and discipline have now been replaced by the skills of management and strategy.

Thus, the relationship between the military and the state becomes symbiotic. Two centuries of total war and mobilization of citizen soldiers linked the military establishment to their civilian governments. The two structures became interdependent, influencing each other in relation to war, strategy, diplomacy, and the conduct of international conflict. The 'civilian' and the 'military' could not remain separate bureaucratic structures or 'minds' professing different orientations. The cleavage in states where the professional soldier type developed was no longer vertical between 'soldiers' and 'civilians'. The conflict became horizontal—over political and ideological orientations between and within the 'soldier' and 'civilian' establishments, as well as a political–bureaucratic struggle over the determination and implementation of national security policy.

There are a few marked characteristics of regimes in the post-World War II era. One, that military regimes were established only in weak states; two, that the coup zone is composed of Latin American, African, Asian and Islamic independent states. (There are only three European states in the *successful* coup zone: Greece, Spain, and Portugal.) And, three, none of the super and major world powers are dominated by military regimes. What is remarkable about the superpowers, and the major powers (China, Western Europe and Japan), is that the role of the military in national security affairs runs from dominant (China, USSR) to influential (US and Western Europe). There is only one exception to the national security pattern where the military wields considerable influence on national security matters while the regime is non-military and democratic—Israel.[3]

Huntington was clearly the first to demonstrate the fusionist theory of military and national security and the emergence of the military as an influential political group in the making of national security policy. Thus, in the political conditions which emerged after World War II the strategy of deterrence changed both the external and domestic environments of states. The strategy of deterrence propelled the creation of what some exaggeratedly term the emergence of the national security state. Harold Lasswell, who claimed that the military's new skills assured their ascendency, despite the fact that his 1941 thesis on the 'Garrison State' was proved wrong, insists on the contemporary validity of the 'Garrison State' model.. Strategic decisions have brought about structural changes in both the military organization and the organization of security. According to Huntington, national security is primarily a matter of negotiations conducted among the different executive agencies wherein both the military and the other partners share in the making and implementing of national security policy (including Congress), and can be explained on the basis of the fusionist bureaucratic politics model. It is, therefore, significant for students of modern military institutions to observe that the *politics of the professionals* (also known as bureaucratic-politics) is fusionist in theory. What characterizes the American joint chiefs is that notwithstanding the fusionist theory, only a few chairmen (the exceptions being a few activists such as Radford, Taylor, and Lemay), have mixed politics and strategy. 'The FCS members, since World War II, have sought to maintain the neat and formal division between "policy" decisions, which they participated in only as advisers, and "military" decisions in the subordinate area of administration and implementation, over which they claimed authority.'[4] This could not be said of the Soviet and Chinese senior military. In the case of the USSR, despite three decades of Stalinist suppression, the Soviet military has become predominant in the making and implementing of national security policy.

In the Soviet case, the role played by the military in the making of national security policy is closely linked to their endeavour to maintain the integrity of military professionalism. The Soviet military achieved professional autonomy, participating in the making of national security policy, and in conceiving the doctrines of deterrence and advocating its auxiliary weaponry. Nevertheless, although the Soviet military are predominant (especially in weapon system procurement policy), they are not the *single* or *decisive* voice any more than their American colleagues, as the cases of Czechoslovakia (1968) and the Six Day War demonstrate.[5]

Thomas writes that 'while the Soviet military have of necessity been drawn into policy making, because of the strategic and national security implications of the current major foreign policy problems confronting the Soviet Union, they not only do not have the decisive voice in formulating policy, but in many instances, have basic reservations about the external policies fashioned and executed by the current political leadership.'[6]

The military establish their influence in national security policy according to the *type* of national security policies prescribed by civilian authorities. Military influence is not necessarily proportional to military power or military content of strategy. Military power and foreign intervention were higher under Kennedy and Johnson than under Eisenhower and Nixon. The soldiers were more influential under the latter pair than the former. 'In the modern super power the professional and the strategist converge. Thus, one could establish the political inflence of the military over *preferred* national security policy. In fact, Betts clearly demonstrates that, in general, military recommendations on the use of force were neither more nor less aggressive than those of the principal civilian policy makers.[7]

Although we cannot establish a precise measurement of the influence and the power wielded by the military over national security policy, there is little doubt that an analysis of the role and behaviour of the military in the making of national security and foreign policy decisions over a long period of time does explain the relative influence of the military. Betts's tabulation of military advice in Cold War crises clearly demonstrates that *relative to the advice of principal civilian policy makers*, military recommendations on intervention were *equally* aggressive in a majority of cases. Some military advisers (e.g. field commanders) had a tendency to give relatively *more* aggressive advice, but others (e.g. Chiefs of Staff) often were *less* aggressive than civilian advisers. In tactical escalation, i.e. after the decision on intervention, has been made however, military advisers had a much higher tendency to be more aggressive than their civilian advisers.

The decision to use force in foreign policy crises depends on the evaluation of alternative options for attaining the Administration's goals. Nevertheless, Betts clearly demonstrates that in the three areas of influence, policy (ends), strategy (programme) and tactics (means), the influence of the military on *policy* is minimal (with very few exceptions). The policies of containment, rollback, or neo-isolationism in the last three decades were conceived, designed and proclaimed by civilians. In the area of strategy, and primarily in tactics, the military does wield more influence. On the making of policy and of military strategy the US Senior Command wields more influence than on declared policy and strategy, where it wields only indirect influence. 'Military advice in Cold War crises was,' writes Betts, 'overall, more aggressive than timid, only rarely shrinking from confrontation.' But when compared to the predominant view of civilian advisers, or presidential predisposition, the soldiers' views were echoes as often as choices. Although there were indeed ample instances of military recommendations urging more force than the Administrations wished to apply, there were other instances—fewer, but still substantial—where military advice led civilians back from the brink.[8]

'The diversity of military recommendations, and the extent of consonance with civilian opinion, account for much of the conclusion that professional military officials *did not dominate* decisions on the use of force' (italics mine). In fact, the influence of the military was greatest when its proposals were negative—i.e. it recommended against the use of certain types of force. The military wielded negligible influence on declared policy, indirect influence on military strategy and force structure, but direct influence on implementation, especially in crisis situations.[9]

The following chart summarizes the influence of the military in the US, the USSR, China and Israel (the latter a state in permanent war dominated by civilians) over policy, strategy and tactics in national security policy-making and implementation.

Influence of Military over National Security Policy Making and Implementation

Country	*Policy*	*Strategy*	*Tactics*
USA	Indirect	Indirect	Direct
Israel	Indirect	Direct	Direct
USSR	Indirect	Direct	Direct
China	Direct & Joint with CCP	Direct & Joint with CCP	Indirect

In Israel the IDF wields indirect influence over the use of force (policy) considerable influence over strategy, but as both the wars of 1967 and 1973 demonstrate, *indirect* influence over the decision to resort to the use of force.

In both the USSR and in Israel, the military wields considerable influence over strategy and only *indirect* influence over the use of force. Only in China does the military dominate policy jointly with the CCP. In the USSR and the US the politics of the military (bureaucratic–politics) is dependent on the type of deterrence policy and its corollary military strategy. The more ambitious the policy, the greater is the military influence in the two superpowers. In the USSR the more serious the crisis, the greater the influence of the military. The case of China is different, where the relationship between the Party and the army goes back to the beginning of Chinese Communism. The Chinese revolution was nurtured in the bosom of the army, and the army has served as its defender over five decades of Communist rule. The nature of the Chinese Communists' struggle—the CCP's dependence on the military between 1927 and 1949—dictated the nature and the relationship, known as party-army, in Communist China. The extraordinary role played by the army in the cultural revolution, as well as in the post

GPCR era, also demonstrates the special fusion between party and army in China.[10]

The military in China, in contradistinction to the USSR and not unlike the US, is autonomous—but unlike in the US it wields predominant influence not only in the making of national security policy, but on Chinese society generally. 'The army thus remains [1973] a central and highly influential element in the coalition that stands on top of China's power structure.' The case of Israel defies several models. It defies the 'garrison state' model, the ill-defined concept of 'militarism', Andreski's model of population/military proportion ratio and other popular suppositions that a powerful military institution *ipso facto either creates military regimes or destroys civilian control.*[11]

The Agranat Commission on the 1973 war demonstrated the absence of clear normative delineation between the military and political functions in Israel and would actually lead one to believe that the civil–military equilibrium was tilted toward the military, in view of the fact, that the most senior military personnel were reprimanded while the political leadership, especially the Minister of Defence, was exonerated by the Commission. Nevertheless, the Commission's omission, according to its terms of reference, is that it restricted itself to an analysis of the *conduct of the military at war.* Had it been given an extensive mandate to investigate the general conduct of the war, it would inevitably have reached the conclusion that the political leadership, not the military, erred in judgment, and that it was the responsibility of the political leadership, not the military, to implement mobilization so as to be ready to cancel out a surprise attack.[12] Thus, the powerful military establishment, not always in harmony with its civilian authority, does not attempt to tilt the balance in its favour, despite its remarkable power. To explain civil–military relations in the US, the USSR, China, and Israel, an analysis of bureaucratic–politics would yield considerable understanding on the *relative* and *relevant* power of the military in the area of national security.

Yet an analysis of the above must clearly distinguish Israel and the US from China and the USSR, where the military may join in an effort to *renovate* or alter the current leadership despite its essential commitment to political authority. In the US and Israel, the military influence is restricted to the making and implementation of national security policy. In the political–electoral arena its influence, per se, is prohibited and nil. The role of the military in supporting the American and Israeli regimes is non-existent.

NOTES

1. Amos Perlmutter, 'The Presidential Political Center and Foreign Policy,' *World Politics*, Vol. XXVII, Oct 1974, No. 1, pp. 87-106.
2. Richard Betts, 'Soldiers, Statesmen, and the Decision To Go To War, 1945-1975,' unpublished dissertation (Government, Harvard University, 1975), pp. 1-45.
3. Amos Perlmutter, ed., '*The Political Influence of the Military*, (forthcoming), Yale University Press, 1978).
4. Betts, 'Soldiers', p. 12.
5. John Erickson, *Soviet Military Power*, Royal United Services Institute for Defense Studies, Whitehall, London, 1971.
6. John R. Thomas, 'Soviet Foreign Policy and the Military', *Survey*, Summer 1971, Vol 17, No. 8, p. 154.
7. Betts, *ibid.*, p. 175.
8. *Ibid.*, p. 209.
9. *Ibid.*, p. 445.
10. Ellis Joffe, 'The Chinese Army After the Cultural Revolution: The Effects of Intervention' *The Chinese Quarterly* 55, July-Sept. 1973, pp. 450-477.
11. Amos Perlmutter, *The Military and Politics in Modern Times*, (Yale University Press, 1977).
12. Amos Perlmutter, 'Israel's Fourth War, October 1973', *ORBIS*, Vol. XIX, Summer 1975, pp. 457-460.

Epilogue: Entebbe 1976

It is significant that one of the IDF's most politically judicious and militarily brilliant acts was characterized by the total absence of adventurist motivations which, under different conditions, in other politics, could certainly have been the case. The Entebbe rescue was far from a simple exercise, and it certainly required a well-executed military operation, involving imagination, skill, incisive command, highly disciplined troops, expert execution of orders, and superior intelligence. Also necessary was total political and military control, and the Entebbe operation is thus a model of this kind of control over the successful planning and use of military force. Here the Israeli conduct of the Entebbe operation once more bears out Mosca's dictum that the mark of an advanced and stable civilization and polity is *political* domination over military instruments.

Space does not permit an account of the operational details of Entebbe. They have already been covered by at least three 'instant' books and several journalistic accounts, although these, unfortunately, are largely incomplete, draw upon unreliable sources and proffer irrelevant interpretations.[1] Of greater interest to students of politics are the processes and the control mechanisms involved in this daring and politically sensitive military operation. From the moment it was learned that the plane had been hijacked, the Israeli cabinet had full responsibility for decision-making concerning all aspects of negotiations and subsequent political action. In fact, the cabinet, the highest executive authority of the State of Israel, operated in three capacities: as a crisis management body, as an operational problem-solving structure, and as a forum for securing national consensus. To fulfil the first function, the cabinet was immediately transformed into an ad hoc executive team made up of the three senior cabinet members, the Prime Minister (Rabin), the Defence Minister (Peres), and the Foreign Minister (Allon). On the initiative of the Prime Minister, Chief of Staff General Gur was invited to act as the military adviser to the Cabinet, and especially the Prime Minister and the Defence Minister. Gur has played this role since the formation of the IDF, although the exact nature of the relationship has varied with the personal styles of successive Prime Ministers and Defence Ministers. In the Entebbe operation General Gur served as the ideal professional—the expert who provides his superiors with options.

In order to perform this function, General Gur established within the High Command his own crisis management team, a special committee headed by the Deputy Chief of Staff, General Y. Adam. Under General Adam's supervision, two teams of officers produced a stream of different (and sometimes conflicting) military operational options, which were presented to the Chief of Staff, who then brought them to the Cabinet crisis management team for consideration. This free flow of political and military information, brilliantly managed by Rabin, made the Cabinet privy to the best possible professional advice and provided the military with the greatest possible administrative and operational freedom of action.[2]

Next an operational structure was established between civilian and military authorities. Once the decision had been made, the clear division of labour between the political leaders and the military permitted the brilliant execution of this militarily complex and politically sensitive operation. Unquestionably the case of Entebbe demonstrated that the institutionalization of the High Command by Ben Gurion and the Haganah before him had created an informal structural arrangement that provided an efficient procedure for handling complex military-political operations that ensured civilian dominance over the process. Ben Gurion had preferred the advice of the Chief of Staff and had left the cabinet ignorant of key military operations, including the decision to go to war in 1956. Prime Minister Eshkol and Defence Minister Dayan, better managers than Ben Gurion, gave the military the freedom of action necessary for choosing the best options. The 1954–55 fiasco came about precisely because Lavon destroyed the delicate communication network that links Israeli civilian and military authorities and ensures a co-operative working relationship between Chief of Staff, Prime Minister and Defence Minister. In Israel the proper and constitutional procedures of civil–military relations are not contained in any legal document, but through a process of political and informal institutionalization, control structures, and procedures that have evolved to handle complex military operations; personal and institutional frameworks have also been formed which enable political authorities to oversee the use of force.

The Entebbe operation, in fact, clearly demonstrates the fusionist model, political and bureaucratic (military). The IDF did not interfere with the political decision-making machinery and the political authorities did not dictate options to the IDF professionals. The choice of the most appropriate military option rested throughout the crisis with the executive of the cabinet (the crisis management team), and the Prime Minister's successful orchestration of the political and military instruments made it possible for the IDF to deploy its maximum capabilities.

Third, the cabinet operated as a national consensus highest authority. Prime Minister Rabin consulted with the leaders of the opposition throughout the crisis. Both the cabinet, the parties, and key members of Parliament were apprised of the day-by-day events. This type of securing national consensus did not exist in Israel before 1973. Some of the 1973 lessons must have been learned. Also it must have been the crisis of authority which made Rabin and his cabinet think of the need to secure the support of the opposition, so that if the operation and the management of the crisis had collapsed, the blame would not have been solely directed at Rabin.

Entebbe was a classic exercise in military professionalism: an operation executed brilliantly by a military whose complete responsibility to its patron—the state embodied in the regime —was unquestioned. The most successful military professional act is one that maximizes the military's expertise, and the most successful political act is one that takes advantage of freedom of action and the available instruments (bureaucratic and military) without compromising either the purpose or the experience of the instruments. Operation Jonathan (Entebbe) represents the accumulated experience of three decades. Those years established the principle that civilian control of the military (objective control) is not achieved at the expense of military professionalism and that the confidence of the military in its civilian authorities produces the most brilliant execution of military purpose. Granted, not all the IDF and political chiefs in Israel have followed this principle. Enough have, however, for Israel to have achieved a balanced and efficient relationship between the civilian authorities and a professionally autonomous but politically dependent military establishment—a rather rare combination in any modern polity and especially noteworthy in a state under a permanent state of siege.

NOTES

1. List of books on Entebbe, see William Stevenson, *90 Minutes at Entebbe*, Corgi, 1976; Yehuda Offer, *Operation Thunder: The Entebbe Raid*, Penguin, 1976; and Tony Williamson, *Counterstrike Entebbe*, Collins, 1976.
2. I am grateful for this information to the knowledgeable military editor of *Haaretz*, Zeev Schiff.

INDEX